TRUSTEES, TRUSTEESHIP, AND THE PUBLIC GOOD

Trustees, Trusteeship, and the Public Good

ISSUES OF ACCOUNTABILITY FOR HOSPITALS, MUSEUMS, UNIVERSITIES, AND LIBRARIES

JAMES C. BAUGHMAN
Foreword by William W. Crook

Q

QUORUM BOOKS

NEW YORK • WESTPORT, CONNECTICUT • LONDON

Library of Congress Cataloging-in-Publication Data

Baughman, James C.
    Trustees, trusteeship, and the public good.

    Includes index.
    1. Charitable uses, trusts, and foundations—
United States.   2. Public trustees—United States.
I. Title.
KF740.B38   1987   346.73'064   86-25574
                           347.30664
ISBN 0-89930-195-9 (lib. bdg. : alk. paper)

Library of Congress Catalog Card Number: 86-25574
ISBN: 0-89930-195-9

First published in 1987 by Quorum Books

Greenwood Press, Inc.
88 Post Road West, Westport, Connecticut 06881

Printed in the United States of America

The paper used in this book complies with the
Permanent Paper Standard issued by the National
Information Standards Organization (Z39.48-1984).

10   9   8   7   6   5   4   3   2   1

To
KENNETH R. SHAFFER
A Friend

CONTENTS

FOREWORD

This book is a fascinating account of trusteeship for the public good, presented within a readable, anecdotal structure rather than organized strictly on the basis of first principles in the manner of treatises and hornbooks. Fiduciary first principles, as they apply to public trusts, are, of course, the real subject of this book, and their importance soon emerges. As you experience the fascinating situations of the cases, you may be amazed, as I was, how in so many situations the principal actors could be so blind or so indifferent to their own conflicts of interest, self-dealing, improper applications of property or funds, and other transgressions. The cases illustrate how far seemingly normal people can stray when blinded by their own self-interest. Although most trustees are not guilty of such wrongdoing, wrong is more interesting than rectitude. And, as in this treatment, *right* may be defined in reference to wrong.

Trustees of public charities and public officials generally should find this book interesting and relevant reading. Their attorneys and other attorneys should be similarly interested, although some may find the approach somewhat popularized in the absence of the usual measure of legal phraseology. This trade-off simply makes the book more readable for more people. So, the general reader wishing to be well informed about matters affecting us all should enjoy this popular yet detailed treatment of public charities.

To my knowledge, there is no book as successful in meeting the need that Professor Baughman has met with this work, which is enthusiastically delivered and contains much valuable information.

—William W. Crook

PREFACE

At every turn, life embodies experience. It was out of my life experiences in a
fiduciary capacity that this book emerged and grew. As a local participant in
decisions involving the use of charitable funds controlled by trustees, I have
become acutely aware of the changing relative strengths of power among boards
of trustees, administrators, the public, and the courts. I am concerned about the
general misconceptions of our vital charitable institutions that the country at
large historically has had, but most particularly about trustees who have often
utterly misunderstood the roles of institutions for which they serve. That this is
true is borne out by increasing litigation concerning the nature of trusteeships.

This book is intended to be a readable exposition, not a legal treatise, of the
juridical status of both trustees and charitable institutions in terms of their relation
to the public good. It is written for trustees of libraries, hospitals, museums,
colleges and universities, and so forth, and for the interested public in general.

The material is presented in real-life scenarios—the experiences of trustees.
Selected to be exemplary (not definitive or exhaustive), the cases identify legal
problems and issues, illustrating the interrelatedness of the cases and problems
in the management of charitable institutions. An attempt has been made to provide
the reader with the setting and background for each case, in order to facilitate
a fuller, richer understanding of the factors that contributed to the dilemma.

Although this book attempts to bring together the disparate literature about
the role of the trustee, the cases themselves have been gathered principally from
court decisions, journal articles, and newspaper stories. This required examining
the complaints made by attorneys general and decisions made by courts of law.
I should hasten to add that the book contains no incidents, references, or material
from any institution with which I am or have been associated, either as an
employee or as a board member.

Because it is such a provocative topic, this book contains an unusual number
of footnotes, which the casual reader can ignore. But for readers who might
wish to see the footnotes, which provide the authority and documentation, they
appear in a section at the end of the book organized by chapter.

It is realized that in treating this topic from a case study approach with names, dates, events, and places, a few individuals may be disturbed or perhaps embarrassed, but it should be quickly added that the overall goal is to be helpful to nonprofit trustees in the fulfillment of their mission. It is my sincere hope that those, like myself, who have faced the awesome responsibilities of fiduciary obligations will find the road somewhat easier to travel, having walked it with their eyes more open.

I am indebted to many individuals, although it would be impossible to thank or even mention everyone who has been generous with his or her time and thoughtful criticism. I should like to mention, however, two individuals who have worked closely with me over the period of my work. They are William Crook, Esq., member of the Massachusetts and Michigan bars, and Attorney Marita Driscoll, member of the Massachusetts Bar. Even though these individuals were generous with their time and help and gave much good advice for improvement in the manuscript, the final responsibility for the book and its content, of course, lies with me.

Special mention needs to be made of the Boston University Libraries and especially the Law Library of Boston University. David Grahek, Esq., a member of the Massachusetts Bar, gave unselfishly of his time and knowledge. I shall always be grateful to him and to Boston University for its commitment to serve the public good by generously making its library resources available to others.

I should like to thank Assistant Attorney General Christine Hehmeyer Rosso, Chief of the Charitable Trusts and Solicitations Division of the state of Illinois, for granting a personal interview and for sharing a wealth of materials relative to Illinois trust law and cases. Her suggestions were invaluable.

So many people were gracious and prompt in supplying necessary materials— judges, law firms, clerks of courts, administrators, government officials, professional associations, and so on.

I acknowledge with grateful appreciation the financial support of the Hollowell Research Fund. Without this grant supporting the project and the proposed reporting of the findings, this book would not have been possible.

And finally, a special thanks goes to my wife and children who have patiently supported me throughout this creative process. Like a charitable institution, a book is an act of faith. When I was not available to go to museums, galleries, or even football games, they always understood. Writing a book is a commitment. They understood this, and I shall be eternally grateful to them.

INTRODUCTION

The changes, accelerating over several decades, are beginning to emerge in a clear-cut phenomenon: the court is showing an increasing willingness to examine and correct when necessary the actions of trustees. In the process, the court is demonstrating that it has the ultimate power, the final say. This ultimate control is being increasingly recognized and used as a means to force trustees of charitable property to serve the public good (their mandate), rather than specialized interests or projects that either are inconsistent with the organization's avowed purposes or possibly skirt legal responsibilities.

In the broadest sense, the term *charitable trust* embodies all charitable entities, whether they are constituted as a trust or a corporation. As such, the trustees of charitable trusts are common-law trustees; that is, they are officers of the court or the state, which, in turn, makes the trustees accountable to the court or the state in a way above and beyond the general public.

SOME EXAMPLES

A hallmark example of court control of a college board of trustees' actions occurred when the Board of Wilson College, Chambersburg, Pennsylvania, announced that the school would close forever on 30 June 1979. Subsequently, the Orphan's Court of Pennsylvania enjoined the trustees from closing the college until the trustees had court approval.

A federal judge of the District of Columbia ordered the trustees of a private charitable hospital to develop a written policy statement governing investment of the hospital's liquid assets. The court also ordered that the trustees read the court order and attest to having done so. Judge Gerhard Gesell did not want to leave room for doubt.

The attorney general of New York created guidelines for the deaccessioning of precious art objects for all New York museums because of public criticism of the actions of the Metropolitan Museum's board of trustees in New York City.

Recently, dissatisfaction with deaccessioning procedures at Harvard's Fogg Art Museum resulted in changing a planned course of action involving the sale of art objects to assure an adequate source of operating revenue. Public pressure, coupled with the insistence of a professional association's resolution, wrought a change in fiscal planning without formal legal action.

The Massachusetts Supreme Judicial Court considered the complaint of the attorney general against the board of trustees of the Hahnemann Hospital (Brighton, Massachusetts) for its contemplated sale of the nonprofit hospital to a forprofit corporation.

In Paterson, New Jersey, a group of citizens protested the sale of art from the Paterson Free Public Library that had been left in trust. The court halted the sale, and the decision has had a salutary effect on other charities holding property in trust for the public's benefit and enjoyment.

In an era characterized by increasing public scrutiny and accompanying legal liability, members of boards of trustees and their agents must recognize their goals, status, purpose, and real powers in society.

The individuals who compose the governing boards of nonprofit organizations are often called trustees, although other terms are used—directors, managers, regents, governors, convenors, members of the corporation, incorporators, and so on. Regardless of title, their duties and responsibilities remain alike in substance; custom, charter, and donative instruments make the real difference.

For clarity and convenience throughout this book, the word *trustee* means any individual, group of individuals, corporation, or other legal entity that holds legal title to property for any charitable use. The authority and power of trustees to manage the charitable property for the public good as vested in their enfranchisement is the subject of this book.

1

AMERICA'S CHARITABLE
ENTERPRISE

> Government alone cannot solve our massive and complex problems. We
> need the input of the private sector—the input of individual initiative which
> has been the great strength of this country from the beginning. We are a
> pluralistic society. Philanthropy is a means, not an end in itself. It provides
> funds to make individual initiative effective, in other words to make the
> private nonprofit sector an effective supplement to governmental effort.
>
> John D. Rockefeller III, *The Nonprofit Organization Handbook*, 1980

To utter the naked statistic that hospitals, museums, colleges and universities,
libraries, and other similar nonprofit institutions constitute 11 percent of our
national wealth may be interesting, even startling. (Not included in this percentage figure are the many enterprises that serve comparable purposes but are
proprietary, that is, exist for profit.) Further, if one were to add like institutions
created and controlled by local municipalities, the individual states, the federal
government, and other political units, the percentage of nonprofit property in
terms of national wealth would be astounding. All you have to do is look at
your own community to observe the vast number of institutions that operate for
direct educational, public health, and related purposes in comparison to the
community as a whole.

THE THIRD SECTOR

The size of the nonprofit Third Sector, representing the privately managed
charitable institutions in American society, is indeed big. It consists of many
entities, including orchestras, professional associations, civic groups, social-
service organizations, and religious groups. Some of the more obvious examples
are museums, colleges and universities, hospitals, and libraries. Some of the
world's finest treasures and most valuable resources lie within these institutions:
the Fogg Museum of Harvard University; the Metropolitan Museum of Art (New

York); the J. Paul Getty Museum (Malibu, California); Yale University (New Haven, Connecticut); Princeton University (Princeton, New Jersey); University of Chicago, Newberry Library (Chicago); Henry E. Huntington Library (San Marino, California); Folger Shakespeare Library (Washington, D.C.); Boston Athenaeum; Mount Sinai Medical Center (New York City); Mayo Clinic (Rochester, Minnesota); Massachusetts General Hospital (Boston, Massachusetts); Bellevue Hospital (New York City); New Haven (Connecticut) Hospital, and many others.

Each of these institutions has the unique distinction—as do all charitable institutions—of existing to serve its ultimate beneficiary: the public.

Periodically, city, county, and state politicians bemoan the increasing amount of tax-exempt property that increases the tax burden on individuals and business enterprises. Concern is increasing throughout the country that the size of such institutions affects our lives by encroaching on the quality of life in residential areas and/or on the value of business districts. From time to time one finds an article or two in the popular press questioning whether nonprofit groups are worth their keep; an example from *U.S. News and World Report* is entitled "Nonprofit Groups: Are They Worth Their Tax Breaks?"[1]

Now look to the other side of the coin: if our colleges and universities, hospitals, museums, libraries, and others were by some political or physical catastrophe to disappear, what would be left? Virtually nothing. The form of our government derives directly from the effect of such institutions. They, not government, establish the high quality of our lives in this country. Many people say they are the vital instruments of life itself.

If these institutions are so important, one would expect that they would be governed by a pervasive public scrutiny that would ensure that they are each providing everything appropriate to the people for whom they have been created and for whom they serve. Looking through the *Congressional Record* at a single day's transactions, one finds our national legislative bodies occasionally concerned with issues of international and national significance to us all.

On the other hand, one finds a great deal of concern, for example, with the extinction of mud turtles in the Mississippi Valley, the increasing subsidization of tobacco growers in the southlands, or with resolutions honoring an aging movie actor or a courageous young boy who pulled a friend from a lion's cage in New York. Indeed, one does not have to look for these reports in the *Congressional Record*; any newspaper will do.

What about our major charitable institutions? How much scrutiny do they get? How much space is allotted to them in the *Congressional Record*, the press, or your own local newspaper? There is a great deal about intercollegiate sports and hero athletes and coaches, a rather constant paragraph or two about a president who has resigned, and nowadays, more increasingly, about protests and strikes over salaries and working conditions of staff members in these institutions, or perhaps demonstrations against investments in South Africa. How much space is devoted to evaluating programs of these institutions? How much space is devoted to the quality of their teachers; surgeons, physicians, nurses, technicians; their curators and librarians? Not least, how often do you see an evaluation of their total service? Not too often.

Does this mean that these nonprofit institutions are not important? Is their contribution to life of little value? The answer to this question is no. Perhaps the paucity of reporting on charitable organizations can be explained by their form of government. Nonprofit institutions exist principally not as open political bodies, as commonly conceived, but through a phenomenon of Anglo-American tradition known as trusteeship.

THE CLOAK OF PRIVACY

Charitable trustees tend to clothe themselves in the cloak of privacy, although their private nature relates more to the institution's management than to its use, which is public. One can find out more about a public corporation that is listed on the New York Stock Exchange, or for that matter any stock exchange, than about a nonprofit organization. The board of trustees of a charitable organization is often a self-perpetuating group of individuals—principally business and professional people, who meet in private and do not publish accounts of their business.

With the exception of jurisdictions that have applicable open-meeting laws for public institutions, many of the nation's great charitable institutions are cloaked in secrecy. Most trustee meetings are held behind closed doors with the press excluded. This condoned secrecy separates trustees from the people they are mandated to serve. The public's right to know is seriously blighted because even the press is denied access to charitable trustees' activities. This reduces trustee accountability to the public.

RELIEVING THE BURDENS OF GOVERNMENT

The American people support both independent nonprofit organizations and governmental programs through various tax measures for a significant number of reasons. The American public accepts these two types of charitable endeavors, perhaps based on the assumption that the independent nonprofit sector not only alleviates some of the burdens of government but also is free to experiment with new and creative ideas and programs that would not be as easy, or even possible, otherwise.

In another sense, support for independent organizations exists because of the traditional basic suspicion of authority—especially governmental authority, which is often seen as remote and negative in character. A recent survey by the Institute for Social Research at the University of Michigan, which conducts the most widely accepted survey research of attitudes toward government, states that only 33 percent of the people polled believe the government in Washington can be trusted to do what is right all or most of the time. Former surveys indicated that only 25 percent trusted the government. In general, the American public remains predominantly negative toward government and public officials.[2]

CHARITY

The English Tudor rulers, especially Elizabeth I, hated and feared poverty and vagabondage because they unsettled the whole society. During the reign of Elizabeth I, specific legislation—the Statute of Charitable Uses, popularly known as the Statute of Elizabeth—was passed, defining and establishing and also guiding for centuries the development of the charitable trust. Just as the Tudors, who had a concern for the public order, lent warm support to "private" charity,[3] American society has continued the process.

The California Supreme Court has identified criteria for determining if a bequest to an institution is charitable. The test is as follows: (1) its aims and accomplishments are of religious, educational, political, or general social interest to mankind; (2) the ultimate recipients constitute either the community as a whole or an unascertainable and indefinite portion thereof.[4]

Charities are by definition public in the sense that they are devoted to benefiting the public at large. The term *public charity* is used, but the word *public* in the phrase adds nothing. Marion Fremont-Smith is quite specific on this point when she says: "There can be no such thing as a private charity in law, since a trust or corporation devoted to benefiting one or a few named individuals, even if its stated purpose is to ease their suffering or to improve their mind, . . . is not considered under law to be a charity."[5] A charity is identified by its public nature and unnamed or indefinite beneficiaries.

For clarity's sake a distinction needs to be made between the formal use of the term *charity* and its popular use. In legal parlance, the term *charity* is used to describe nonprofit organizations. In the popular sense, it connotes assistance to the poor, the suffering, or the indigent.

When it comes to the use of the word *charity*, the law does not make a distinction between the rich and poor. Charity does not necessarily mean alms-giving; in a broader sense, it is the use of resources for the benefit of the community "either by bringing their minds or hearts under the influence of education or religion, by relieving their bodies from disease, suffering or constraint, by assisting them to establish themselves in life, or by erecting or maintaining public buildings or works or otherwise lessening the burdens of government."[6]

Charity is a gift to a general public use. It benefits everyone alike under the same laws. The courts have been quite specific on this point. In 1900 the Massachusetts Supreme Judicial Court, for example, held that a bequest to the President and Fellows of Harvard College to be held as a permanent fund with the net income applied for scholarships "is a gift to a *public charitable corporation*," (emphasis added) within the Massachusetts laws relating to the management of charities. The court continued: "That a gift for the promotion of education in Harvard College is a public charity is a proposition too plain to need discussion."[7]

FORMING THE DEMOCRATIC IDEAL

When the colonists came to this country, they brought with them the concept of English common law, including equity jurisprudence. With the signing of the Mayflower Compact in 1620 aboard the ship *Mayflower*, democratic self determination was established as the ideal form of government in all walks of American life, public and private. This democratic control and its related power of the vote have been the driving forces in forming the governing structure for the development and growth of charitable organizations, created mainly as corporate bodies in this country. Thus, the twin processes of English common law and of representative government with its concomitant formal institutional structures have shaped American society as a whole.

Shortly after the Pilgrims landed at Plymouth, the need arose for an institution of higher learning to serve the general good of the colony by educating young men for the ministry. Harvard College was established in 1636, awarding its first bachelor of arts degree in 1642. *The Story of Harvard*, published by the President and Fellows of Harvard College, states: "On [President] Dunster's petition in 1650, the Royal Governor granted the Charter which still guides the University. Thus the President, the Treasurer, and five others were incorporated as 'The President and Fellows of Harvard College,' and given perpetual succession. They are the oldest corporation in the Western Hemisphere."[8]

The steadfast determination of the people to determine the manner in which they were to govern themselves, both publicly and privately, was strongly enunciated in 1791 in the Bill of Rights, the first ten amendments to the U.S. Constitution, enacted as a prohibition on the federal government. Arnaud Marts, formerly president of Bucknell University and foundation director, espoused the importance of Amendments Nine and Ten to charitable organizations. He interpreted these two amendments as the great "freedom to" for the American people, comparing them to the Magna Carta in terms of America's freedom.[9] The two amendments are

Amendment Nine. The enumeration in the Constitution, of certain rights, shall not be construed to deny or disparage others retained by the people.
Amendment Ten. The powers not delegated to the United States by the Constitution, nor prohibited by it to the States, are reserved to the States respectively, or to the people.

As a result, since charitable institutions were not designated in the Constitution as a power of the U.S. government, most of them are chartered under the auspices of a state. It should be noted that the federal government does have the authority to create a charitable enterprise and has done so on occasion—for example, the American Red Cross, which grew out of the First Geneva (or Red Cross) Convention of 1864 and was subsequently reorganized and granted a new charter in 1905 by Congress. This charter established the basic organization of today's American Red Cross.

The American Red Cross and other charitable trusts have become the perfect mechanism for the accumulation of charitable resources organized and distributed through an association. Alexis de Tocqueville, a Frenchman of liberal and democratic convictions, visited America in 1831–1832 to study prisons in the new republic. In his classic work *Democracy in America*, which he published on his return to France, he discerningly wrote:

Americans of all ages, all conditions, and all dispositions constantly form associations . . . . In this manner they found hospitals, prisons, and schools . . . . Wherever at the head of some new undertaking you see the government in France, or a man of rank in England, in the United States you will be sure to find an association.[10]

The associations of which de Tocqueville spoke form an integral part of American society. Charitable institutions stand as an essential web of popular democratic government, giving great force to the general plan of freedom as Americans have come to know it.

CREATING PRESENT-DAY CHARITIES

The phenomenon of forming associations to carry out a charitable purpose continues uninterrupted today. The 1980 *Nonprofit Organization Handbook* states that more than 815,000 private, nonprofit, tax-exempt organizations are registered with the Internal Revenue Service. Each year the IRS denies some 2,300 applications for exempt status and 8,600 are withdrawn voluntarily, but each year the IRS also approves more than 36,000 applications for exempt status for new nonprofit organizations.[11]

The Holocaust Memorial Museum, for example, showing what some described as "the dark side of human civilization," was established in Washington, D.C., in 1984 with private funds. Located near the Washington Monument, the museum focuses on the annual Days of Remembrance for the six million Jews and other countless minority Europeans who were persecuted and murdered under the Third Reich. Perhaps a museum is another way to remind people of the horrors of war and madness, which remain dominant in the minds of so many civilized individuals today.[12]

In another tone, in 1983 the Thomas Cole Foundation, organized by two New York City art dealers, turned Mr. Cole's home, situated in the Catskill Mountains, into a museum. The foundation is a way of honoring Mr. Cole as well as of making productive the Cole homestead, which has been designated as a national historic landmark. Mr. Cole is recognized as the father of the Hudson River school of art.[13]

Wealthy dilettantes—who have the financial means and perhaps ambition and wish to venerate their names—sometimes create a museum in their name. Many join the American tradition when each tacks his or her nameplate over the door of the new museum created with the wealth acquired in business, commerce, and high enterprise.

The money to create a private museum can come from established sources as well as from the nouveau riche. "While old money established the Whitney Museum of American Art and the Solomon R. Guggenheim Museum," writes Fay S. Joyce of the *New York Times*,

new money has given rise to the Hirshhorn Museum and Sculpture Garden in Washington, founded by Joseph H. Hirshhorn, and a number of smaller institutions. These include the Terra Museum of American Art in Evanston, Ill., named for Daniel J. Terra, the founder and head of a chemical company and now President Reagan's Ambassador-at-large for Cultural Affairs, and the Aldrich Museum of Contemporary Art in Ridgefield, Conn., named for the dress designer Larry Aldrich.[14]

Beneficence of this sort, although admittedly serving the public, creates as well a monument unto the donor or creator in the name of charity. All of this is done in the name of benevolence, but not of least importance is the sizable tax deduction that goes with such generosity.

The public contributes as much as, if not more than, the benefactor; but the fact remains that the public is benefiting, since once a charity is created, its property thenceforth in perpetuity exists for no other reason than to serve the public good.

2

THE BOARD AND ITS IMAGES

The characterization of a trustee as a fiduciary is crucial to an understanding
of his duties, and underlies the determination of all of his powers.
Marion R. Fremont-Smith, *Foundations and Government*, 1965

THE POPULAR IMAGE OF THE TRUSTEE

What does it mean to hold a trusteeship in a charitable institution, such as a
hospital, museum, college, university, or library—public or private? What does
it mean to the public—who is presumably served?

It is easy to assume that most trustees of charitable institutions see trusteeship
as an honor bestowed on them in recognition of perhaps wealth, social status,
or their image as obvious successful standouts in the field of large corporations.
Corporate success signifies that they qualify for the right of passage to serve in
prestigious volunteer leadership positions. If questioned about their motivation
for board membership, many would not dare, of course, admit to such reasons
for service. If called on to talk about the role of nonprofit trusteeship, however,
they would likely respond: We own and control the paintings in this museum,
the services of this hospital, the books and paraphernalia of this library, the
classrooms and laboratories of this college or university, and we direct their use
toward those who need access to them as we see fit and as best we can.

The common individuals, the citizens whom charitable trustees serve, will—
if they consider them at all—think of members of a board of trustees as the
power elite: as a stable group of special individuals who have little time for
ordinary people. They are often seen as powerful socialites who control a private
preserve and give a little time (time enough to get pictures in the society column
of the local newspapers) to determine how much, what kind, and under what
conditions the institutions can afford or are inclined to provide in services. The
published announcements of the charitable trustees, who have determined to do
this or not, seem more immutable or unassailable than the laws of nature.

Trustees, by any reasonable standard, are members of the establishment—whether they come from old or new affluence. Their trademark is continuity.

Images of trustees as powerful, influential individuals flow from the long-standing myth that the extent of the benefits the public derives depends on the discretion of the trustee. Actually, the public retains a vital, beneficial interest in such public-service institutions as hospitals, universities, museums, and libraries. Like many activities in a pluralistic society, trustee activity tends to assume mythical qualities and in time fades in clarity and propriety in connection with its original reason for being, in both the trustee's perception and the popular mind.

A number of years ago the late Raymond Hughes, the distinguished president of Iowa State College, who was later a trustee of a charitable enterprise, sardonically observed, "This business of being a college trustee can be a great business, a great pleasure, and a great service." Elaborating further, he noted: "It can also be a very small, useless, and perfunctory performance. A shocking percentage of the . . . men and women serving as trustees . . . controlling our American colleges and universities, know little of their responsibilities and care little about their institutions; perfunctorily attend board meetings, and approve presidential recommendations without understanding or serious consideration."[1]

As one friend deeply interested in trusteeship, remarked to me:

If trustees were really interested in their public obligations and responsibilities in the context of their decision making, one would find them discussing it. I have observed numerous different board meetings in action, and yet scarcely, if ever, does one find this to be the case. They just go on and on until they find their trustee tails in a legal crack.

Symbolic Bodies

In some instances trustees waive their rights as decision makers by standing on ceremony without accepting the inherent responsibilities. In fact, some boards seem to be organized on that basis. An example is the National Wildflower Research Center, a charity organized to promote scientific research. On the occasion of her seventieth birthday, Mrs. Lyndon B. Johnson drew the attention of the American people through press reportage that she was creating a National Wildflower Research Center. "Lady Bird Turns 70, Makes Gift to US," one headline read, and the news item stated that Mrs. Johnson was deeding a sixty-acre parcel of land and was committing $125,000 of her money to be used toward a research laboratory and office for the new center, to be located near Austin, Texas.[2]

To manage the new organization, Mrs. Johnson created a one hundred–member board of trustees, including a number of notable individuals—among them, former president Gerald R. Ford, with actress Helen Hayes and Mrs. Johnson serving as honorary co-chairpersons. Such a large board probably was created more with the intent of bringing wealth, power, and prestige to the scene than to manage efficiently, suggesting that boards of trustees of organizations such as the National Wildflower Research Center (and those of hundreds more) are principally symbolic bodies.

"Boards of trustees of institutions like Brookings [Institution]," according to the social critics Leonard and Mark Silk, "are above all symbolic bodies. What trustees actually do—and usually it is precious little—is far less significant than what they stand for. Appointments are therefore signposts for the interested public, pointing where the institution is moving, or at least hopes to move."[3] It is not inconceivable, however, that with the ever-escalating judicial intervention in the affairs of trustees, the image of the trustee will inevitably and dramatically change.

Why Serve?

Motivation for trusteeship cries out for careful consideration, especially when new appointments are being made to the board.

Does the trustee serve in order to have his or her name on the trustee roster? Does the trustee accept the invitation for social preferment and then go to meetings and automatically vote? Is she or he a professional in the area who feels the need to have a greater span of control, and thus wants to run the operation? Perchance, is the trustee a burnout in the same area who feels the need to compensate for an unsuccessful career aspiration? Parenthetically, taken as a whole, the worst kind of board member is the one who is a specialist in the area, for often this trustee wants things done his or her way and often uses a number of techniques—subtle or otherwise—to achieve control.

Is the trustee purely altruistic? A partial answer is provided by Professor Cyril Houle, who cites Donald McCarty's research study regarding board membership. After Mr. McCarty sorted the individual school board member cases into groups in terms of what seemed to be their major motivation, he found that 46 percent of the cases could be classified as apparently or extremely altruistic, but 54 percent could be identified as being partially or extremely self-interested. Mr. Houle then states, "These findings will come as no great surprise to anyone who knows board members or, for that matter, people!"[4]

In a Twentieth Century Fund report titled *Abuse on Wall Street*, journalist Chris Welles writes forcefully about self-interest:

The basic problem is that all nonprofit institutions, particularly those that receive contributions from affluent donors or investment income from endowments, depend on benefactors from the business world.... Businessmen and those associated with business wealth enable these institutions to survive.... Although these individuals are generally well intentioned, they sometimes have difficulty separating their philanthropic and fiduciary activities from their personal business interests. When they permit the latter to take precedence over the former, the conflict of interest inherent in the situation degenerates into abuse, and the affected nonprofit institution, as well as its beneficiaries, inevitably suffers.[5]

Composition of Boards

Typically, the nonprofit sector in a given area is controlled by boards whose members are from the profit-making sector in the same geographic area and also serve on several other boards. The Cleveland Museum of Fine Arts, one of the nation's most important museums, is a good illustration. "Cleveland, of course, is an extreme example of the interlocking structure of museum boards," writes art critic Grace Glueck, "but even the members of other, less exclusive boards have what might be called a solid community of interests."[6]

The various surveys indicate that trustees, as a group, are cut from the same socioeconomic bolt of cloth. They are by definition members of the establishment. Tens of thousands of individuals serve as trustees, although the precise number is not known and would be difficult to determine, since the average trustee serves on more than one charitable board. A typical trustee profile— although characteristics vary from one type of institution to another—can be developed from various survey data.

Most trustees hold at least a baccalaureate; a significant number hold professional and doctoral degrees. The majority, save public institutions, are fifty years old or older. Most are white males, although the public institutions tend to have more representation from women and minority groups. Even though the proportions may vary by type of institution, the following professions are most prevalent: law, clergy, banking and finance, academic, and the arts. Presidents and board chairpersons of profit-making corporations are well represented.

The survey data thus suggest that boards of trustees of our nation's nonprofit organizations consist in large part of some of the nation's richest and most powerful individuals from the American political, economic, business, industrial, service-oriented, and cultural milieu. As such, they are an amorphous group of power brokers, who sit at the command posts of society, shaping the national destiny by the role they play through nonprofit (as well as profit-making) institutions. They rule America.[7]

Generosity

Because nonprofit organizations depend heavily on the beneficence of the business world and its contacts, it is standard operating procedure to select individuals for reasons of political suasion or prestige. The admitted intention often is to have the trustee play a philanthropic role or perhaps even to legitimatize the charitable organization while playing a reactive role in the decision-making part of institutional management. Some commentators on charities are quite cynical about the relationship between board membership and fund-raising. "Universities and philanthropic institutions," writes social critic Robert Liston in the *Charity Racket*, " . . . raise funds by electing quite a large board of trustees, composed for the most part of wealthy bankers, corporate executives, and professional people. Expertise in educational matters is usually not required or even desirable among trustees, but a fat purse is frequently a prerequisite."[8]

Several anecdotes flow from financial concerns of the nonprofit world. " When I was a candidate for chairman of the board of the Mount Sinai Medical Center in New York City," writes Alfred R. Stern, "one of its trustees pulled me aside to confide: 'I really don't think I'm in favor of your election as chairman. You haven't given Mount Sinai enough money.' "[9] Is trusteeship chiefly cocktail parties and money?

On the college and university side, the late Arnaud C. Marts, president of Bucknell University, cogently wrote in his memoirs how trustees were involved in private generosity for the public good. Bucknell's Old Main had been destroyed by fire, with the remaining gutted structure lingering in the ashes as an eyesore.

At his first trustee meeting as president, Mr. Marts recommended that the board proceed directly to raise the funds necessary to rebuild Old Main. It was immediately and unanimously voted to do so. In his memoirs Mr. Marts wrote:

Naturally, I mentally canvassed the trustees and discovered that I could count on only two of the twenty-five whose generosity could or would reach five figures . . . . This lesson sank in deeply . . . . I . . . resolved that when the next emergency at Bucknell should arise requiring substantial generosity there would be at least twelve or fifteen members of the board of trustees who could do something far more than cast a vote authorizing me to go out and find someone else to provide the funds for doing it. I let it be known among alumni and parents that I would like to learn of men worthy in their own lives and spirits to be trustees of Bucknell University and who were generous to causes providing education for ambitious boys and girls.[10]

President Marts succeeded. During the next financial emergency two years later, when accrediting bodies threatened to withdraw approval of the engineering programs unless the curriculum was reorganized and a new chemical engineering laboratory built, he was ready. "I had a dozen trustees on my reorganized board," he said, "whose generosity would take care of that with little public activity or notice."[11]

With seldom a *rara avis* to be found among them, trustees, therefore, have assumed the same coloration. This is especially true at private institutions that appoint board members because of their wealth, their prominence, or presumed personal contacts for securing money for the institution.

Thomas Hoving, former director of the Metropolitan Museum of Art, expressed this point well when explaining to *New Yorker*'s John McPhee the Metropolitan's loss of the purchase of a great $6 million painting:

We should have reached for it. The reputation of the Metropolitan has always been based on its power to acquire things without reserve. A museum can lose that sort of knife-edge. It's a matter of attitude. If you lose that *one* day of going for the great thing, you can lose a decade. Any trustee should be able to write a check for at least three million dollars and not even feel it.[12]

Elitism for All

Incident after incident reveals that trustees have an establishment homo-geneity—elitism—leaving the door open to the criticism that trustees manifest an inherent insensitivity to the interests of the broader community they serve and represent. Dissenters, however, are demanding a change in the structure, composition, and attitudes of boards of trustees.

During the workers' upheaval at the Metropolitan Museum in New York, Grace Glueck writes that "a clutch of Metropolitan Museum board members held a dinner meeting to discuss new acquisitions in what, with curious aptness, is referred to as the Louis XVI Room." She then tells that the trustees were treated to an invasion of cockroaches that had been poured onto the table by members of the Art Workers Coalition. The dissenters felt that the trustees "were preoccupied with acquiring art rather than with communicating the spirit that produced it."[13]

Work, wealth, wisdom—preferably all three, but at least two of the three—are what the late Henry Wriston, both a college and university president, wanted most from a trustee. President Wriston earnestly believed these criteria to be candid enough and less brutal than a midwestern colleague's three attributes of trusteeship: "Give, Get, or Get Out!"[14]

Contemporary trusteeship carries an awesome but challenging responsibility that suggests that when the onion is peeled, trusteeship is more than cocktail parties and money. The amount of money an individual can muster cannot and should not be the major condition for appointment to a board of trustees in today's world. The public's beneficial interest is too important and the fiduciary responsibilities of board membership too significant for money, family name, or prominence to be the sole criterion for appointment.

Facts often come easily, but wisdom lingers. Wisdom remains as the essential attribute of trusteeship. An effective trustee advances the mission of the nonprofit organization through proper knowledgeable leadership and proven administrative ability. Underpinning this is interest—a desire to be involved and effective. The trustee has the kind of background and intelligence that affords the capacity to make good judgments, demonstrating sharper, more clear thinking than a pe-dantic professional administrator. The trustee must know more than the profes-sional. By way of analogy, the tailor may make suggestions on the fit of the suit, but the buyer makes the final judgment, that is, if the suit is to fit the person—or the situation.

Because knowledge and experience are of paramount importance for trustee effectiveness, the Carnegie Corporation of New York especially emphasized these qualities when testifying before Congress on what it looks for in trustees:

Now what we are looking for in trustees is, to use the broad term, men of affairs, that is men who have a concern for things which we are chartered to do, men who themselves are liberally educated, who are humane and who have a concern for the common good, and above all, who are not so encumbered with other trusteeships that they can't give us time, because we ask a great deal of time from our trustees, and the way we are organized it is necessary that we get it.[15]

Lay membership on boards is critical to ultimate success in meeting charter purposes in a democratic society. President Henry Wriston of Brown University espoused this idea in his classic work *Academic Procession*,[16] which he wrote on his retirement. Roy Sorenson is also specific on this point in his classic little book *The Art of Board Membership*, when he quotes Lewis Meriam of the University of Chicago as follows: "Always and inevitably in a democracy the people must seek the balance between expert service and popular control. Let me close with the thought that, in cases of doubt, they should decide in favor of popular control."[17]

THE LEGAL IMAGE OF THE TRUSTEE

"The common element of all charitable purposes is that they are designed to accomplish objectives which are beneficial to the community."[18] Thus, the legal image of the trustee is quite different from the popular. What is the legal status of the trustee? To whom is the trustee accountable? What set of guidelines shepherd trustee action?

The Legal Status of the Trustee

A clue to answering these questions lies in the recognition of the concept of the charitable trust. Some confusion exists, however, as to the exact interpretation that can be given to the legal status of a charitable trust in a given state because of a series of court decisions over the years when some states did not recognize the juridical convention of the trust. All states now recognize the charitable trust, but the vestiges of confusion linger. One can receive as many different answers as to how the laws are interpreted as there are states to give them.

Charities are, however, by definition public in the sense that they are devoted to benefiting the public at large. The essence of a charitable trust is that the beneficiaries should not be definite.[19] Thus, a charity is identified by its public nature and by unnamed or indefinite beneficiaries.

The confusion can be illustrated by the following two apparently contradictory interpretations of the legal status of trustees regarding the assets of private charitable institutions. In *The Story of Harvard*, its corporate author states, "With wide delegation of authority, the Corporation *owns* and operates Harvard today"[20] (emphasis added). In contrast, a private midwestern university official recently declared that the trustees were only managers of the university's resources, which belong after all to the public. How can two similarly situated universities see their roles so differently? Do they not operate under the same recognized, inherent common-law principles?

A. Lawrence Lowell, a lawyer and the president of Harvard University from 1909 to 1933, put it rather nicely in his 1919–1920 annual report, when he said: "The trustees, or whatever the members of the governing body may be called, although vested with the legal title to the property, are not the representatives of private owners, for there are none. They are custodians, holding the property in trust to promote the objects of the institution."[21] The truth is that the Harvard Corporation, like any similarly situated charitable board, is only the legal owner. The people of Massachusetts retain a beneficial interest in all charitable property, and the ultimate beneficiary of Harvard University is society—not the President and Fellows of Harvard University, its student body, its faculty, or alumni.

The great contribution America has made to the juridical convention of the trust is its corporate nature. The Harvard Corporation, as body corporate and trustee, manages Harvard University and all of its assets, including its $3.6 billion portfolio, for the benefit of the citizens of the Commonwealth of Massachusetts.

Professor Howard L. Oleck has expressed forceful reservation and deep concern about the "danger of the proprietary mentality" of charitable trusteeship. In some cases, organizers, officers, or employees in the for-profit sector are owners, although more often the stockholders are the owners. In the nonprofit sector, however, the proprietary mentality is quite improper, even if the organization was founded and funded entirely by the so-called owner. Mr. Oleck categorically states, "Ownership by management, in most nonprofit organizations, is a flat contradiction of the *pro bono publico* idea that is the essence of (proper) group activity not for profit."[22]

Misunderstanding of the issue is not restricted to trustees and executive officers. The notion persists that the donors maintain an interest in money given to charitable organization. Once a donor makes a gift to a charity of his or her choice, the donor is pretty much out of the picture.

F. Emerson Andrews, formerly Director of the Foundation Library Center, tells about the time that Congress was holding hearings on charitable foundations in the early 1950s. The Select (Cox) Committee of the House called Henry Ford II to testify concerning the Ford Foundation. In an unguarded moment, former Representative Edward Cox made a troublesome statement: "I deem it extraordinary that he should volunteer to come here and give us his views on the questions that we are undertaking to investigate, and I think it is extraordinary that a young man of great wealth like himself should seriously consider himself somewhat as a trustee for the use of the great funds *which are his*."[23] Mr. Ford was quick to correct the misunderstanding, but, regretfully, in some quarters the notion still persists.

F. Emerson Andrews also writes about responses to the congressional Select (Cox) Committee's question "In your opinion, has the public a direct interest in tax-exempt foundations and comparable organizations?" Even though the majority of replies were in the affirmative, he quotes one respondent from the House Hearings as follows:

In our opinion the fact that a foundation has been exempted from taxation does not of itself give any 'direct interest' to the public, any more than the public has a direct interest in Harvard University, Yale University, or any other privately endowed educational institution, or in all of the churches of the United States, by virtue of the fact that those organizations are exempt from taxation.[24]

Karl Meyer, a contemporary commentator on art museums, writes about the public interest in charitable property in *The Art Museum*:

A museum does not "own" but, rather, is the steward of the art it possesses. On this point, common law is explicit: *No charitable institution may "own" corporate property.* A director is accountable by law to his shareholders, and if he is shown to be negligent in managing their property, there are legal consequences to be paid. In a museum, it is the public that are the shareholders and museum trustees are legally accountable for any malfeasance.[25] (Emphasis added)

The Fiduciary Principle

In 1985, when Attorney General Dave Frohnmayer of Oregon sent the annual report form to charitable organizations, he included an open letter to all trustees and directors, which contained the following statement:

Trustees and charitable corporation officers and directors have a fiduciary relationship to the charitable organization, often referred to as the fiduciary's principal. An Oregon court recently summarized the fiduciary's legal obligation as follows:

"A fiduciary is legally bound in equity and good conscience to act in good faith and for the best interests of his principal. A fiduciary's loyalty must be to his principal. Any conduct which is intended to place a fiduciary's own interests or any other party ahead of the best interest of the principal is a breach of the fiduciary's duty."

You are serving in a very worthwhile position which is highly valued by society. However, it is also a position that carries with it important responsibilities and trust.[26]

Fiduciary, in general, means holding or held in trust, and the Latin for trust is *fides*, from which our word *confidential* derives. As a noun, *fiduciary* means one in whom a trust or confidence is reposed. An individual who serves as a charitable trustee owes a fiduciary duty to the public, which reposes confidence in the trustee to manage the charitable trust for the public.

More than a half century ago, Benjamin Cardozo (later Mr. Justice Cardozo), then chief judge of New York, made his now classic statement on the obligation of the trustee as a fiduciary to act fairly in the interests of the beneficiary. He wrote:

Many forms of conduct permissible in a workaday world for those acting at arm's length, are forbidden to those bound by fiduciary ties. A trustee is held to something stricter than the morals of the market place. Not honesty alone, but the punctilio of an honor the most sensitive, is then the standard of behavior. As to this there has developed a tradition that is unbending and inveterate. Uncompromising rigidity has been the attitude of courts of equity when petitioned to undermine the rule of undivided loyalty by the "disintegrating erosion" of particular exceptions . . . . Only thus has the level of conduct for fiduciaries been kept at a level higher than that trodden by the crowd.[27] (Citations omitted)

Equity

In his statement Chief Justice Cardozo mentions courts of equity as opposed to courts of law. The term *courts of equity* refers to courts that administer justice according to the system of "fairness, justness, and right dealing."[28] Equity courts, serving as an alternative to the harsh rules of common law, are sometimes called courts of chancery. Equity is based on a system of rules and principles that originated in England in the fifteenth century, when courts of chancery began to enforce charitable uses or trusts, that is, property left to trustees (legal owners) to use for unnamed beneficiaries (equitable owners). Remedies in equity aim at reparation, as opposed to punishment, and have the added strong feature that future actions conform to the judgment of the court. The late Austin Wakeman Scott, the well-known legal scholar on trusts, has said that if it had not been for the development of separate courts of law and equity, we would probably not have the modern-day trust.[29]

Trustees—with malice toward none, with charity for all—hold an awesome responsibility for which they are legally accountable. Charged with the task of running the charitable organization for the public good, charitable trustees are ultimately accountable to the public.

Structure of Trusteeship

What structural guidelines shepherd trustee action? Beyond the fact that trustees must manage the nonprofit organization for the public good, specific guidelines depend on many complex variables that differ among states and among types of institutions.

Because rules vary from state to state, a trustee must become familiar with the interpretation of the law the courts have given in a particular jurisdiction. A jurisdiction refers to the power of a court to hear and determine a case. Without jurisdiction, the court's judgment is void. At the risk of treading on too many exceptions to the rule, here are a few general ideas.

The two basic organizational structures for private nonprofit institutions are the *charitable trust* and the *charitable corporation*. Leonard DuBoff, the noted legal art scholar, says that charitable trust is governed by common law and statutory rules for trusts, whereas the charitable corporation is purely a creature of statute, and the rules for its conduct will emanate from the state not-for-profit statutes, as interpreted by the courts.[30]

Two theories of ownership have evolved over the years: "trustee owner" and "absolute owner." In the former the public is deemed to hold equitable property interest, whereas in the latter the public does not. In either instance, the trustees must honor a donor's wishes and be accountable.

The concept of the trust, originating in England, carries a dual ownership pattern: a legal owner (who manages the trust without personal monetary profit) and a beneficial owner (who receives the benefit from the trust). In the case of a charitable trust, the beneficial owner is the public at large. The fact that a trust incorporates itself or that a nonprofit organization is incorporated does not destroy the essence of the charitable trust concept—the public character of the charity.

The charitable trust and charitable corporation are not antipodal entities. In both organizational structures the trustee owes a duty of loyalty (faithfulness) and a duty of care (watchful attention). Even though a legal distinction can be drawn between a charitable trust and a charitable corporation, especially in determining the standard of care to which a trustee is held, the rules concerning dedication to public purposes are applicable to both.

The *Restatement (Second) of the Law of Trusts*, a compendium of common law, is quite specific on this point. It reads: "Ordinarily the principles and rules applicable to charitable trusts are applicable to charitable corporations."[31] The form of the charity—trust or corporation—does not destroy the charitable institution's public character, use, or purpose.

In this country neither the Constitution nor its amendments, nor the Congress, nor state legislatures have taken any statutory action that limits or redefines the common law purpose of charitable institutions to serve the public good. The Latin phrase often used for the *public good* is *pro bono publico*.

Structure may seem to obfuscate the common law, and indeed it has in certain courts. But if an organization declares itself to be eleemosynary, or charitable (that is, operating with the sole purpose of serving the public good and with no motivation for profit—proprietary interest), its organizational structure makes no fundamental difference in its legal accountability to use its resources, to manage property, and to exercise its stated purposes in its charter and bylaws for the interests of the public and no other. This is true despite the fact that it may once have been a proprietary institution or that it exists structurally as a corporation or trust or as a quasi arm of government, such as a municipal school board or public university.

This public interest guides trustees in managing the charitable enterprise entrusted to their care. With the special gifts and skills that trustees possess, they hold a legal and ethical responsibility to make the charitable organization useful for the public good—your good and mine.

3

HOSPITALS

The word "hospital," at least in its popular usage, ordinarily denotes a charitable institution .... It is only where income may be used for the profit of the owners that a hospital corporation ceases to be a charity.

In re Pelton's Will, New York Court of Appeals, 1947

Nothing is so permanent as change. Health-care planners will increasingly realize the significance of this proverb as myriad political, social, and economic forces emerge during the next several years. Our conception of health care and how it can best be offered and financed will almost certainly undergo major changes in the next decade. Currently there is a general lack of consensus within the health-care community about such problems as cost, quality, access, and governance. Of deeper concern is the lack of unanimity in terms of resolving the difficulties. In this climate of change, one that possibly threatens the system itself, the policymakers—hospital trustees—will need to shift from a reactive role to one of demonstrable leadership in health-care policy-making.

Medical staffs and hospital administrations often proclaim decision-making responsibilities that clearly are not theirs. Accountability for health care rests squarely on the shoulders of hospital trustees, who are perceived as having no vested interest in the health-care system, because their role is voluntary. Because of their volunteer status, but more importantly because of their fiduciary status to serve the public, trustees are in a position to make informed, unbiased judgments about the future of health-care and hospital policy. This ponderous responsibility calls for courage, informed judgment, and wisdom. Most assuredly the decisions made in a hospital affect the broader community.

In discharging their leadership roles, however, trustees cannot plunge in with imperious or arbitrary decrees, no matter how wise or courageous the decisions may appear. The public retains constitutional and legal rights. As the *Boston Globe* so aptly pointed out during the controversy over the possible sale of the world-renowned psychiatric hospital, McLean Hospital in Belmont, Massachusetts, "The trustees of all institutions involved should remind themselves that they are exactly that—trustees—and move with great caution."[1]

Hospital trustees, like all charitable trustees, hold a responsibility for the public good, and when trustees violate this public trust, the courts have demonstrated their willingness to intervene. As the New Hampshire Supreme Court states, "More recently courts have recognized that the public has a substantial interest in the operation of private hospitals and that of necessity in the public interest some measure of control by the courts is called for."[2] The decision of the New Hampshire Supreme Court is clear despite the independent status of nonprofit hospitals, for they still have the duty to account to the court. In accounting to the court, trustees are expected to render clear, unequivocal statements.

Regardless of the manner in which a hospital was created, whether by private bill by a legislature or under a franchise granted pursuant to a general not-for-profit code authorizing a charter, nonprofit (private) hospitals are legally classified as public charities because they are devoted to public health without private gain and are supported by nontaxable endowments solicited from the public. It may be added that this is true of all eleemosynary institutions, that is, hospitals, museums, colleges, universities, libraries, and so on.

Thus, to be effective, trustees must be courageous enough to take the lead in forging policy for the future, but at the same time they must be cautious enough to act within the limits of their fiduciary duties. The first several cases that follow offer insight into basic principles and constraints of hospital trusteeship. They also discuss who has the right to bring suit should conflict develop.

THE CHARTER

Central to a charitable organization's activities is its charter. As the governing instrument the charter determines what the charitable organization can or cannot do. Various terms may be used to describe the organic document of a charitable organization, such as *charter, articles of incorporation, certificate of incorporation, articles of association, articles of organization*, and *articles of agreement*. They all mean essentially the same thing.

The broad provisions of statutes permitting the establishment of charitable corporations allow charter charitable purposes to be stated in quite general terms—for example: the welfare of humankind. Even though the management of a charitable enterprise is afforded a great deal of discretion, there are also limits. A charter granted to a charitable corporation is not an unlimited license.

Hospital management determines how hospitals interpret their charters to deliver health-care services. It is now quite fashionable for hospitals to change from nonprofit to profit-making status through lease and other arrangements, often without appropriate consideration for the public interest. The outcome is still uncertain in terms of whether this trend meets fiduciary obligations to the public or even whether this is the best way to deliver health care at the lowest cost. It is currently a hot issue.

Operating in an environment marked with considerable inflation and ever-escalating costs, trustees of nonprofit (charitable) hospitals are joining the divestiture carousel ride to for-profit status. The movement to the profit-making takeover of nonprofit hospitals is based in part on the belief that the profit-making sector is, as some economists proclaim, more efficient because the profit sector has the appropriate incentives to be responsive to market forces. Recent research, however, has begun to punch holes in this so-called commonsensible business argument.

The public interest in hospitals carries a legal concern in terms of both the uses and benefits of hospital property. One of the earlier and more interesting examples of this new trend is the case of the Queen of Angels Hospital[3] (hereafter, Queen or *Queen*), whose board of directors attempted to change the hospital's charitable purpose.

To Know the Hawk from the Handsaw: Queen of Angels Hospital, Los Angeles, California

The Powers Granted. As a nonprofit corporation chartered in 1927, Queen's articles of incorporation state that the corporation's purposes are to establish, own, maintain, and operate a hospital in the City of Los Angeles. In 1971 Queen's board of directors decided to lease the hospital to a private, profit-making corporation for at least twenty-five years. The minimum annual rental guaranteed Queen was $1 million per year. Queen intended to use a substantial portion of this money to establish medical clinics in Los Angeles, which would dispense free medical care, aid, and advice to the needy. Another portion of the lease funds were to be used to set up a retirement plan for an unincorporated religious association that had offered free services (valued at $16 million) to the hospital over the years.

The attorney general of California, however, objected to both the lease arrangement and the retirement plan. In response to the attorney general, Queen's board of directors filed a petition for declaratory relief. (A petition for declaratory relief is a legal procedure that permits trustees to seek instructions from a court. The court's action is sometimes referred to as a declaratory judgment.)

The purpose of the board's action was to determine not only the validity of the lease agreement between Queen and the private hospital corporation but also the legality of the retirement plan agreement between Queen and the religious association. (Many, but not all, actions involving charities are for declaratory judgments.)

From the beginning no one disputed that an outpatient clinic was functionally equivalent to a hospital. However, the attorney general contended that "under its articles of incorporation, Queen held its assets in trust primarily for the purpose of operating a hospital, and the use of those assets exclusively for outpatient clinics would constitute an abandonment of Queen's primary charitable purpose and a diversion of charitable assets."[4] Citing a previous case, the California

Supreme Court declared that the rules governing the use of assets of charitable organizations are well established. "All the assets of a corporation organized solely for charitable purposes must be deemed to be impressed with a charitable trust by virtue of the express declaration of the corporation's purposes . . . ."[5]

Applying this rationale, the court stated that the issue in *Queen* was not whether clinics were equal to or better than operating a hospital, but whether clinics were authorized by its charter. The question was not whether Queen could use some of its assets or the proceeds from the operation of the hospital for purposes other than running a hospital—it certainly could and had been doing so. The question was whether it could cease to perform the primary purpose for which it was organized. The court would not allow Queen, created for the purposes of establishing and running a hospital, to discontinue operation in favor of establishing neighborhood clinics, despite the fact that they were charitable in nature.

To cease operation as a hospital and become a clinic would constitute a breach of trust, which occurs when there is a violation of duty by a trustee either by omission or commission. Thus, if the board of directors were to consummate the deal, it would be performing acts beyond those authorized by its charter. When a board of trustees acts beyond its expressed or implied powers, the act or agreement may be held to be *ultra vires*, that is, beyond the powers granted (discussed below).

Sound Business Judgment. The second major issue in the case focused on the multimillion-dollar claim for the value of past services rendered, submitted by the religious association shortly after the board of directors had decided to lease the hospital. The board had settled the claim with the association by establishing a retirement plan for its members. This was to be funded with a portion of the lease proceeds.

Concerning the board's obligations, the court said: "Although the claim for compensation for past services was made in good faith and was not a dishonest claim, 'there was no basis for such claim . . . .' The compromise of the claim— e.g., the retirement plan—'was not a proper exercise of sound business judgment or of the fiduciary duties of Queens' Board.' "[6] Thus, the court held that Queen had no lawful obligation to repay the religious association, that the compromise agreement was invalid, that the retirement plan was invalid, and that if implemented, the plan would constitute a diversion of charitable assets.

The case leaves little doubt that trustees, while acting in good faith, must realize the legal limits of their authority and discretion. Board members in their fiduciary capacity have obligations not only to the public at large but also to the charitable organization's purpose as granted in the charter. The court will not generally interfere with the internal management of charitable trusts unless there are acts complained of as fraudulent, illegal, or *ultra vires*. In this case, the attorney general blew the whistle.

Just as a plasterer and a carpenter need to know a hawk from a handsaw, so should the trustee know the tools of trusteeship. One trustee tool is the charter with its accompanying scope of authority. Not only can the corporation be held liable for acting beyond the scope of its authority but also individual members may be individually responsible for *ultra vires* acts when they exceed the powers of the corporation for individual gain or profit.

ULTRA VIRES

Many legal doctrines, such as *ultra vires*, apply similarly to governmental and nongovernmental institutions, but there can be a difference between for-profit and nonprofit institutions. The doctrine of *ultra vires* serves as a good example for demonstrating how for-profit corporate case law can differ from the law applicable to nonprofit corporations. "*Ultra vires*, although nearly completely dead as a business corporation theory," according to Lizabeth Moody, "has a continuing vitality in the realm of the nonprofit corporations where purposes are central to the whole concept."[7] This concept suggests possible serious repercussions if hospitals become for-profit business.

Queen illustrates the principle of *ultra vires* in the instance of a charitable nongovernmental hospital; the Callaway Memorial Hospital[8] (Callaway) case demonstrates the use of the principle in a governmental charitable hospital, governed by state statute.

Buyer Beware: Callaway Memorial Hospital, Fulton, Missouri

Scope of Powers. Callaway, organized as a county hospital by the County of Callaway, Missouri, issued notes "with recourse"—a term used in endorsing negotiable instruments by which the endorser indicates that the individual remains liable for payment of the instrument. The Fulton National Bank purchased sixty-two notes, and on maturity the bank made demand for payment. When the hospital did not pay, the bank sued to recover alleged losses of $26,404.35 with 8 percent interest.

In 1967 the Supreme Court of Missouri held that Callaway, as an arm of county government, had no authority to endorse with recourse notes executed by the hospital. "There is no authority," declared the court, "whatever in our statutes which would permit the hospital to endorse these notes with recourse."[9] The court then held that such endorsements were *ultra vires* and void. The law of Missouri is clear that all contracts with municipalities must be in writing and be authorized by law. The bank, the purchaser of the notes, could not seek recovery of payment made under contract even though the hospital may have received a benefit. A contract entered into by a municipality beyond the scope of its powers is void.

It's a Matter of Law. In the eyes of the law the Callaway incident is analogous to the situation involving a minor who is presumed not to have the capacity to enter into certain relationships (for example, contracts), and therefore the courts will intervene to protect the minor just as it interdicted the bank from the recovery of alleged losses. It is of interest to note that the court never verified the bank's claim as to the actual dollar amount the hospital allegedly owed on the note, for the point of law took precedence over everything else.

Along with the hospital, the individual trustees were sued; however, the court reasoned that they had not endorsed the notes, either as individuals or on behalf of the hospital, and they received no consideration.[10] The court decided that the trustees, as individuals, were not liable. On the other hand, had there been personal gain by the trustees, the outcome might have been different.

THE ATTORNEY GENERAL—THE GATEKEEPER

As noted in the Queen case, it was the attorney general who objected to the decisions made by the board of directors. The rationale for this follows. Unlike a private trust with named beneficiaries, the charitable trust with unnamed beneficiaries is almost always enforced by a representative of the public: the attorney general of the state or a county law officer. His or her powers generally extend equally to charitable corporations and to charitable trusts because "in both cases the Attorney General can maintain a suit to prevent a diversion of the property to other purposes than those for which it was given; and in both cases the doctrine of cy pres is applicable."[11] (*Cy pres* refers to the legal procedure that equity will use to substitute another charitable object believed to approach the original purpose as closely as possible when a charity is or becomes illegal or impossible or impractical vis-à-vis fulfillment. The courts, however, are careful in making sure the charitable objects cannot be carried out, and the court will find a similar charitable purpose within the general intent of the donor.)

The next case, *Holt v. College of Osteopathic Physicians and Surgeons* (hereafter, *Holt*), describes the attorney general's role with the following comment:

Since there is usually no one willing to assume the burdens of a legal action, or who could properly represent the interests of the trust or the public, the Attorney General has been empowered to oversee charities as the representative of the public, a practice having its origins in early common law.[12]

The attorney general's enforcement powers antedate the passing of the famous Statute of Elizabeth in 1601. In this regard, Professor Austin Wakeman Scott comments:

In England the records show that even before the enactment of the Statute of Charitable Uses in 1601 suits were brought by the Attorney-General to enforce charitable trusts. The community has an interest in the enforcement of such trusts and the Attorney General represents the community in seeing that the trusts are properly performed . . . . The suit may be brought by the Attorney General on his own initiative, or it may be brought by him on the relation of a third person. The relator need not have any direct interest in the enforcement of the trust.[13]

Traditionally, public supervision of charitable property has been delegated to the English attorney general to be performed as an exercise of his *parens patriae* powers. The term *parens patriae* (parent of his country) was used in England to refer to the monarch's duty to protect property devoted to charitable uses, although that duty was executed by the attorney general who represented the Crown. In this country *parens patriae* refers to the people of the state. Following the English tradition, the attorney general represents the interests of the state in enforcing charitable funds.

As the common law devolved on the states and federal government, the attorney general came to represent the state and its interests in charities. He or she holds a prerogative right not only to protect but also to enforce all charities, as well as to represent interests of the community at large. These are the ancient powers of guardianship over persons under disability and of protectorship of the public interest in charities.[14]

The broad powers of the attorney general are summarized by Austin Scott as follows:

Not only may the Attorney General bring a proceeding to enforce a charitable trust or to enforce the obligations of a charitable corporation, but he is ordinarily a necessary party and is entitled to be heard, when a proceeding is brought for permission to deviate from the terms of the trust, or to apply the doctrine of cy pres. So too he is entitled to be heard in a proceeding to terminate a charitable trust, or in a proceeding to approve a compromise. However, in all these matters his consent or nonconsent, though important, is not binding on the court.[15]

Although the legal status of charitable organizations has changed with respect to standards of conventional tort law (civil wrong) or to the standards of fiduciary (trust) responsibility, the role of the attorney general in the enforcement of charities has not. In some jurisdictions such as Illinois, where the attorney general is a constitutional officer, the powers of this officer over charitable trusts cannot be cut back or abrogated; they can only be strengthened and expanded by the legislature.[16]

MINORITY TRUSTEES' RIGHT TO SUE

Getting the Cold Shoulder from the Majority: College of Osteopathic Physicians and Surgeons, Fullerton, California

Cotrustees Bring Suit. In 1964 a minority group of three trustees of the College of Osteopathic Physicians and Surgeons[17] (hereafter, COPS) gained the court's approval over the attorney general's objections to maintain a suit against the majority trustees of the charitable corporation. The principle in this case, that minority trustees of a nonprofit corporation may bring suit, has now been codified in California. On the other hand, the new nonprofit corporation law abrogates the application of the trustee's rules of the California Civil Code and to that extent overrules *Holt*.[18] It may be added, however, that where the statutes are silent, the courts will probably analogize from trust law.

COPS, at the time, held assets in excess of $1.5 million in trust. The minority contended that the majority threatened to divert the assets of COPS to purposes other than those for which it had been created and for which COPS had in the past solicited and received funds in trust. They sought to have the court interpret the trust's charitable purposes, as well as to decide whether the conduct of the majority trustees would be contrary to these purposes and therefore a breach of charitable trust.

The court, however, dismissed the case, sustaining a formal objection of the majority trustees that the minority trustees had not stated sufficient grounds to bring an action. The minority trustees appealed the lower court's decision to the California Supreme Court, which held that the minority trustees did have sufficient grounds for a suit. Although the court never made a decision on the alleged violation of corporate purposes, the court's in-depth treatment of the case can be instructive to trustees.

Two major questions emerged from this case: (1) Were the majority trustees in violation of the charitable purposes of COPS? (2) Did the three minority trustees have the right to sue the corporation without the consent of the attorney general?

As background information for addressing the first question, the distinction between *allopathic* and *osteopathic* medicine must be clarified.

Allopathic medicine is the generally accepted medical method of the mainstream health-care establishment. Osteopathic medicine emphasizes medical treatment by manipulation of the bones and muscles, although it includes all types of medical and physical therapy. In an osteopathic school students are educated and trained in the principles of osteopathic medicine. These methods are not taught at medical schools teaching the allopathic theory of medicine. Physicians receiving their training at osteopathic schools are known as osteopaths, and they make up a separate and distinct profession although practicing the diagnosis and treatment of all human ailments.[19]

The charter of COPS states its purposes to be the following:

To establish, maintain, carry on and conduct an osteopathic medical and surgical college, in which all branches of learning, and instruction which now pertain or which may in the future pertain to the science and art of health maintenance; prevention, relief and recovery from disease, as well as any or all academic subjects desirable or necessary as a foundation for the teaching of such branches.[20]

From the time of its incorporation in 1914, COPS continuously operated an osteopathic medical and surgical college that prepared individuals to enter osteopathic medicine. Throughout its existence COPS presented itself as a medical institution whose *raison d'être* was to provide training in osteopathic medicine.

On such grounds, COPS received benefactions for its chartered purposes. The American Osteopathic Association, a national organization whose objective is the furtherance of osteopathic medicine and surgery in the United States, had on application from COPS awarded scholarship funds and research grants.

Canceling an Identity. In the litigation, the minority charged that the majority trustees had made application to the Association of American Medical Colleges and to the Council on Medical Education and Hospitals of the American Medical Association to become an approved allopathic medical school, rather than remaining an osteopathic medical college. The majority also had resolved to amend the charter of COPS to change the name of the school, deleting the word *osteopathic* so as to have only residual identity as an osteopathic hospital.

These acts, the minority trustees alleged, were "abandoning and repudiating the charitable purpose of COPS to conduct an osteopathic medical and surgical college and to convert COPS into a school teaching nonosteopathic medicine and surgery according to the allopathic school of medicine."[21]

Filing an answer to the minority trustees' complaint, the attorney general, as the defendant, denied that trust assets were being diverted from their charitable purpose. But the court held that "although the public in general may benefit from any number of charitable purposes, charitable contributions must be used only for the purposes for which they were received in trust."[22] The public interest is a necessary condition, but it is not sufficient in determining the use of charitable bequests.

The other major issue the court resolved centered on the following question: Did the three minority trustees have the capacity to sue the corporation without the consent of the attorney general? The law varies from state to state as to whether the attorney general has the exclusive right to bring suit.

The dispute over the issue emanated from the earlier Pepperdine case,[23] in which the California District Court of Appeal held that "the assets of a charitable corporation, in the final analysis, belong to the state and a suit for their recovery can be maintained only by the officer designated by law."[24] Subsequently, in 1960, legal scholar Kenneth Karst published a classic paper titled "The Efficiency of the Charitable Dollar,"[25] in which he severely criticized the Pepperdine decision.

When this issue emerged again in *Holt*, the defendant trustees, clinging to the holding in *Pepperdine*, took the position that the attorney general was the only person empowered to bring suit in cases involving charitable organizations.[26]

In deciding the question of whether minority trustees could sue majority trustees without this consent, the court said, "The prevailing view of other jurisdictions is that the Attorney General does not have exclusive power to enforce a charitable trust and that a trustee or other person having a sufficient special interest may also bring an action for this purpose"[27] (citations omitted).

Thus, in *Holt* the court held that the minority trustees had the capacity to bring action on behalf of COPS against the majority trustees to enjoin any breach of trust that was threatened.[28] Rationalizing that trustees possess a special vantage point because of their deep knowledge of the affairs of the charitable enterprise they administer, the court, citing Karst, said: "The charity's own representative has at least as much interest in preserving the charitable funds as does the Attorney General who represents the general public. The cotrustee is also in the best position to learn about breaches of trust and to bring the relevant facts to a court's attention."[29]

As often is the case, the majority trustees argued in their defense that the safeguards afforded by corporate law in the area of privately owned corporations were applicable. But the court reasoned that charitable trustees as fiduciaries had a special interest wholly unlike that of a private corporate shareholder, making the differences between private and charitable corporations as an analogy valueless.[30]

Kenneth Karst vigorously maintains that the "law should recognize that the charitable trust and the charitable corporation have more in common with each other than each has with its private counterpart. The important differences among charities relate not to their form but to their function."[31]

The majority trustees also built their defense, at least in part, on the distinction between a charitable corporation and a charitable trust. They contended that "members of a governing board of a charitable corporation are not truly trustees and that a different rule applies to them."[32]

Holt offers a cogent discussion for the common law basis of charitable institutions. As in *Holt*, litigants often attempt to draw a distinction between a charitable trust and a charitable corporation.

Trust Versus Corporation. A charitable trust may be distinguished from a charitable corporation by origin and by its governance. A trust's origin is court created, being governed by common law (case law) and statutory rules for trusts. The corporation's governance, however, is purely a creature of statute, and the rules for its conduct generally emanate from the state not-for-profit corporation statutes and applicable trust law (as interpreted by the courts). An extensive body of literature on the distinction is available. The principal difference is that trustees of a charitable trust exist as individuals (although they take action as a group), but trustees or directors of charitable corporations exist as body corporate. The principal reason for incorporating is to protect individual trustees from legal action. When action is brought (unless, for example, there is fraudulent or illegal behavior on the part of an individual trustee), the action is against the corporation itself, rather than against the individual trustee.

Austin Scott states that "in the case of a charitable corporation the members of the board of management, whether called directors or trustees, are not trustees in the strict sense. The title to the property is in the corporate entity and not in the individuals who constitute the board."[33] However, the trustees of a corporation are responsible for the management of corporate affairs, and as such they "are in a fiduciary relation not merely to the institution itself but to the beneficiaries of the trust administered by the institution."[34]

Marion Fremont-Smith expresses deep concern about the fiduciary responsibilities and the legal milieu. She writes:

Some attorneys argue that the fiduciary duties of corporate directors are not as strict as those of trustees; they often rely improperly on court decisions rendered when some of the states did not recognize the validity of charitable trusts to establish the basis for a difference. [She advocates that] this problem must be solved by the development of a body of case law or by the enactment of legislation clearly stating that differences of form are immaterial in determining the duties of charitable fiduciaries.[35]

Recognizing that trustees of a charitable corporation do not have all the attributes of a trustee of a charitable trust, the California Supreme Court in *Holt* said that the trustees of a charitable corporation do not individually hold legal title to corporate property and are not personally liable for corporate liabilities. In either instance, however, the individual trustees are the people solely responsible for administering the trust assets, and in both cases they are fiduciaries in performing their trust duties.

Citing the classic statement from the *Restatement (Second) of Trusts* that "rules governing charitable trusts ordinarily apply to charitable corporations," the court decided that since minority trustees of a charitable trust were empowered to bring suit, there was no reason for the minority trustees of a charitable corporation not being able to do likewise.[36]

PROFIT AND NONPROFIT WEBS

The Aborted Hospital Sale: McLean Hospital, Belmont, Massachusetts

The McLean Hospital, a prestigious charitable psychiatric hospital in Belmont, Massachusetts, was founded in 1811. It was the third mental hospital in the United States and the first in New England. In November 1983, bowing to intense pressure, the chairman of the board of trustees of McLean Hospital Corporation declared in a news conference that the sale of the prestigious 328–bed McLean Hospital, a nonprofit hospital, to a profit-making chain was off. The proposed sale fizzled out because of a torrent of fiery opposition from almost every quarter.

Before 1980 the Massachusetts General Hospital Corporation (MGHC) held legal responsibility for both the McLean and Massachusetts General (MGH) hospitals. In 1980 two new corporations were formed: one for Massachusetts General Hospital and one for McLean Hospital. Even though each corporation had its own board, the membership composition of each was the same twelve individuals. MGHC, serving as the parent corporation, was the sole membership corporation of both MGH and McLean. Its major responsibilities were appointing trustees, managing endowment funds, and fund-raising.[37]

Concern Expressed. In its own sphere of health care, each hospital is regarded as among the best in the world. The then-proposed sale of McLean to the Hospital Corporation of America (HCA), a profit-making, Nashville-based corporation, raised the hackles of many individuals and groups—particularly the Harvard Medical School Faculty—because McLean is a major teaching center in psychiatry for the Harvard Medical School, and many doctors hold joint appointments with the two institutions. A report by a faculty advisory committee to the administration of the Harvard Medical School urged rejection of the sale to HCA "on the grounds that it would be destructive for the school to enter an agreement strongly opposed by faculty at both McLean and MGH."[38]

The medical staff's concerns were buttressed by Dr. Arnold S. Relman, editor of the *New England Journal of Medicine*, a vehement opponent of the proposed sale. Dr. Relman published an artfully worded editorial[39] against the sale in the *Journal*. He also printed a special article[40] reporting a comparative study based on data gathered in California showing that price, not management efficiency, made profits. Both articles were timely and, of course, devastating to the proponents of the sale of McLean.

Dr. Relman emphatically warned the faculty advisory committee about the possibility of "serious conflicts of interest" should Harvard tie up with a for-profit health-care company in a medical or research agreement. The medical staff reflected on the fact that teaching hospitals should not be influenced by the motivation for profit. Had the sale been consummated, McLean would have been owned and managed by a profit-based corporation whose accountability was to shareholders who received dividend checks. The medical staff rejected the notion of profit status for McLean because it represented a "violation of the public trust."[41]

HCA is currently strong. But what about the future? Divestiture, breakup, relocation, reorganization—each is a real possibility under adverse circumstances. Were such conditions to occur, the posture of a for-profit corporation during a period of financial exigencies would be necessarily different from that of a not-for-profit corporation. Accountability is to the stockholder in a for-profit enterprise, not to the public as is the case in a nonprofit organization in which the public interest is the foremost consideration. McLean, although not a poor person's hospital, since only 2 percent of its patients receive assistance in the form of reduced rates or free care, is still a charitable hospital chartered to operate for the public good.

In fact, as the chairman of the board declared, McLean was neither broke nor even near the point of bankruptcy. Moreover, it was in the early stages of a $28 million capital fund-raising campaign.

The *Boston Globe* reported the price tag for McLean to be a rich $40 to $60 million.[42] Thus, one of the world's most prestigious psychiatric hospitals would have been wafted from the nonprofit to the profit sector with the only apparent justification, according to the press, being the need to raise some fast cash for

MGH "bricks and mortar."[43] Surely a public trust entails more than the swish of a pen!

The Real Issue. Stripped to the bare bones, the sale of McLean not only would have been a fat plum for HCA, adding immeasurable distinction to its growing chain of profit-making hospitals, but also would have meant divesting MGHC (and thereby the citizens of the Commonwealth of Massachusetts) of one of its most precious treasures—in favor of enriching the treasury of MGH in Boston.

The contemplated sale at first seemed to carry all the friendly colors, but on closer inspection the Jolly Roger became more apparent, and the whole deal began to sour as prominent citizens and leading opinion makers began to question its efficacy—much as one would question the efficacy of a drug formerly popular in use but now of questionable value. This questioning in turn led to a ground swell of caustic criticism in the press and elsewhere. The board of trustees wisely decided to call off the sale before running the risk of being hoisted on its own petard.

Even though the public in general may benefit from any number of charitable purposes, charitable contributions must be used only for the purpose for which they were received in trust. Over the years McLean had represented to the public that it was a mental health hospital, and funds had been solicited from the public for McLean and mental health purposes. Such acts bind the trustees to the primary purpose of operating a mental health hospital. As the court observed in *Queen*, " . . . The character of an institution is to be determined, not alone by the powers of the corporation as defined in its charter, but also by the manner of conducting its activities."[44]

Using the proceeds from the sale of McLean for MGH, while benefiting the public interest, may not have fulfilled the articles of incorporation requirements. Perhaps the most significant factor in the contemplated sale of McLean was not the possible threat of formal action by the attorney general, but rather the public pressure brought to bear on the trustees, nurtured in large part by an adverse press, which threatened a serious loss of public image. Public perception became a potent force in encouraging the McLean governing board to reconsider its fiduciary duties as a charitable trustee.

Recent Developments at McLean. Almost before the dust settled from the tiff over the sale of McLean, the trustees whipped up a new plan. In December 1985 the McLean trustees secured a $30 million tax-exempt bond from the Massachusetts Health and Educational Facilities Authority (MHEFA), a body politic and corporate and public instrumentality of the Commonwealth of Massachusetts. (In short, MHEFA is a state agency that arranges tax-exempt bond issues for qualified nonprofit corporations.)[45]

Barely two months later McLean announced a breathtaking plan, in the offing for more than eighteen months: that it was forming a joint venture with American Medical International (AMI) of Beverly Hills, California, a profit-making corporation. The name of the new joint corporation was the McLean Health Services,

Inc. (MHS). Another, but new, corporate angel appeared on the horizon in connection with the 328–bed mental hospital. In making the announcement, the trustees stated that $11 million would be made available through the new corporation (MHS) to McLean, and that these new funds would be comingled with the $30 million tax-exempt bonds garnered from MHEFA in order to move forward with new construction and renovations.[46]

Under the agreement the trustees assured that "McLean Hospital [would] remain an independent, non-profit corporation governed by the McLean Hospital Corporation Board of Trustees."[47] Just as with the former proposed sale to HCA, the joint venture represented a pleasing, savory plum for AMI because the deal carried McLean's prestige and good will. This rather nice gift was openly admitted.

Dr. Francis de Marneffe, general director for McLean, said, "While McLean and its staff offer one of the most prestigious mental programs in the country, AMI provides the partnership with strong organizational resources, including marketing expertise, insurance products and services, and advanced information services."[48] About this latest development Dr. Relman

predicted that the venture could face "a tough balancing act" to avoid conflicts of interest.
. . . Academic health centers are all under siege. This arrangement is clearly preferable to a sale or a lease, clearly more financially advantageous. Nevertheless, there are disturbing implications. American International is buying Harvard's reputation and Harvard's skill. There will be powerful pressures on McLean staff to cooperate with McLean Health Services.[49]

As noted in the MHEFA bond issue, dated 12 December 1985, McLean outlined the key points of the agreement with AMI. Some are as follows:

1. McLean will retain its status as a not-for-profit corporation under Internal Revenue Code section 501(c)(3); will remain an affiliate of the Massachusetts General Hospital [MGH] and will continue as a teaching hospital affiliated with the Harvard Medical School . . . .

3. It is contemplated that the new corporation will be initially capitalized at $11.0 million, $8.0 million provided by AMI, $3.0 million provided by McLean. This $11.0 million will be used to purchase from McLean access to the McLean staff, programs and goodwill. Additional working capital requirements, as needed, will be contributed by each party in a manner to be determined . . . .

5. *Profits*, if any, from the new corporation [McLean Health Services, Inc.] will be shared equally by AMI and McLean.[50] (Emphasis added)

The prospectus also notes that the excess of revenues over expenditures for the years 1983 through 1985 are $2.4 million, $2.6 million, and $3.1 million, respectively.[51] There appears to be a comfortable margin in the immediate future to meet financial obligations.

FUTURE DIRECTIONS FOR CHARITABLE HOSPITALS

Legal Scholar Howard Oleck cautions that the mixing of profit and nonprofit purposes and operations not only produces a hypocritical scheme for self-enrichment in the name of the public interest but also creates a regulatory nightmare for state and federal regulatory agencies.[52] The moment of critical concern in profit and nonprofit ventures will likely center on conflict of interest, that is, breach of trust.

Further, how long the law will allow tax-exempt institutions to engage in profit-making schemes is a matter for the IRS and the Congress. Perhaps they will come forward with regulations and laws to end this possible abuse, as they did with foundation hypocrisy a decade or two ago.

Because the beneficiaries of charitable trusts are indefinite or unnamed—which is the essence of a charitable trust—few individuals ever think of their beneficial interests, leaving to trustees the operation of charitable enterprises with little interference. The public has come to accept the trustee *maxim*: "What we do is noble—regardless!" However, Chris Welles aptly warns, "Unless trustees of nonprofit institutions take the initiative in purging their organizations of conflict-of-interest problems, they may eventually face a new wave of public criticism, legal challenges, and perhaps even new federal legislation."[53]

The Pennsylvania Supreme Court once lucidly noted, "Every dollar a public institution saves in tax levy becomes an extra stone in the heavy sack the Commonwealth piles on every taxpayer's back."[54] The common-law status of charitable institutions must be reaffirmed. It forbids business purposes in a nonprofit enterprise. When a profit is turned in any entity, the enterprise ceases to be a charity. If a nonprofit institution wishes to retain its special privileges, such as tax-exemption, it should disgorge itself of any relationship with a profit-making corporation. Taxpayers should not be expected to help finance dividend checks.

A Flaw in the Plan: Hahnemann Hospital, Brighton, Massachusetts

Redesigning a Charity. Important as the philosophical question is about quality health care being offered for its own sake as opposed to profit making, the concern in the Hahnemann case is with the trustees' right to sell all, or substantially all, of the nonprofit hospital's property to a for-profit corporation. It was the first time such a question arose in the Massachusetts courts.

The Massachusetts attorney general sought to enjoin the sale of all the assets, including the hospital's goodwill and license to provide hospital care, because he believed that such a transaction exceeded the trustees' authority. He also felt this to be equivalent to closing the hospital's affairs (that is, corporate dissolution), which the attorney general maintained needed court approval.

Even though the state supreme court held that the trustees retained the right to sell the hospital, they still may have needed court approval to finalize the sale. Further, the trustees could not use the funds derived from the sale in any way that would be violative of the original Mary Ida Converse Trust (Converse trust) instrument established in 1932, which provided much of the original funding for the hospital, constructed in 1939 and 1940.[55] Also, the probate court authorized several payments out of trust principal to finance modernization of the hospital's physical facilities.

Leslie Espinoza, assistant state attorney general, reaffirmed the public nature of a charitable hospital when she said, "As a charitable institution, Hahnemann Hospital belongs to the public, not to the board (of trustees)." In bringing the suit, the attorney general's office was acting on behalf of the public.[56]

John Cornish, chief counsel for Hahnemann Hospital and a member of the board of trustees, argued that "the hospital has a legal right to sell its assets and that continued good management of the hospital and donation of the proceeds from the $3 million sale to charitable organizations will provide the greatest public benefit."[57]

The Attorney General's Complaint. The good management of the hospital had been in question for several years. From 1970 to 1979 there were gains and losses, but from 1980 to 1982 there was a deficit. The trustees, in their financial plight, contracted with a profit-making hospital firm to manage the hospital with the option to purchase the hospital outright in the future. After turning the situation around financially, the profit-making firm began to exercise its option under the purchase and sales agreement with the Hahnemann trustees.[58] The trustees amended the articles of organization in 1985 to include, among other things, grant-making purposes for "any activity that promotes the health of the general public."[59]

The attorney general learned about the sale through the secretary of state's office when the trustees filed to amend their corporate charter to permit the sale. He therefore brought suit, alleging, among other things, that the debt "was caused by the Board of Trustees' failure to properly manage the corporation and by the Board of Trustees' failure to diligently protect the assets of the Hahnemann Hospital."[60]

Deciding the Issues. One significant aspect of the court's decision was the integrity of the Converse trust. The relationship of this trust with the hospital's articles of organization was of paramount importance. The Converse trust specified the conditions under which the trust could be aligned with the Hahnemann Hospital. In substance, the Converse trust directed support either for a hospital or a convalescent home. There was no provision for support of activities that would promote the general health of the public.

With the absence of a general health provision in the Converse trust instrument, the court held that the trustees could not use any of the funds raised through the sale, or any assets in their possession prior to September 1985, in connection with this newly stated purpose. Funds raised prior to the reorganization in September 1985 were gifts to the Hahnemann Hospital as it was then chartered to operate. This money was held in trust, to be used only for the purposes specified in the Converse trust. Any postsale funds raised after the adoption of the new articles of organization could of course be used for the reconstituted purposes. The court's use of the Converse trust instrument, allowing it to take precedence over the general laws, is a real red-letter day for both donors and the public.

Court Dicta. Of particular importance in the Hahnemann case are the dicta (court opinion as opposed to decision) issued by the Massachusetts Supreme Judicial Court (MSJC). The court said that the reading of the law by the board of trustees to mean a free hand in the use of unrestricted funds by the simple act of amending the articles of organization

would, in effect, grant to charitable corporations unfettered discretion to apply funds to any charitable purpose. By simply amending its charter purposes, a charitable corporation would itself be able to exercise the power to devote funds to new charitable purposes whenever the trustees decided to do so, without any requirement that the new purposes be similar and not contradictory.[61]

The court reasoned that such an interpretation by the trustees about the public, the law, and the attorney general vitiated long-standing trust principles. The public could not be certain that their gifts would be used for similar charitable purposes. Further, by merely restructuring itself, the charitable corporation could evade the law that requires court approval for dissolution. And finally, such a reading would eviscerate the attorney general's power and responsibility to supervise and enforce charitable trusts, forestalling breaches of trust.

The Public's Concern. As far as the general public is concerned, at issue in the Hahnemann case is the authority and power of trustees to use endowment and other funds. Donors want to make bequests to hospitals, but they also want to be assured that their gifts are going to be used for the purposes for which they were given. The MSJC, presumably aware of this legitimate donor concern, upheld the viability of the gift instrument whose provisions had been incorporated into the articles of organization.

Although the general laws permit trustees great latitude in decision making—especially when the gift instrument is silent—trustees cannot, as a matter of course, notwithstanding the general laws, ignore gift instruments and charters. When a trust is legally sound and in accord with public policy, it will be enforced. The MSJC, while recognizing the importance of the role of trustees and giving them great discretion, was, on the other hand, shaking its finger at the trustees, reminding them that they had fiduciary responsibilities under the law. The court made it clear that the Hahnemann trustees would violate their fiduciary duties to the hospital if they caused the hospital to violate its duty to the trust.

The Hahnemann case suggests that despite the fact that volunteer, nonprofit trustees may tire from the toil and burden of trusteeship, they simply cannot fold up their tents and go home, turning hospital assets into reconstituted chartered purposes. Trustees hold assets in trust for the purposes for which the trust was created. Trustees, therefore, have the duty to administer the trust in line with the donor's wishes for the public's beneficial interest.

BYLAWS

Consistent with the notion that charitable hospitals must operate in line with their charters and the public good, the courts have demonstrated a proclivity toward reviewing internal operations—even bylaws—if a possible violation is reported. The following case demonstrates not the diversion of charitable assets (which involves the attorney general) but the interpretation of a charitable hospital's bylaws (as the result of a personal grievance).

The Eternal Bylaw: Newcomb Hospital, Vineland, New Jersey

Medical Staff Privileges. The board of trustees and the medical staff of the Newcomb Hospital in Vineland, New Jersey, refused to issue or even to consider an application by Dr. Paul A. Greisman for admission as a member of the courtesy medical staff. This action deprived him of the customary use of the hospital's facilities and services extended to such members. Dr. Greisman took his grievance to court. Both the hospital and its board were named as defendants in the case, as was the medical staff, an unincorporated association, which held a fiduciary relation to the citizens of New Jersey and was accountable at law for its actions, just as the trustees were.

The net effect of the Greisman case[62] is that private charitable organizations may have organizational law (bylaws), but it must be in line with public policy. If it is not, the court will not hesitate to enter the case; and if in the court's judgment it is against public policy, the court will strike down the bylaw, as in this case.

As the parties agreed in the case, the basic issue to be resolved was the reasonableness of a bylaw requirement that included as basic qualifications for membership on the hospital courtesy staff that the applicant be (1) a graduate of a medical school approved by the American Medical Association and (2) a full or associate member of the county medical society. This presented a "catch-22" situation, since Dr. Greisman was a graduate of the Philadelphia College of Osteopathy, and his application to the county medical society was automatically never acted on.

Clearly, Dr. Greisman did not fulfill the hospital's basic qualifications. Dr. Greisman, however, was fully licensed to practice by the New Jersey State Board of Medical Examiners. The quarrel, fittingly summarized by the New Jersey Supreme Court, was as follows: "Viewed realistically, our proper concern here is whether the hospital had the right to exclude consideration of the plantiff [Dr. Greisman], solely because he was a doctor of osteopathy and had not been admitted, because of his osteopathic schooling, to his County Medical Society."[63]

The American Medical Association no longer openly discriminates against osteopathic medicine, but for a number of years it rejected schools of osteopathy because of differences in medical beliefs and policies. Dr. Greisman alleged that the basic qualifications were arbitrary, capricious, unreasonable, and void as against the public policy of the state of New Jersey.[64] The hospital did not question Dr. Greisman's personal or professional qualifications; it rested its case on the bylaw that required candidates to be graduates of accredited American Medical Association schools and to be members of the county medical society.

Public Versus Private Status. The trustees asserted that "the Newcomb Hospital is a private rather than a public hospital, that it may in its discretion exclude physicians from its medical staff, and that no legal ground exists for judicial interference with its refusal to consider the plantiff's [Dr. Greisman's] application for membership."[65]

In response the Supreme Court of New Jersey reasoned as follows:

They [hospitals, such as Newcomb] are private in the sense that they are nongovernmental but they are hardly private in other senses. Newcomb is a nonprofit organization dedicated by its certificate of incorporation to the vital public use of serving the sick and injured, its funds are in good measure received from public sources and through public solicitation, and its tax benefits are received because of its nonprofit and nonprivate aspects. It constitutes a virtual monopoly in the area in which it functions and it is in no position to claim immunity from public supervision and control because of its allegedly private nature. Indeed, in the development of the law, activities much less public than the hospital activities of Newcomb, have commonly been subjected to judicial (as well as legislative) supervision and control to the extent necessary to satisfy the felt needs of the times.[66] (Citation omitted.)

Hospitals and the Public Good. The court rightfully observed that throughout "the course of history, judges have often applied the common law so as to regulate private businesses and professions for the common good."[67] The court also noted that specific legislation had been passed in different states to supervise private businesses and professions for the public good; thus, the current situation demonstrably shows that events have gone far beyond the early common law.[68]

About the bylaw the lower court's opinion reads:

The bylaw of the defendants [Newcomb Hospital] which purports to require membership in the Cumberland County Medical Society as a basic requirement or preliminary qualification for admission to the medical staff of the Newcomb Hospital is void *per se* as contrary to the public policy and public welfare of our State.

Secondly, the bylaw of defendants which purports to require *the plantiff Dr. Greisman* to be a graduate of a medical school approved by the American Medical Association, *insofar as it applies* to the *plantiff*, contravenes the public policy of this State and the true interests of justice.[69] (Citations omitted)

The court relied on an earlier case in which the Middlesex County Medical Society had taken the position that it was a private organization whose admissions policy was immune from judicial review. The supreme court, however, reasoned that "the Society was not a voluntary membership association in which the public had little or no concern but was, rather, an association in which the public was vitally concerned and which was engaged in activities directly affecting the health and welfare of the people."[70] The court struck down the arbitrary membership requirement of the medical society, since the society engaged in an activity of public concern.

The New Jersey Supreme Court struck down the Newcomb Hospital bylaw. Dr. Greisman became eligible for courtesy medical staff privileges.

In the concluding paragraph the New Jersey Supreme Court summarized the role of hospitals in society and the trustees' fiduciary obligations.

Hospital officials are properly vested with large measures of managing discretion and to the extent that they exert their efforts toward the elevation of hospital standards and higher medical care, they will receive broad judicial support. But they must never lose sight of the fact that the hospitals are operated not for *private* ends but for the benefit of the public, and that their existence is for the purpose of faithfully furnishing facilities to the members of the medical profession in aid of their service to the public. They must recognize that their powers, particularly those relating to the selection of staff members, are powers in trust which are always to be dealt with as such. While reasonable and constructive exercises of judgment should be honored, courts would indeed be remiss if they declined to intervene where, as here, the powers were invoked at the threshold to preclude an application for staff membership, not because of any lack of individual merit, but for a reason unrelated to sound hospital standards and not in furtherance of the common good.[71]

It may be said, and with emphasis, that boards have been forewarned about bylaws that work against the public good. Standards are evolving in this important management area that make it increasingly difficult for trustees to proclaim they did not understand or were not aware.

THE DONOR

Trustees enjoy great latitude in discharging their fiduciary duties. As fiduciaries, however, they do not have carte blanche in terms of what they see as "best" for the public interest. Not only must prudent trustees remain faithful to the specific purposes for which the charitable organization is chartered but trustees also owe a duty to the donor. Trustees must adhere to the donor's wishes in terms of both the trust's purposes and its expressed terms. Such adherence is mandatory until or unless a court of proper jurisdiction instructs otherwise. Since the beneficiaries of a charitable trust are unnamed, rarely is there a watchdog to guarantee loyal performance. Thus, proper conduct for a trustee often rests with the trustee's own integrity, peer trustee pressure, or external authority.

Sometimes in determining what is best, it is necessary for trustees to receive instructions from a court to make certain what has been uncertain. The purpose of such instructions is to enable trustees to discharge their duties properly under the terms of the trust and to protect the trustees in the discharge of these duties. Again, the attorney general is a necessary and proper party in the process.[72]

A Connecticut Yankee in Superior Court: Hartford Hospital, Hartford, Connecticut

Trustee Discretion. In his will, Frederick S. Bliss,[73] a wealthy benefactor, created in 1943 a life estate for his sister, Grace E. Bliss, who was the income beneficiary for the remainder of her life. Mr. Bliss died in 1943, followed by his sister in 1966 at the age of approximately 102 years. Bliss had directed that on his sister's death, the trustee—Connecticut Bank and Trust Company—divide the trust into three equal parts, two of which were to be given to the Hartford Hospital for the construction of a new wing to be known as the Bliss wing. A portion of the remaining third was to be used for the maintenance of a free bed or beds at the Hartford Hospital to benefit individuals requiring hospital care, as the trustee in its "absolute discretion may appoint or select" pending approval of the hospital. The will further specified that any unexpended income not required for free beds was to be paid to the hospital for its uses and purposes.

None of the income from the free bed fund established after the death of Grace E. Bliss, however, was ever used for free bed purposes. Instead the trustee paid the entire income from the free bed fund to the hospital, which held it in an "invested income fund" to meet building costs associated with the Bliss wing.

The upshot of the matter is that the trustee in 1971, supported by the hospital, requested the court to grant permission to transfer the income from the free bed fund to the building fund for the Bliss wing. On a directive from the probate court, the trustee sought an interpretation of the terms of the will from the superior court with regard to the trustee's administration of the free bed fund. Both the trustee and the hospital had determined that, given current conditions, sufficient funds were available for free beds for worthy persons and that the construction of the Bliss wing was more urgent.

The trustee's officer in charge of the Bliss account testified that

in exercising its discretion the trustee took into consideration the resources available to potential recipients of free bed grants, including group insurance, medicare, and welfare benefits, and also took into consideration the overwhelming emphasis in the Bliss will on the construction of the Bliss wing—almost two thirds of the residuary estate being devoted to the Bliss wing.[74]

Honoring the Donor's Wishes. The Connecticut attorney general, who by state law represents the public interest in the protection of any gifts, legacies, or devises intended for public or charitable purposes, was a named defendant in the case. His position was that "the record discloses not only a complete failure on the part of the trustee to comply with the wishes and directions of the testator as to the use of the fund income for free bed purposes but also a complete failure by the trustee to take positive steps of any nature whatsoever to carry out the purposes of the trust."[75] The testimony presented at the hearing supported the attorney general's position.

Some commentators have been audacious enough to state that the "American courts have perhaps too much respect for the whims of donors and too little respect for the public interest."[76] But the wishes of a donor in charitable bequests (unless they are illegal or impossible to fulfill) are generally honored by the courts. Trustees, as fiduciaries, are under an obligation to act in terms of the expressed wishes of the donor until a court of competent jurisdiction directs otherwise.

Central to the argument in the Bliss case was the trustee's contention that "the completeness of the discretion" given to the trustee in the administration of the trust could not be more broadly expressed.

The court, on the other hand, said that "absolute discretion" in the act of appointing or selecting, and the use of such language by the settlor, does not in itself become unlimited.

"Simply stated, the trustee is given no dispositive, as distinguished from administrative, power."[77] Trustees may propose, but the court disposes—in short, the exercise of power by trustees is circumscribed. Although the donor may say "in their absolute discretion," the court has the final authority, not the donor or the trustee.

As a matter of law, the court made it clear that it would not give unbridled authority to trustees. This case clearly emphasizes the fact, as the court states, that "trustees have no powers not expressly or impliedly conferred on them by the terms of the trust. Their obligation to obey the instructions of the donor of the trust is the cornerstone upon which all other duties rest"[78] (citation omitted).

Best Bib and Tucker: Shriners' Hospital, St. Louis, Missouri

Accumulation of Assets. In his last will and testament, Corry T. Meeker created a trust in which he provided that after named relatives were deceased, the residual of his estate be placed in a charitable trust to support the activities of two hospitals that provided medical care for crippled children. Mr. Meeker's will provided that 25 percent of the annual income be added to the principal of the trust and invested and reinvested.

Controversy arose over the 25 percent accumulation provision, which, because the trust was set up as charity, was to continue in perpetuity. Prior case law had indicated that 100 percent perpetual accumulation of income by a charitable trust was contrary to the public good, since funds then accumulated forever and never became available for public use.

The trustees of the Meeker trust sought instructions from the court about possible improper accumulation of income as provided in Mr. Meeker's will.

The trial court held that the accumulation provision was valid and that the donor's wishes should be adhered to.

Shriners' Hospital for Crippled Children (hereafter, Shriners) contested the trial court's decision on the grounds that "the perpetual accumulation of income by a charitable trust [was] against the public policy and common law of Missouri."[79] Shriners sought to have the 25 percent accumulation provision abolished so all of its entitlement under the trust would come to it without any accumulation.

In 1977, the appeals court observed that what Shriners "argues, in effect, is that it disagrees with what is 'best.' "[80] The court reasoned that to direct the trustees to take action contrary to the wishes of the donor would be to defeat the donor's expressed intentions, especially when there had been no evidence presented that some action by a court limiting accumulations was necessary either to satisfy the public interest or to preserve the purpose of the trust.

The appeals court held that the Meeker will did not provide for "perpetual accumulation" with its 25 percent accumulation provision. The accumulation provision, therefore, was not void *ab initio* (from the beginning), but rather was mandatory on the trustees and was to be enforced until evidence was provided to the contrary and a court of equity decreed otherwise. The direction for accumulation was valid; therefore, it was enforced.

The Powers of the Court of Equity. The Meeker case drives home the point that ultimately what is "best" is a matter for the courts to decide—not the trustees. As the court said:

All charitable trusts are subject to the broad powers of the courts of equity to secure the maximum possible benefit to the public and to carry out insofar as possible the intent of the donor . . . . While the trustees are bound by the mandatory directions contained in the trust instrument, the court "is not bound by the instructions of the settlor, but may direct, prohibit, or vary accumulations, and may reconsider decisions made by it with regard to such matters."[81] (Citations omitted)

DUTIES OF CARE AND LOYALTY

Other constraints inherent in fiduciary responsibility center around internal management and personal integrity. These constraints can be divided into two general categories: (1) the duty of care, relating to the management aspect of the institution, and (2) the duty of loyalty, concerned with self-dealing. The duties of care and loyalty are of utmost importance for any trustee, and a breach of either is extremely serious business.

The Sibley Hospital Case (hereafter Stern case or *Stern*)[82] shows graphically what can happen to the integrity of a board of trustees when some of its members and officers are perhaps interested in power, self-aggrandizement, and prestige rather than in the exercise of fiduciary powers to carry out their mission.

Hog-tying the Board on Investments: Sibley Memorial Hospital, Washington, D.C.

The Background. In 1891 a missionary society established the Lucy Webb Hayes National Training School for Deaconesses and Missionaries, mainly for the purpose of providing health-care services to the poor in the nation's capital. Incorporated in 1894 as a nonprofit charitable corporation, the school built, during the following year, the Sibley Memorial Hospital (hereafter, Sibley) to further its charitable mission.

In the mid–1950s Sibley merged with another charity, the Hahnemann Hospital. (The name Hahnemann Hospital is coincidental with the Hahnemann Hospital in Massachusetts. Several hospitals were named in honor of Samuel Friedrich Hahnemann, a German physician who lived from 1755 to 1843 and who founded the homeopathic method of treating disease.) Hahnemann was retained as a separate corporate entity solely for the purpose of receiving certain charitable contributions under the terms of the wills and trust agreements that predated the merger. The Sibley board of trustees also constituted Hahnemann's board.

After the merger of the two hospitals and in preparation for a new hospital building, the Sibley board adopted new bylaws to accommodate the mushrooming and more complex hospital affairs. The new bylaws provided for a board of trustees to number twenty-five to thirty members with the proviso that the full board meet at least twice each year. An executive committee was authorized to represent the full board between meetings in such matters as, for example, opening checking accounts, approving the budget, renewing mortgages, and entering into contracts. (A board may create and authorize committees to act between meetings on its behalf, but actions by its committees have no authority until they are ratified by the full board in an appropriately scheduled meeting.)

Two committees were also created to handle financial matters: a finance committee and an investment committee. The finance committee was responsible for reviewing the budget and regularly reporting on the amount of cash available for investments. The management of investments was to be supervised by the investment committee, although it was expected that the two committees would work closely together.

Neither the finance committee nor the investment committee ever met, despite the fact that member trustees were elected annually to serve on both committees; nor did the full board supervise financial matters as a body corporate, creating a perfect set of conditions for the growth of festering financial health problems. The Sibley board and its finance and investment committees simply ignored their bylaws, allowing two trustee officers to hog-tie the full board, resulting in questionable financial practices later discovered by a group of angry patients who challenged various aspects of the hospital's fiscal management.

The hospital's financial and budgetary affairs were handled almost exclusively by Mr. Donald R. Ernst, a trustee and board treasurer, along with Dr. John M.

Orem, a trustee and hospital administrator, and a few other officers apparently aware of Mr. Ernst's investment policies.

At the trial the defendant trustees admitted that "they approved Ernst's recommendations as a matter of course, rarely if ever read the relevant details of audits critically, and generally left investment decisions to the presumed expertise of Mr. Ernst. Several also commented that the Treasurer regarded their suggestions as 'interference' in these matters and none forced the issue."[83]

The Claims. Under this regime several questionable practices occurred. First, Sibley took out a long-term construction loan from a consortium of local banks. And the hospital renewed the loan despite the fact that there were large, unused balances—sufficient to pay off the loan without totally impairing the hospital's ability to meet obligations—on deposit in the same banks to which the debt was owed. Second, several trustees held responsible positions in local banking institutions in which inordinate amounts of money—far in excess of capital or operating requirements—were kept on deposit. These moneys, in checking or savings accounts, allegedly drew inadequate or no interest. Third, the hospital employed as an investment adviser, a corporation whose chairman and principal stockholder was a hospital trustee at the time of retention. He was also a member of the investment committee and had urged and may have voted in favor of the recommendation.

A trustee's total abdication of the supervisory role is improper under traditional principles. Yet the board abdicated its responsibility by failing to assume an identifiable supervisory role over investment policy and hospital fiscal management in general. Further, the treasurer far exceeded his authority with respect to accepted trustee practice. Even though it may be proper for a board to appoint a committee of its members to deal with the investment of the corporation's funds, the board must use due diligence in supervising the actions of those officers, employees, or outside experts to whom the responsibility for making day-to-day financial or investment decisions has been delegated. If the board fails to supervise what it has delegated, then it may be adjudged to be in default of its fiduciary duty to manage the fiscal and investment affairs of the charitable enterprise entrusted to its care.[84]

In 1974 the court observed in *Stern* that a corporate director who failed to acquire the information necessary to supervise investment policy or who consistently failed even to attend meetings at which such policies were considered had violated his or her fiduciary duty to the corporation.[85] But the Sibley board as body corporate (the only way a board can take action) simply lacked the courage to set things right. It is always easier to go along and not make waves. The Sibley trustees, who later became defendants, could have avoided the nasty ensuing legal jeopardy and public embarrassment they experienced if only they had said: "We are a board—body corporate—and as such act only in corpus at a legally constituted meeting of the board. That's the way things are and are going to be, for it is the only sensible and proper way to do business." Again, many difficulties arise in board affairs because the corpus concept is violated.

It may be added that many problems arise in board business from the general disrespect of the concept of a board as an entity. The only time one is a member of a board, whether public or private, is when the individual is sitting in the corpus of a board meeting. The board may authorize committees, and a trustee may act in that capacity, but the member cannot exceed the expressed authorization of the board's resolution or its bylaws. A board member, when not sitting in the corpus of a board, should respect the fact that she or he is merely an individual whose opinion is no more important than any other individual's.

Upon the death of Dr. Orem and following some severe internal fracases that led to the dismissal of personnel, the president of the board finally decided to activate both the finance and investment committees that had not met for more than ten years. Yet the treasurer continued to dominate decision making, and he discouraged, or at times flatly refused, inquiries by other trustees in investment matters. Only after his death did the board begin to exercise investment policy and fiscal management in general. However, this was too little too late because the damage had already been done.

Bringing Suit. Believing that they had been bilked as a result of fiscal mismanagement, an angry group of patients commenced a class action suit in the federal court of the District of Columbia. (A class action suit is litigation brought by a proper party representing a usually large number of injured parties.) The court would not allow the patients to proceed on antitrust grounds, but it did permit the patients to maintain a suit for alleged breach of trust to prevent further injury to the hospital. The fact that the court granted the patients standing to sue is highly significant. This appears to be an unusual holding.

The patients claimed that they had been damaged by being required to pay excessive amounts for hospital services caused by the trustees' alleged self-dealing and overreaching. Essentially, the five defendant trustees were charged with mismanagement, nonmanagement, and self-dealing. (Mismanagement occurs when board members allow personal interest to interfere with their duties. Nonmanagement happens when trustees do not do their jobs. Self-dealing arises when trustees use trust property for their own benefit.)

The two principal contentions in the patients' complaint were "that the defendant trustees conspired to enrich themselves and certain financial institutions with which they were affiliated by favoring those institutions in financial dealings with the Hospital, and that they breached their fiduciary duties of care and loyalty in the management of Sibley's funds."[86] The conspiratorial claim failed for lack of proof, but the court did find serious breaches of duty on the part of the trustees.

The Court Creates Guidelines. By creating a set of principles against which to measure trustee behavior in fiscal affairs, the court formulated explicit guidelines for trustees to follow. The court held that a trustee of a charitable hospital organized under the Non-profit Corporation Act of the District of Columbia was in default of his or her fiduciary duty to manage the fiscal and investment affairs of the hospital if it had been shown by a preponderance of evidence that

- while assigned to a particular financial or investment committee of the board, the trustee failed to supervise the actions of the personnel to whom had been delegated the responsibility for making day-to-day financial decisions; or

- the trustee knowingly permitted the hospital to enter into a business transaction with him/herself or with any organization in which the trustee then had a substantial interest or held a position as trustee, director, etc., *without having previously informed the board* of that interest or position and of any significant reasons why the transactions might not be in the best interest of the hospital; or

- except as required by the preceding paragraph, the trustee actively participated in or voted in favor of a decision by the board or subcommittee to transact business with him/herself or any organization in which the trustee then had a substantial interest or held a position; or

- the trustee otherwise failed to perform his/her duties honestly, in good faith, and with a reasonable amount of diligence and care.[87]

The Court Decides. Based on these guidelines, the court found that even though no conspiracy existed between the trustees and the financial institutions with which they were affiliated, since the funds had been handled almost exclusively by the now-deceased treasurer, there was evidence that each defendant trustee had breached "his fiduciary duty to supervise the management of Sibley's investments."[88] The court concluded that all the trustees had "in the past failed to exercise even the most cursory supervision over the handling of Hospital funds and failed to establish and carry out a defined policy."[89] Judge Gerhard Gesell elaborated further: "It is clear that all of the defendant trustees have, at one time or another, affirmatively approved self-dealing transactions."[90]

But Judge Gesell also reasoned, "The function of equity is not to punish but merely to take such action as the Court in its discretion deems necessary to prevent the recurrence of improper conduct."[91] The relief, while firm, was not punitive and was fashioned to a series of injunctions designed to insure a clean break between the past and the future.

The court decreed that the appropriate committees and officers of the hospital present to the full board a written policy statement governing investments and the use of idle cash in the hospital's bank accounts. The court also ordered the establishment of a procedure for the periodic reexamination of existing investments and other financial arrangements to insure compliance with board policies. The judge also required all trustees to disclose their affiliations with banks, saving and loan associations, and investment firms doing business with the hospital and ordered that all current financial arrangements should be reviewed by disinterested members of the board to ascertain if these arrangements were in the hospital's best interests.

Stopping short of removing any of the trustees from office, which he had the authority to do, Judge Gesell reasoned that this would be unduly harsh under the circumstances, considering the long service and the age and illness of the trustees. "It is therefore unnecessary to interfere by order of removal or dis-qualifications with a transition that is necessarily already taking place due to other immutable factors."[92]

Cautioning the board with respect to the selection of new members, the court displayed its full awareness of the ambitious nature of some individuals who aspired to be trustees when Judge Gesell warned:

> It is obvious that, in due course, new trustees must come to the Board of this Hospital, some of whom will be affiliated with banks, savings and loan associations and other financial institutions. The tendency of representatives of such institutions is often to seek business in return for advice and assistance rendered as trustees. *It must be made absolutely clear that Board membership carries no right to preferential treatment in the placement or handling of the Hospital's investments and business accounts.*[93] (Emphasis added)

To ensure that his orders were not misunderstood or ignored, Judge Gesell ordered each current board member and all board members appointed for the next five years to read his order and signify that they had done so either by signing the order or by affirming that they had done so in the minutes of a board meeting.

Adding an ounce of prevention, the court boldly advised that new trustees be appointed who did not have direct business affiliation with the hospital; the court did not wish to see Sibley's board of trustees once again hog-tied because of possible conflicts of interest resulting in breach of fiduciary duty. A board united in interests, beliefs, and tastes is itself a solution to the most troubling problem of court intervention.

A Postscript. The legal premises on which the court fashioned its remedy are important for all trustees, whether it be a hospital, college, university, library, museum, or any other eleemosynary institution. Some selected premises are as follows:

- The charitable corporation is a relatively new legal entity which does not fit neatly into the established common law categories of corporation and trust . . . . The modern trend is to apply corporate rather than trust principles in determining the liability of the directors of charitable corporations, because their functions are virtually indistinguishable from those of their "pure" corporate counterparts. [Author's note: it may be added that this is court dicta, and no citations were offered.]
- Both trustees and corporate directors are liable for losses occasioned by their negligent mismanagement of investments. However, the degree of care required appears to differ in many jurisdictions. A trustee is uniformly held to a high standard of care and will be held liable for simple negligence, while a director must often have committed "gross negligence" or otherwise be guilty of more than mere mistakes of judgment.
- This distinction may amount to little more than a recognition of the fact that corporate directors have many areas of responsibility, while the traditional trustee is often charged only with the management of the trust funds and can therefore be expected to devote more time and expertise to that task. Since the board members of most large charitable

corporations fall within the corporate rather than the trust model, being charged with the operation of ongoing businesses, it has been said that they should only be held to the less stringent corporate standard of care. More specifically, directors of charitable corporations are required to exercise ordinary and reasonable care in the performance of their duties, exhibiting honesty and good faith.

- . . . A corporate director, on the other hand, may delegate his investment responsibility to fellow directors, corporate officers, or even outsiders, but he must continue to exercise general supervision over the activities of his delegates. Once again, the rule for charitable corporations is closer to the traditional corporate rule: directors should at least be permitted to delegate investment decisions to a committee of board members, so long as *all* directors assume the responsibility for supervising such committees by periodically scrutinizing their work.

- . . . A director whose failure to supervise permits negligent mismanagement by others to go unchecked has committed an independent wrong against the corporation; he is not merely an accessory under an attenuated theory of *respondeat superior* or constructive notice.

- . . . A director should not only disclose his interlocking responsibilities but also refrain from voting on or otherwise influencing a corporate decision to transact business with a company in which he has a significant interest or control.[94] (Citations omitted)

CONFLICT OF INTEREST

Because of the strong presence of business people on charitable boards, conflict of interest issues occasionally surface. These individuals tend to apply profit-making corporate rules to the charitable enterprise. Forgetting the clarion call of charitable trusteeship to a loftier, selfless code of ethical behavior, forgetting that this code mandates complete disclosure of any possible self-interest in a transaction, these individuals can all too easily be trapped in the net of their own ambitions and their hazy confusion of profit-making rules versus nonprofit rules. When necessary, cotrustees must show courage by questioning possible conflict of interest of fellow trustees—an essential procedure to avoid grief, shame, and broken confidences for all concerned. In a nutshell, conflict of interest arises where the "regard for one duty leads to disregard of another."[95]

It is imperative that trustees use utmost discretion in dealing with charitable property to avoid even the suggestion of conflict of interest. As fiduciaries, trustees "must subordinate their individual and private interests to their duty to the corporation whenever the two conflict."[96]

A trust is more than a relation between a trustee and a beneficiary. It is a legal institution involving the courts and its officers (the trustees), who have a duty to act in terms of the best interest of the beneficiary. More specifically, a "fiduciary relationship," according to Austin Scott, "involves a duty on the part of the fiduciary to act for the benefit of the other party to the relation as to matters within the scope of the relation."[97] The trustee is under a duty not to profit at the expense of the beneficiary.

A fiduciary relationship should be distinguished from a merely confidential relation, such as between an attorney and client or between a physician and patient. More formal accountability exists in a fiduciary relationship.

Since, as noted, so many trustees come from the business community and high enterprise, they often carry with them into the charitable governance situation a proprietary mentality quite inappropriate, and it is against this that caution must be taken. Howard Oleck forcefully writes:

Some trustees and officers of nonprofit organizations develop what can be called a "proprietary" attitude, as though they were owners of the organization, not its servants. The improper and reprehensible nature of such an attitude, and of the decisions that flow from it, are obvious.

It is well for such persons to be reminded of the law applicable to high-handed use of managerial status. Statutes governing false statements, entries, or reports, of course, are stringent, and misconduct results in personal liability . . . .

Any arrangement or contract of the organization in which a situation of conflicting loyalties is found will be subjected to strict scrutiny by the courts. Then the persons who seek to maintain the transaction must maintain the burden of proof of its propriety.[98]

The case *Gilbert v. McLeod Infirmary*[99] (hereafter, *Gilbert*), occurring in South Carolina in 1951, serves as a good example of conflict of interest in a charitable corporation.

But Butter Wouldn't Melt in Their Mouths: McLeod Infirmary, Florence, South Carolina

A Wrinkle Develops in the Plan. In *Gilbert*, two minority trustees brought suit against the McLeod Infirmary, its chairman, and others, requesting the court to void the proposed sale of part of the hospital's real estate to J. B. Aiken, a hospital trustee, for $50,000 for the purpose of constructing an apartment building. The facts of the case revealed that three separate Aiken corporations were involved in the proposed sale: Aiken Loan & Security Company for mortgage insurance; J. B. Aiken, as mortgagee; and J. B. Aiken (sponsor) on behalf of Florence Apartments, Inc., as mortgagor. The attorney for the latter was stated in the application to be R. B. Fulton, who also served as a McLeod Infirmary trustee.[100]

Mr. Aiken broached the matter of the property to the chairman and one other trustee on 26 October, and as a result a hasty meeting of the executive committee was scheduled the next day. The executive committee, with one member absent who was not notified of the meeting, met with Mr. Aiken, although he was not a member of the executive committee, to consider the proposal to sell the hospital property. The executive committee unanimously approved the sale and authorized the chairperson to call a special meeting of the full board of trustees for the next evening to consider approving the executive committee's recommendation, although curiously enough, the constitution of the board required written notice for such a meeting.

On 28 October the board met with eight of the twelve trustees in attendance, including the two interested trustees. The board considered the resolution of the executive committee to sell the property. The members present at the meeting unanimously adopted the resolution and authorized the chairperson and secretary to proceed with arrangements for the sale. The majority of members signed the option attached to the resolution. Two members of the board were out of town at the time of the meeting and were not notified of the meeting or of its purpose. (They became the plaintiffs in the case). Further, the minutes contained no notation of the interested trustees having disqualified themselves from voting, nor was there a record of a vote except that it was unanimous.

As might have been expected, a great deal of flack developed over the sale within the medical staff, who unanimously joined in a written petition of protest against the sale. That in turn led to the formation of cleavages, consolidations, and cliques in the community.

Concerning the attorney-trustee's role, the court said that it was "fully aware of the high character and standing of Mr. Fulton at the bar, but because of the facts which have been mentioned we think he should have disqualified himself . . . and refrained from voting. Not only did he vote; he engaged in the debate and was further active to the extent of making motions."[101]

Trustee Self-dealing. The well-established rule against self-dealing was stated in *Gilbert* as follows:

[W]hen a director, in selling corporate property to himself, represents or joins in the representation of the corporation, the transaction is voidable at the option of the corporation, or others suing in its behalf, merely upon proof of the fact stated; but when the purchasing director abstains from participation in behalf of the corporation and it is properly represented by others who are personally disinterested, the transaction will stand under attack if the director made full disclosure, paid full value, and the corporation has not been imposed upon; and the burden is upon the director to establish these requisites by evidence.[102]

As a matter of law, it is firmly established in South Carolina that

a person occupying a place of trust should not put himself in a position in which self-interest conflicts with any duty he owes to those for whom he acts; and as a general rule he will not be permitted to make a profit by purchasing or leasing the property of those toward whom he occupies a fiduciary relation without affirmatively showing full disclosure and fair dealing. Upon this principle it is held that a director who exercises a controlling influence over codirectors cannot defend a purchase by him of corporate property on the ground that his action was approved by them.[103]

Courts are particularly stern in cases of abuse of office and conflict of interest (breach of trust) and will make their points clear, as, for example, in *Gilbert*, when the South Carolina Supreme Court held that the facts presented to the court were of such a nature to warrant overturning the lower court's decision, to invalidate in equity the close corporate result, and to void the sale. "There is no finding of actual fraud or fraudulent intent; indeed, we think Mr. Aiken was innocent of that; but his conduct failed to measure up to the high standard required by the law of one in his *fiduciary* relation to the hospital" (emphasis added).[104] Applying corporate law, the result was the same as if trust law had been used. "The directors or other members of the managing board are sometimes called trustees," declared the South Carolina Supreme Court. "Their legal position is the same no matter by what name they are called, whether directors, trustees, or governors."[105]

The Double-barreled Shot: The Marin County Hospital District, California

The Fairness Test. In some states, statutes exist that forbid conflict of interest under any circumstances, despite disclosure or meeting the fairness test. Statutes of this kind are aimed at the mischief that can arise when a public officer is sworn to a duty to represent the public interest as opposed to a private pecuniary interest. Conflict of interest may be actual or potential. A 1978 California court decision, using the conflict of interest statute, barred a nonprofit private hospital president from serving on an elected governmental hospital board.[106]

The Health and Safety Code of California is a conflict of interest statute making certain people ineligible to hold office as a director of a public hospital district. The code reads: "No person who is a director or an officer of, or who occupies any management position or office whatsoever, on the administrative staff of any such private hospital, shall be eligible for or hold any district office or any management position or office whatsoever in any district hospital."[107]

The Challenged Election. Mr. George Monardo, who was elected to the board of directors of the Marin Hospital District, was also president of the Ralph K. Davies Medical Center, a nonprofit private hospital located in San Francisco. The fuss developed when Marin Hospital District electors challenged Mr. Monardo's election to the board, and he contended that the code applied only to proprietary hospitals and that he was, therefore, eligible to serve on the public governmental board.

The California Court of Appeal concluded that the Health and Safety Code "[made] officers or directors, or managers of private nonprofit hospitals, as well as private proprietary hospitals, serving the same area as a public hospital ineligible to serve on the public hospital's board of directors."[108] Giving the broadest interpretation that it could to the statute and to the mischief at which it was aimed, the court established that the legislation's intent was to identify individuals perceived as having a potential conflict of interest.

OPEN MEETING LAW (ACCOUNTABILITY)

It is difficult to gain any in-depth understanding of charitable organizations because they are in the main allowed to operate in almost complete secrecy. The trustees of nongovernmental charitable organizations are frequently self-perpetuating bodies of prominent citizens, with a healthy representation from the business community, who conduct their affairs in private and do not publish accounts of their actions. Even in the instance of charities sponsored by government, which operate in most jurisdictions under sunshine laws—laws that require open meetings of governmental agencies and departments—it is possible for the real business to go on in executive sessions behind closed doors. The minutes of those deliberately closed-door meetings and the secret deals struck are often either nonexistent or never made public.

Fortunately, the press closely monitors the open meeting law and does from time to time voraciously challenge its lack of enforcement by public officials, either through pithy editorials or even complaints directly to governing boards or perhaps to appropriate governmental authority. Nongovernmental charities, however, escape close public scrutiny because they are generally not subject to open meeting laws even if they perchance receive public monies, because such monies are not determinative.

The Sun Does Not Always Shine Brightly: Leonard Morse Hospital, Natick, Massachusetts

Interpreting the Statute. The pertinence of the Massachusetts open meeting law cropped up in connection with the Leonard Morse Hospital[109] (hereafter, Morse), a charitable hospital organized originally in 1893 as a charitable trust and reorganized as a charitable corporation in 1916 by a special act of the legislature.

The issue squarely raised in this case is whether the board of trustees of Morse is a "governmental body" within the meaning of the open meeting law. The statute reads that "all meetings of a governmental body shall be open to the public." The statute defines a governmental body as "every board, commission, committee or subcommittee of any district, city, region or town, however elected, appointed or otherwise constituted."[110]

Morse was established under the will of Mary Ann Morse, who died in 1891. The town of Natick, Massachusetts, in 1893 voted to accept the devise (terms) and bequest. The will provided, among other things, that the town hold legal title to the hospital; that the hospital shall be under the care, control, and management of a board of trustees to number seven; and that the trustees be residents of Natick and elected by the legal voters of the town. Morse trustees are still elected by popular vote in the general town elections.[111]

Cherishing their private status, the trustees denied permission for the press to attend meetings. In turn, the press complained to the district attorney, alleging that the board had been violating Massachusetts open meeting statute. The district attorney, the public official who enforces the open meeting law, directed the trustees to comply with the statute. Upon receiving the trustees' reply that the board of Morse was not subject to the statute, the district attorney brought suit.

Whetting Accountability. In reversing the trial court's decision, which favored the district attorney, the Massachusetts Supreme Judicial Court stopped short of offering its own definition of a governmental body: "We are aware of no judicial decision in Massachusetts addressing the nature or extent of the meaning of the term 'governmental body' as used" in the statute.[112] Despite the facts that the board was elected by the legal voters of the town, that the hospital had received support from the town through appropriations and bonds, and that legal title to the hospital was vested in the town, the court held that the board of trustees of the hospital was not a governmental body within the meaning of the open meeting law.

Part of the rationale for this ruling was that the board of trustees of a charitable institution does not possess powers common to most governmental agencies, including the power to tax, the power to take property by eminent domain, the power to regulate coercively individual and group conduct, or the power to control other agencies—all definite powers of civil government.[113]

Even though the decision went in favor of the hospital trustees, the fact that the issue has been raised should serve notice to charitable trustees that the public is interested in accountability. The water has begun to drop on the trustee secrecy stone. Just as the undertow caught governmental bodies by surprise when open meeting laws were first enacted, so may nongovernmental charitable trustees find themselves in a similar situation in the near future. Common law remains in force until statutory law replaces it. It could be, with the mood of the public for strong accountability of public assets, that the community at large may demand that legislatures act to curb charitable trustee secrecy, inasmuch as any charity is impressed with a public use. As the old French proverb runs, an individual forewarned is worth two.

REGULATORY AUTHORITY AND ALLOCATION OF RESOURCES

The Morse hospital case reaffirms the private nature of nonprofit independent hospital boards of trustees. They may conduct hospital affairs behind closed doors, but such a privilege does not give trustees a blank check to do what they please. They cannot, in the final analysis, escape accountability for the supervision and management of the hospital entrusted to their care: this is a responsibility of theirs and theirs alone.

Accountability manifests itself in yet another constraint placed on trustees—regulatory authority. Decisions of private independent boards of trustees are subject to governmental authority through three sources of law: (1) common law (court-made law from individual case decisions), (2) statutory law (written law originating in legislatures), and (3) administrative rules and regulations (mandates emanating from the executive side of government). Most governmental business is conducted in the open, including deliberative sessions of its administrative agencies and boards. This is one of the few times the public is able to gain insight into what private hospital trustees are up to. In addition, the state possesses the power, for example, to stop hospital construction—even though private hospital trustees have the money and have voted in a duly constituted meeting to build the facility—if the state deems the project not to be in the public's best interest.

Recently, a Massachusetts Senate oversight committee criticized the Public Health Council, the Department of Public Health's top policy body, for its leniency in approving hospital expansion and construction projects that shot up hospital capital spending by millions of dollars. The report said that hospitals in Massachusetts spent a record $300 million on new construction in 1983—$70 million more than in the previous year—and then passed the bill along to patients in the form of higher health-care costs. The legislature did not act to stop the construction, but it brought pressure to bear on a statutory committee that had the power to act.

Oftentimes the state also has the power to regulate such medical practices as transplant procedures. However, policy is set by trustees, whose major duties include the allocation of resources, both human and money, to achieve the objectives of the institution as expressed either implicitly or explicitly in its charter. Trustees need to evaluate the privileges granted to them that say in effect "the greatest good for the greatest number." Herein lies the challenge for the future.

Tough Road Ahead: Massachusetts General Hospital, Boston, Massachusetts

Transplant Sweepstakes. On Thursday, 13 September 1984, at 4:00 P.M., the New England Donor Bank received a call from Bermuda about a possible donor, a young traffic accident victim. By midnight the first surgical team from Boston was removing the donor's lymph nodes to be flown back immediately by chartered plane to Boston for tissue-matching tests. At 4:00 A.M., another Boston team of surgeons arrived in Bermuda, ready for action. At 11:00 A.M., after the donor was declared dead, the team began removing the heart, which was rushed by ambulance to a waiting chartered plane already cleared for takeoff. Less than 2 hours later (hearts remain viable for only 3 to 4 hours), at 3:30 P.M., the surgical team was back in Boston starting the 3¼-hour transplant operation at Brigham and Women's Hospital, then the only hospital in Massachusetts, by state mandate, that could perform this medical procedure.[114] The uproar over transplantations that erupted in Boston shows the commotion that can develop when considering the public good in relation to individual hospital concerns.

Resulting from the state's regulatory decisions on transplantations, a maelstrom quickly developed in Boston. As each hospital jockeyed to gain state approval to perform the high-prestige but costly transplant operations, an acrimonious public debate between the state regulatory bodies and the interested hospitals reached new intensity with each move of the medical transplant board.

More than usual competition, albeit ostensibly disguised, was conspicuous as the participants vied for potential state approval. Why? The stakes were high: money, power, and politics were at the heart of the storm. Reputations, professional preferment, full hospital wards, and physicians' annual income of $150,000 to $400,000 or more were part of the grand sweepstakes.

Hospitals—like other institutions—tend to act in terms of institutional self-interest. With medical service as a primary value, individual hospitals make their mark by serving their patients. Hospital governance, financing, and patterns of development and use are intrinsically intertwined with their institutional aspirations and constraints. At times and in some hospitals, institutional self-seeking takes forms of vanity, such as poising themselves to be participants in the world center for liver transplantation, with the intent of distinguishing themselves from their perhaps envious sister institutions. Indeed, sometimes institutional vanity takes the form of nourishing ever more distinguished medical staffs who obtain not only a national but international reputation in hopes of attracting gifts and gifts in kind. It is much easier to attract money for high-prestige medical procedures than it is for public health. A board of trustees is astutely attuned to this reality. Who wants to give money for public health? People will give for heart transplants—it's instant money and instant fame.

Somehow it isn't flashy to give money for research in such public health problems as venereal diseases. Herpes simplex type 2, for example, affects millions—and currently still is incurable. Until recently, it took three to six days to diagnose. As the result of recent research, diagnosis takes twenty minutes. When this important breakthrough occurred, it barely received mention in the press. Articles about programs in this direction, tucked away in the dark recesses of the newspaper, pale beside such banner headlines as "Mass. Woman, 23, Gets New Heart; 5th Recipient in N.E."[115]

It is, therefore, relatively easy for a board of trustees to rationalize that even though venereal disease and AIDS are certainly important public health matters, we are going to leave them to others. We feel that our job is advancing research with such high-prestige items as heart, liver, pancreas, and so on, transplants.

Of particular interest in the heated public debate that erupted in the press was the conspicuous absence of direct involvement, in the sense of public leadership, of the various concerned hospital trustees as a body corporate. Preferring to keep their anonymity and dignity, they gave their "spirited horses" (the general administrators) their heads in taking the public limelight on the issue of transplants. Yet the resolution of the problem was unmistakenly a trustee responsibility.

The State's Interest. Stinging criticism from public officials serves to remind trustees that their obligation to the public good goes beyond just treading water or staying out of trouble. Trustees (not medical staff personnel) are answerable for policy. Professional medical aspirations do not exempt boards from accountability. If the medical staff wishes to conduct certain new technological medical procedures, the board of trustees must make the decision. However, in states like Massachusetts that exercise a high degree of regulation and control over hospitals and the health-care industry, state approval is often necessary before moving forward with new and unusual medical treatment.

Lured by the possibility of surefire success and by intense pressure from their respective medical staffs, in 1984 several hospitals in Boston—a city that likes to consider itself the medical Athens of the world—poised themselves solidly to be the world's leader in liver transplants. Four large hospitals—the highest number for any one city—gained state approval for liver transplant surgery, one of the most complicated, most surgically demanding, and most expensive of all current operative procedures. Data supplied by the hospitals show that a liver transplant operation can take from 22 to 24 hours, requires 35 to 50 people, uses up to 100 units of blood, and involves a long hospital stay. Some physicians have said that liver transplants can exceed $200,000 per operation.[116] Not of least importance are the postoperative drugs necessary in liver transplants to keep the body from rejecting the foreign tissue. Costs for these drugs can run to $100,000 or more a year; those cures have hidden costs.

Of particular interest here, however, is not cost per se, but the basis on which the state was saying no to some hospitals on transplantation.

The Commonwealth granted permission to four hospitals to do liver transplants, but it gave permission to only one hospital (at least temporarily) to do heart transplants. The rival hospitals were unhappy, protesting the task force's recommendation. However, George Annas, professor at Boston University's School of Public Health and chairman of the task force, wanted to limit heart transplants to one hospital. He felt that this approach "[put] the public interest ahead of individual institutional concerns."[117]

The State Department of Public Health, interested in hospital services for the greatest good for the greatest number, became concerned with what it believed to be other higher-priority health-care issues, especially the possibility of curtailed services to the poor as a result of the costly transplantation procedures. From the beginning of the regulatory debate, the task force on transplants recommended that the state should approach transplantation cautiously so as not to divert resources intended for other higher-priority health-care services. Therein lay the state's concern for the public good.

As state officials were beginning to bring down the regulatory screws on the basis of the public good vis-à-vis transplants, Boston's mayor began audaciously expressing deep concern for infant mortality in Roxbury and Dorchester—two areas of the city with significant numbers of poor people. The Department of Public Health issued statistics showing that the infant mortality rate in Boston was 15.8 deaths for every 1000 live births compared to the state average of 10.1 per 1000. Mayor Raymond L. Flynn asserted, "No society can claim to be just and compassionate when it abandons its commitment to its infant children."[118]

Within a stone's throw of the great hospitals vying for state approval for costly transplant procedures to benefit so few is a lack of basic health care for tens of thousands of people—the poor. Senator Edward L. Burke, a member of the state task force on transplantation, cut to the core of the matter when he said: "God bless the people who get new hearts and livers . . . . But I'm concerned about people living within the shadows of these institutions who cannot get good primary and secondary care."[119]

The essence of the matter is illustrated in the liver transplant controversy. In granting permission to selected hospitals to perform liver transplants, the state specified in its regulatory guidelines that hospitals "shall not, as a consequence of its undertaking a liver transplantation program, reduce the amount of free care provided to nonliver transplant patients."[120] ("Free care" refers to hospital services provided by the various hospitals for the poor who neither can pay nor have medical insurance.) The hospitals balked, insisting that the phrase *nonliver transplant* be deleted, which would, of course, allow hospitals to use free-care budgets for liver transplants.

The state regulators were not alone in their objections; the medical community was also critical. " 'It's unrealistic to think that you can add new technologies and not have someone else suffer,' protested Dr. Mitchell T. Rabkin, president of Beth Israel Hospital. 'It's a sham, it's a snare, it's a delusion, because the hospitals which said they would do this [not charge additionally] said they would do it for only one year. They are willing to sacrifice something else in order to get on the merry-go-round.' "[121]

Preventive Pathology. Particularly noteworthy in the regulatory travail was Massachusetts General Hospital's (MGH) involvement. MGH is a Harvard-affiliated hospital, and the Harvard Medical School is dedicated to preventive medicine and public health. Proof of this is in the Harvard Medical School's deep interest in Health Maintenance Organizations (HMOs). The Harvard Community Health Plan (HCHP) emanated from Harvard.

When the heart transplant medical phenomenon first hit the headlines in 1967, with the first successful transplant operation by Dr. Christiaan Barnard of Capetown, South Africa, who became world famous overnight, MGH made the purposeful decision not to move forward with such medical technology. Over the years MGH reaffirmed this bold position.

As recently as 1980 MGH issued a three-page press release stating, in effect, that even though such research had intrinsic importance, success was doubtful, and it would serve only a limited number of people at enormous cost.[122] (Estimates of heart transplant operation costs range from $75,000 to $150,000 or more.)

"To turn away even one potential cardiac transplantation patient is a very trying course to follow," the trustees said in a statement explaining their decision. "Yet in an age where technology so pervades the medical community, there is a clear responsibility to evaluate new procedures in terms of the greatest good for the greatest number."[123]

In substance, MGH preferred to spend money on public health matters rather than enormous sums on rare and isolated cases with little impact on the public good. It was an extraordinarily bold decision for the lay hospital trustees to make. Standing firm with great courage, the trustees withstood intense pressure from all sides, notably the medical staff, which had given nearly unanimous approval for the transplant project at MGH. The *Boston Globe* wrote about the decision as follows: "The trustees' decision is reportedly the first time that the lay governing board has refused to allow doctors there to adopt a new procedure."[124]

One major dissenting medical voice on the General Executive Committee, which represented the medical leadership at MGH, was Dr. Alexander Leaf, the chief of medicine. Dr. Leaf felt the hospital should devote more resources to preventive medicine rather than treating them with expensive down-the-line technologies.

"We keep telling ourselves we have to make tough allocation decisions and now we've come up to one and we've made it," said MGH Chief of Medicine Alexander Leaf, who staunchly opposes heart transplants and was the lone dissenting voice of the medical staff this time around. "Then people say, 'What's wrong with you? You're not innovative.' Well, I think we're going to have to do much more of this in the next 10 years."[125]

The Dilemma. The situtation, however, changed dramatically almost overnight with the Federal Food and Drug Administration's decision (November 1983) to license the drug cyclosporine for general use on a national basis. The drug reportedly significantly improved organ transplant results by helping prevent the body from rejecting the foreign tissue.[126] With the general availability of the drug, hospitals everywhere wanted to get on the transplant bandwagon. But barely a few months after this startling announcement, the press reported that the drug cyclosporine, despite its proclaimed usefulness for transplants, was extremely dangerous to the kidneys. An article in the *New England Journal of Medicine* reported that an individual who had received this drug was apt to experience kidney failure and the inevitable kidney dialysis—a medical program underwritten by the federal government. In response to this, Dr. Bryan D. Myers, who directed the study, said, "We think that in the coming years, a good proportion of the remainder [that is, transplants] are going to do the same."[127]

The substance of the heart transplant issue, however, centers around tightening hospital budgets. The bottom line is this: Can government through regulatory procedures keep nonprofit independent hospitals from invading their free-care budgets to pay for costly new technologies? The question can be asked in another form: Are the funds necessary for transplant operations justifiable in terms of the public good, which is the avowed basic principle on which hospitals are established? This is an issue trustees need to think about. Trustees—not medical staffs—need to evaluate the privileges they have under their charters that come with *pro bono publico*. This is a matter of judgment, conviction, and courage.

While the decision-making process continues to forge the path through unexplored territory, concerned trustees have an obligation to assume leadership, to discuss these issues with the public in line with their public trust, to evaluate all aspects of these complex issues, to stand strong behind decisions made with forthrightness and integrity—in short, to forge the future for the greatest good for the greatest number.

The road ahead for trustees is fraught with tensions involving public policy issues and advancing modern society with its accompanying technological innovations. Much will benefit humankind, but trustees will need to see clearly, like Robert Frost, how to travel the two diverging roads in a yellow wood to find the one less traveled that will make all the difference in health-care services.[128]

SUMMARY

In the current climate of change in the health-care field, hospital trustees must shift from a reactive role to one of leadership in health-care policy-making. They hold a responsibility for the public good. When this public trust is violated, the courts have demonstrated a willingness to intervene. A great deal of discretion is afforded the management of a charitable enterprise, but there are limits.

In the Queen of Angels Hospital case, the California Supreme Court held that a nonprofit corporation could not cease to perform the primary purpose for which it had been organized, running a hospital, and instead establish and run neighborhood clinics, even though charitable. Furthermore, the court held the board had no power to settle a baseless claim for compensation for past services with a retirement plan, as it would be a diversion of charitable assets. The acts were *ultra vires*.

In the Callaway case the Missouri Supreme Court held that a contract entered by a county hospital as an arm of a municipality was beyond the scope of its powers and thus void.

The charitable trust with unnamed beneficiaries is almost always enforced by a representative of the public, the state attorney general or a county law officer. This official's powers extend equally to charitable corporations and to charitable trusts. The attorney general represents the state and its interests in charities. She or he holds a prerogative not only to protect but also to enforce all charities as well as to represent interests of the community at large.

In the Holt case the California Supreme Court held that trustees of a medical college holding a minority view had the right to sue the corporation without the consent of the attorney general. The majority trustees intended to change the charitable purpose from the teaching of osteopathic to allopathic medicine.

In the McLean Hospital situation, public opinion in Massachusetts brought about the cancelation of the sale of a charitable psychiatric hospital to a profit-making hospital corporation. However, this plan has since been replaced by one in which the hospital will enter a joint venture with another profit-making hospital corporation.

In the Hahnemann Hospital case, the Massachusetts Supreme Judicial Court decided that a board of trustees retains the right to sell its main asset (the hospital). But the Court stated that the sale may need formal Court approval and that the subsequent use of funds cannot be violative of the gift instrument (the Converse trust).

In the Greisman case the New Jersey Supreme Court struck down a bylaw of a private charitable hospital, which was considered to be against public policy. The bylaw had effectively denied membership on the hospital's courtesy staff to a doctor because he was trained in osteopathic medicine.

Trustees enjoy great latitude in discharging their fiduciary duties, but they have not been given carte blanche in terms of what they see as best for the public interest. Not only must they remain faithful to the specific purposes for which the charitable organization is chartered but they also owe a duty to the donor. Trustees must adhere to the donor's wishes in terms of both the purposes of the trust and its expressed terms until or unless a court of proper jurisdiction instructs otherwise.

In the Bliss case the Connecticut Superior Court directed a trustee to obey the instructions of the trust's donor to use a portion of the income to maintain free hospital beds rather than devote it to a building fund. Despite the granting of "absolute discretion" to appoint or select, the trustee, according to the court, has only administrative discretion; the court always retains the dispositive discretion.

In the Meeker case a Missouri appeals court directed that the trustees follow the donor's wishes and continue to accumulate 25 percent of the annual income of a trust rather than make all the annual income available to the beneficiary. The court emphasized that ultimately what was best was a matter for the courts to decide, not the trustees.

In the Sibley Hospital, or Stern case, a federal district court in the District of Columbia created a set of principles against which to measure trustee behavior in fiscal affairs and formulated explicit guidelines for the trustees to follow. This action came about as a result of the abdication by the board of a charitable hospital of its supervisory role over investment policy and fiscal management in general. It may be proper for a board to appoint a committee of its members to deal with the investments of the corporation's funds, but the board must use due diligence in supervising the actions of those officers, employees, or outside experts to whom the responsibility for making day-to-day financial or investment decisions has been delegated.

The trustee must use utmost discretion in dealing with charitable property to avoid even the suggestion of conflict of interest. As a fiduciary the trustee is under a duty not to profit at the expense of the beneficiary.

In the Gilbert case the South Carolina Supreme Court found a fiduciary relationship between a hospital trustee and the hospital he served and thus voided a sale of hospital assets to the trustee even without a finding of fraud or fraudulent intent.

In the Monardo case a California court applied a broad interpretation to a conflict of interest statute and barred a nonprofit private hospital officer from serving on an elected governmental hospital board.

In the Leonard Morse Hospital case, the Massachusetts Supreme Judicial Court disagreed with the argument of the district attorney that the hospital's board of trustees of the hospital was a "governmental body" within the meaning of the state open meeting law. However, the mere fact that the subject was raised indicates the growing public sentiment for accountability of charitable assets.

Decisions of private independent boards of trustees are subject to governmental authority through three sources of law: common law, statutory law, and administrative regulations. However, policy is set by trustees; their major duties include the allocation of resources, human and financial, to achieve the objectives of the institution as expressed either implicitly or explicitly in its charter. Trustees need to evaluate the privileges that have been granted them in terms of the greatest good for the greatest number. Concerned trustees have an obligation to assume leadership, to discuss these issues with the public in line with their public trust, to evaluate all aspects of the issues, and to stand behind decisions made with forthrightness and integrity.

4

COLLEGES AND UNIVERSITIES

The trustees of the University are vested by its charter of incorporation with the power to conduct its affairs and are not subject to the interference of the state in that control in absence of an abuse of their fiduciary duties.

In re Antioch University, District of Columbia
Court of Appeals, 1980

INTRODUCTION

The governance of academic institutions is curious to the point of being picturesque. If you ask members of the faculty, who runs a university? they will probably say, the faculty, of course. If you ask an administrative officer—particularly the chief administrative officer—the response will likely be, the president, of course. If you ask a member of the board of trustees, the response will probably be a little less assured and a little less hardy, but along these lines: Well, the faculty takes care of the academic aspects of the university. The president has the obligation to keep the whole place moving along smoothly, but of course it is the board of trustees who makes the final decision.

The significance of this latter response is that it is contrary to both common (court decisions) and statutory (legislative) law, which clearly states to a great extent that the board of trustees is the university. Trustees are inclined, however, to be less assertive that they are indeed the beginning and end of the university and as such are fully responsible to the public they serve. Further, they have the duty to see that charitable property is not diverted from the public purposes for which it was entrusted to their care and that no one realizes an unwarranted gain. The examples of intrusion of the courts into the affairs of colleges and universities (that is, their boards of trustees, public or private, through common or statutory law) are so varied and numerous that even a fairly lengthy, single chapter in a small book can provide only a few illustrations.

President Benjamin Wheeler's Story

Confusion about who governs colleges and universities is not new. Picture this. President Benjamin Ide Wheeler of the University of California, upon becoming the Roosevelt Professor at the University of Berlin for 1909–10, was introduced to Wilhelm II, kaiser of Germany, by an eminent German professor, Adolph Harnack. In making the introduction, Professor Harnack began by saying: "Will Your Majesty graciously receive our distinguished guest from the United States. He fitly bears the title of 'Exchange Professor,' since he comes from a monarchy within a republic to a republic within a monarchy."[1] So went the introduction, and so go the myths suffusing American and German university governance; both tend to overlook the real governance situation.

Even though faculties in neither country have any final say, the American professoriat continues to believe that the Germans have more control. Historically, faculties of German universities have governed themselves by controlling their internal affairs. German professors do have a major voice in curricular matters, and their senior members possess lifetime tenure. The influence of the ministry of education remains dominant, however. Two critical powers retained by the ministry of education keep the important governing rights in the hands of the state, not the faculty. These are the control of finances, including the preparation and approval of budgets and the management of endowments and buildings, and also the appointment of all holders of salaried academic posts.[2]

In the United States, faculties are in substance governed by trustees and their president, and presidents are appointed by boards of trustees. In Germany presidents are elected by their respective faculties. The freedom essentially ascribed to German university professors is ostensibly a myth.

The Powers That Be

Beyond the mythology of university governance in other countries, today's board-to-the-bench syndrome personifies trustee failings, such as inertia, several kinds of ignorance, nonperformance, and confusion and uncertainty about their appropriate role. On occasion one finds a trustee who is willing to state the importance of taking more control over academic decision-making. Such a maverick trustee, however, is more than likely to be quarantined by the majority until the individual absorbs the group's *modus operandi* and behaves more to the liking of the majority of the board.

One need only observe a trustees' meeting to learn how often ill-informed and unprepared trustees are to meet their fiduciary obligations at common or statutory law. At the American Academy of Arts and Sciences' second conference on the governance of universities, Jeff Greenfield, then assistant to the mayor of New York City, commented:

I have been to board of regents meetings at the University of Wisconsin and they are simply a joke. The expertise is all on the side of the administrators. There is no way the regents can provide an effective check because they do not have the information. The regents are as vulnerable as any welfare mother in a ghetto trying to confront some white-collar planner who has all the facts at his disposal. The result is downright immoral.[3]

Administrators sometimes deliberately keep their trustees uninformed because they have an inherent insecurity and perhaps even a deep-seated guilt about the kind of ship they are running. This, in turn, leads to the sophistic belief that the less the trustees know, the easier "my" job as president will be. Such a myopic view of the presidency is commonplace and perhaps even condoned, because it makes the trustee's job so much easier, especially when the trustee serves for social status or advantage. The result may be less discussion in board meetings, where it is more comfortable for everyone to talk about the surging "bull" or sagging "bear" market instead.

There are, however, other situations that are quite different. At one small liberal arts college for women, the board of trustees takes a strong interest and plays a deep and continuing role in the college's affairs. Several committees within the board are active, and the college is able to raise substantial funds when needed. Some board meeting time is devoted to the portfolio when the Finance Committee gives a report, but the time allotment is kept in perspective, and other committees receive appropriate attention. Instead of dwelling on how much money can be made, there is cogent discussion of the portfolio in terms of how it can enhance the quality of education for young people.

Committee reports are discussed knowledgeably, because each board member has read the report before the meeting. The college president does not drone on about trivialities of the college and campus life in general; the board would not tolerate such an approach. The board demands and receives a president who has presence, not only on the campus but beyond. This board is alive, the college is doing well, the faculty is highly motivated and doing outstanding teaching and research, and the student body is of high quality.

It is in the best interest of the college to foster boards of this repute. A crown jewel of any college is its board of trustees—sparkling, glistening with activism and visibility. Good boards do exist; all too frequently, however, the rubber-stamp kind also exists, to the detriment of the college or university. Witness the mushrooming litigation in which boards find themselves embroiled for lack of attention to the management of the colleges entrusted to their care.

The governance of academic institutions is often characterized by a discrete misunderstanding of egos, with administrators and faculty usually claiming a responsibility they in fact do not have. Trustees find themselves more comfortable evading a responsibility that is clearly theirs alone. For this reason, the research base for this study was difficult, since no institution wanted to see its legal conflicts and their resolution in print. Such institutional litigations are generally not published in the professional literature; when they are, they are reported in the most indefinite and ambiguous terms so as not to offend "the powers that be." The Wilson College case that follows represents an exception.

RESTRUCTURING BOARDS OF TRUSTEES

The College That Refused to Die: Wilson College,
Chambersburg, Pennsylvania

Let's Keep It Entre Nous. The surprise announcement about the fate of Wilson
College, a small women's institution in Chambersburg, Pennsylvania, came at
a mandatory all-college meeting on 19 February 1979. "Wilson College shall
close at the end of the current semester"[4] were the words that fell from the lips
of Martha B. Walker, chairperson of the board of trustees (hereafter, board).
The student newspaper *Billboard* reported initial student reaction: "Upon hearing
this, my heart dropped to its very depths. Cries of pain and sorrow rose from
the lower level of the hall. I turned to one of my friends and asked, 'Are we
dreaming?' And she had tears rolling down her cheeks."[5]

At a support rally following the closure announcement, Gretchen Van Ness,
president of the student government association, threw down the gauntlet to the
board when she said: "The decision to close the college at the end of this academic
year comes as a shock to all of us. We realize there are problems, some of them
very serious, but we refuse to accept the Board of Trustees' decision that there
are no viable solutions."[6]

Ms. Van Ness challenged the rulers to account to the ruled. She said in
substance that there were limits to trustee power under their enfranchisement
because all corporations, public or private, derived their authority to act as a
corporation from the state, through the charter, and that trustees were under an
obligation to operate within their charter for the public good.

The board of Wilson College had agreed from the beginning of the discussions
on closure that the whole matter should be kept strictly confidential. The reason
given was that a rumor of possible closing would trigger a decline in applicants
and place great strain on the already deteriorating situation; such a rumor in the
Philadelphia papers during the previous year had already been suspected of
creating a drop in applications that year. Thus, the board's announcement of its
well-kept secret stunned the Wilson community and others.

The announcement cited two developments that had led to the board's decision:
(1) the declining rate of contributions from individuals, foundations, and corporations and (2) the inability of the college to attract enough students for the
next freshman class.[7] While publicly denying that the college was going bankrupt,
the board was in substance saying that it was.

Wilson's situation in the spring of 1979 polarized around fiscal pressures
created by a drastically curtailed enrollment situation. For several years running,
the spartan endowment of the college had been invaded to cover annual operating
deficits until there was little more than $300,000 remaining in unrestricted funds.
The board was in the precarious financial position of finding it almost impossible
to borrow money despite the fact that more than $4 million in restricted endow-

ment and scholarship funds remained, not including the almost $10 million book value of College realty and equipment.[8]

The fiscal/enrollment picture, exacerbated by the board's apparent inability, or perhaps refusal, to make an informed judgment on the situation, had deteriorated to a costly 5-to-1 student-faculty ratio. This was described by some "as high and unsupportable, and luxurious," as the "normal ratio for a small private women's college is 10 to 12 students per faculty member." The number of freshmen had shrunk from a peak of 252 in 1965 to only 55 in 1978, with a total enrollment of 214 on 1 February 1979 on a campus adequate for 650 students. The answer to the crisis, the board believed, was to close the college, placing all remaining assets in a foundation for the general purpose of fostering "liberal education of women for excellence, for leadership, for service."[9]

The alumnae, stunned and angered by the decision, prevailed on the trustees to think again. On 10 March 1979, however, "the Board reconfirmed its previous decision to close Wilson College effective June 30, 1979."[10]

A number of devout alumnae swiftly formalized their disappointment and anger into a Save Wilson Committee. They succeeded in convincing the Franklin County Pennsylvania Court of Common Pleas, Orphans Court Division, Chambersburg, Pennsylvania, that the case be heard. The alumnae began to raise $1 million to help their beleaguered college. The petitioners (the individuals who presented the petition to the court) in the Wilson College case (*Zehner v. Alexander*) filed a class action suit. The suit charged the board with numerous counts of mismanagement, including the following: (1) failure to implement the Middle States accreditation report, (2) failure to recruit new students or to use alumnae in the recruitment effort, (3) failure to curtail expenditure in view of income, (4) failure to reorganize and maintain a competent and effective administrative staff, (5) failure to devise and implement a plan for faculty retrenchment.[11]

Noteworthy is the fact that the petitioners sought neither punitive damages nor individual trustee personal liability for any mismanagement, nor the deprivation of any special status the college had previously enjoyed. The alumnae, however, sought court supervision over the college's operation, the removal of the trustees, appointment of new trustees, and the reversal of the closure decision.[12]

The board's unpropitious announcement envenomed the college's constituencies. In the melee that followed, an unrelenting barrage of charges and countercharges shot wildly around the Wilson campus and into the media. The trustees entrenched themselves behind the motto "death with dignity," while the alumnae, students, former trustees, donors, and others became as determined to keep Wilson open as the board was to close it.

Bringing Truth to Light. The showdown came during the week of 7 May 1979, during hearings at the Franklin County Common Pleas Court. Students, faculty, alumnae, and friends of Wilson College jammed the courtroom as the Save Wilson Committee presented its case to prevent the 110-year-old Wilson

College from closing on 30 June. The burden of proof lay squarely on the Wilson board. In effect, they had to justify their 17 February decision on the basis that "it was impractical or impossible to continue Wilson College."[13]

On 25 May 1979 a little known, but courageous judge jolted the Wilson board with his decision, which also sent judicial shock waves throughout the higher education milieu. Judge John W. Keller, in an 87–page judicial opinion, which included 276 specific findings of fact and 21 different conclusions of law, found that the trustees had been seriously misled by the president; had permitted mismanagement of the college, especially in the critical area of admissions; and had failed to bring their expertise to the board.[14]

Reversing the 17 February decision of the Wilson College board to close the liberal arts college, as well as taking the highly unusual judicial action of removing two trustees from office, the court stated:

The difficult days that lie ahead for Wilson College, its governing board, its alumnae and its student body are obvious. However, we doubt that those future days are any more fraught with peril, any more risky, any more doomed to failure than the conditions and circumstances which confronted the incorporators 110 years ago.[15]

The court held that the fulfillment of the charter purposes were neither impossible nor impractical, though in jeopardy as a result of the improvident and precipitous decision of the board of trustees on 17 February 1979. The untimely closure decision seriously impacted other areas as well, for example, the recruitment program, the ongoing academic and financial integrity of the college, and the credibility of the college as a functioning educational institution. The damage incurred was extremely serious.[16]

Assuming the trustees honestly believed it was impossible or impractical for Wilson to continue as an institution of higher learning, they simply were not aware that under Pennsylvania law they needed approval to end or alter the corporation in its current form. It is astounding that the president "was not advised by counsel that only the Court had authority to decide whether the College would be closed."[17] Revealing of the trustees' naïveté was their denial to the court that proceeding with closure necessitated amending the college's Articles of Incorporation, securing a court order to divert (change the use of) the assets committed to Wilson College, or instituting any *cy pres* (nearness) proceeding of any type. Even more amazing is the fact that the trustees also denied the existence of the court's "supervisory powers" to conclude that the actions of the trustees were improper.

The Establishment Reacts. The higher education establishment quickly denounced Judge Keller's bold judicial decision. Ms. Elisabeth Clarkson, an alumna and trustee of Wilson who later became chairperson of the restructured board, said, "Much commentary about Judge Keller seemed to me truly mean-spirited."[18] An editorial cited by Ms. Clarkson from the journal *Change* in part reads:

The judge's *decree nisi* [a provisional decree that becomes absolute unless cause be shown against it] consists of a schoolmasterish potpourri of managerial nit-picking and some outright ludicrous assumptions. Over 60 paragraphs alone are devoted to a detailed recitation of the functioning or malfunctioning of Wilson's Admissions Office, including a count of admission reply cards.[19]

In discussing the notion that the judge was the villain in the case, Ms. Clarkson observed:

Though most people wouldn't have bet on the Save Wilson plaintiffs' winning the decision, several trustees began to wonder as the evidence mounted of administrative ineptitude or insensitivity, disaster in the Admissions department which they had not known about, a record of poor human relations, plus an instance of altered board minutes with a whiff of cloak-and-dagger about it.[20]

Writing for the *New York Times*, Fred Hechinger hit the nail on the head: "Perhaps the real reason why the Wilson College case alarmed so many college trustees is that Judge Keller said what board members prefer not to hear. He told the Wilson board bluntly that it had not done its job. It had failed, he said, to inform itself about the institution's management."[21]

Following the court's decision a majority of the remaining trustees chose to resign. Because the controversy caused so much comment nationwide, the Association of Governing Boards of Universities and Colleges analyzed the situation in *AGB Reports*.[22] The review cleared Judge Keller from any abuse of judicial authority in the matter.

Even though some people may have viewed the court's intervention as unnecessary judicial intrusion, the court considered its involvement a means of enforcing the law regarding fiduciary obligations of Wilson's trustees. Joseph Gies, editor of publications for the Association of Governing Boards, writes in *AGB Reports* as follows: "This new board and the new president it appointed found themselves confronted, amid all their other problems, with a severe public relations handicap: the instant negative reaction of their peers in Pennsylvania and around the country to the shock of Judge Keller's decision, almost universally perceived as *governmental intrusion*"[23] (emphasis added).

Judge Keller challenged the trustees to demonstrate the same courage that the founding trustees of the college had displayed when they asked for subscriptions from Franklin County residents to establish the college. "Wilson was a pioneer college, the beginning of a great movement in the United States," declared Dr. Paul Swain Havens, president emeritus of Wilson College, "and it has continued without a break since its founding."[24]

Serving the Public Interest. The Wilson College case serves to jog awareness that we are a nation of laws, and no one—not even trustees—is above it. It also cogently illustrates several general principles that should guide trustee behavior, regardless of the particular type of charitable institution.

The source of authority in a charitable institution is the same as that in the democratic state itself: the citizenry. As professor Cyril Houle writes:

A board is never the sole master of its own organization. The outside influences brought to bear on it vary from situation to situation, but, in general, they include laws, the wishes of the constituency, constitutional provisions, traditions, commitments made to other agencies or associations, and regulations established by some higher authority such as a national association.[25]

Fiduciary responsibility centers around a legal relationship between the trustees and the public—the entity whom the trustees serve. In terms of substantive law, which defines the rights and obligations of individuals, trustees have a right to manage the charitable property, but they also have a duty to manage the charitable organization for the public's benefit. "A trustee in a nonprofit institution holds a position of public trust. As a fiduciary, the trustee serves the institution and the public to which the institution is dedicated."[26] In rendering his decision, Judge Keller properly recognized the interest the public had in its charities when he said, "the implementation of the decision to close Wilson College without prior approval of the Court attempted to deprive the public, represented by the Attorney General as parens patriae, of an opportunity to comment upon or protest the decision."[27]

More specifically, trustees must fulfill the unique mandate of the charter— the privilege granted by the government—under which that particular charitable institution was founded. The charter specifies the purpose of the charitable institution, which takes its place in a complex of other charitable organizations— each with a purpose and each contributing to a network of nonprofit services to the public. If a charitable organization exceeds the bounds of its charter or what is permissible under applicable law, it engages in an *ultra vires* act. For example, a charitable organization chartered as a nonprofit organization to provide orchestral music through public performances cannot engage in political action activities, even though those activities may be nonprofit. If it did, the board would be exceeding the bounds of its chartered activities. The charter defines and delimits the powers of the trustees. Through this instrument, usually granted by the state through its secretary of state's office, trustees fulfill their fiduciary responsibilities for the public good.

Within this framework the court stated that "the trustees of Wilson College have a fiduciary responsibility to the College to fulfill the mandate of its charter, viz. that it be a teaching institution."[28]

The fiduciary responsibility of the board of trustees requires it to use all assets of the college in the continuance of the college as an institution of higher learning and as a teaching institution until its charter purposes become impossible to fulfill, which is precisely the question that Judge Keller raised in his opening remarks.[29]

The court then proceeded to educate the trustees—something the court felt the president of the college should have done—to meet their fiduciary responsibilities in accordance with common and statutory law.

The court held that the trustees "could determine that the corporation should discontinue its chartered non-profit activities; but it had no lawful right to set a termination date for those non-profit activities or take any steps toward the implementation of that termination decision until Court approval had been secured."[30] The court also held that "without prior Court approval the Board of Trustees of Wilson College had no lawful right to determine what disposition should be made of the assets of the non-profit corporation."[31]

Failure to understand this led to some serious consequences. According to the court: "By implementing the decision to close Wilson College, the trustees attempted to essentially deprive the Court of its power to review the recommendation of the Board and to approve or disapprove the proposed diversion of college assets from a teaching institution to some other charitable use."[32] On the issue of the existence of court supervisory power, it was made abundantly clear that trustees cannot take on a regal aura, usurping the court's supervisory authority over charitable institutions. On this point the court was quite specific, citing Pennsylvania Supreme Court rules, which state that the Orphans' Court has jurisdiction to hear such cases. Judge Keller also cited several lower court decisions—and Wilson was a lower court ruling—indicating that "the scope of the rule contemplates that that authority extends to all *internal* matters of nonprofit corporations for charitable purposes"[33] (emphasis added).

The court's scrutiny of the internal affairs of Wilson College revealed some aspects of trusteeship that warrant careful consideration by trustees in general. After examining the general financial picture of the college, the court found that "the College is not bankrupt or near that fiscal disaster point. The assets far exceed the established or presently known potential liabilities."[34]

The court also found that the projection of a 1979 freshman class of 164 students after receiving an estimated 11,000 inquiries was not warranted on the basis of any facts submitted. The *Wilson College Alumnae Newsletter* reported that Judge Keller heard sworn testimony that "1,500 second requests for specific information about Wilson College were left unanswered for five months on a shelf of the Admissions Office."[35] About this, the court said, "The failure of the Director of Admissions . . . is inexplicable and inexcusable."[36] The court then noted, "All evidence establishes the Director of Admissions was not competent to perform the duties of his office, and the student recruitment program of the College suffered accordingly."[37] The court observed, "The President of the College failed in her responsibility to adequately supervise the Director of Admissions in the discharge of his mission."[38]

One of the most telling moments on the management of the college appeared in the findings as follows:

The failure of the President and Chairman Walker to inform the Board, the student body and the alumnae of the evident failure of the widely touted successful admissions program in early January 1979 was an unreasonable nondisclosure, improper and irresponsible; and it directly contributed to the Board's panic reaction and sense of urgency to close [the college] at the February 3, 1979 meeting[39] [when the Board became aware of the pending enrollment crisis].

Thus, "those members of the Board of Trustees who voted in favor of the resolution to conclude the operation of the College in its present form, establish a Foundation, and fund it with the remaining assets of the College acted precipitously without sufficient or valid information and consequently irresponsibly."[40]

Learning Lessons. The *New York Times* wrote that the judge had "declared the college's management bankrupt but not its treasury."[41] The Wilson trustees were not, and are not, alone in their general misunderstanding of the vital area of fiscal/enrollment management. Such misunderstanding is as ordinary as a common cold.

Colleges experiencing enrollment difficulties are often operated on a management-by-crisis basis. The situation often stems from the board's failure not only to evaluate the effectiveness of its chief executive officer but also to inform itself properly of the college's mission and activities. Both the board of trustees and the college president need to be visible in appropriate realms in order to attract gifts and students. In general, the president will work with the public sector to raise money and attract students, and the trustees will work on the level of trustee to trustee with foundations, corporations, and other entities that offer grants.

One important lesson to be learned from the Wilson case is that when boards authorize committee or consultant reports to assist in decision making, the board must give thoughtful consideration to them. Trustees simply cannot reject these reports out of hand without stating cogent reasons in a board meeting for their actions, because accountability is a prime consideration in trusteeship.

The Wilson board commissioned reports, then failed to act on them. Taking notice of this, the court wrote that both a major consultant report (the Moon Report) and the Middle States Association accreditation report had been virtually ignored. The Moon Report "is an extraordinarily well-written analysis of the problem areas of Wilson College and comprehensive proposals for the correction of the same. It is written to be read and understood by persons whose education and training is [sic] not necessarily in the field of college administration."[42]

After receiving the report, the board took minimal action on it by appointing an implementation committee at one of its meetings. Subsequently, however, there was "no evidence that the Board via its implementation committee, any other committee, or as a full Board took any action to monitor progress toward the implementation of the recommendations of the Moon Report following the November 1974 meeting."[43] In the end, this inattention to the management of the college became devastating to the trustees' defense because they failed to exercise the kind of judgment expected of a trustee in a fiduciary capacity.

Removing Trustees. Although stopping short of removing the entire board (because the evidence did not support such a move), the court did remove two trustees: Dr. Mary Patterson McPherson, president of Bryn Mawr College, and Dr. Margaret Waggoner, president of Wilson College, who was a ''member of the Board of Trustees, and not an ex-officio member.''[44]

In Dr. McPherson's case, two basic problems surfaced.

Dr. Mary Patterson McPherson shall be removed from the Board of Directors of Wilson College due to the patent conflict of interest existing between Bryn Mawr College where she is the chief executive officer and Wilson College; and due to her failure to exercise her recognized expertise as a director of Wilson College.[45]

The first problem dealt with the fact that a trustee of a nonprofit corporation may not have any interest conflicting with the interest of the corporation. In this regard, Judge Keller reasoned that both colleges, located in the same geographic area, must compete for women students out of the national pool of students.

According to J. Thomas Menaker, lawyer for the Wilson trustees, ''the order marked the first time a judge had found that a conflict of interest was created when the president of one college served on the board of another.''[46]

The second problem addressed the issue of bringing personal expertise to a board. The court said, ''The law requires trustees of a non-profit corporation to bring to the board to which they are elected or appointed that expertise which can reasonably be expected considering their training, experience and background; for the duties and responsibilities of such trustees may not be taken lightly.''[47]

''Miss McPherson,'' according to *The Chronicle of Higher Education*, ''said she and many of the other trustees thought enrollment had declined because the college 'is geographically remote, it is a single-sex institution, and it has a traditional curriculum,' and because 'Pennsylvania has more institutions than are necessary.' ''[48]

Even though Dr. McPherson claimed it was not her position as trustee to run the admissions office on a day-to-day basis, the court was noting that she had ignored a vital part of her job as a trustee: she had failed to inquire adequately about admissions.[49]

Ms. Clarkson commented about this in an *AGB Reports* article:

Judge Keller spoke here of Dr. McPherson's expert knowledge in Admissions, and it is distinctly possible that she might have been a great deal more critical and outspoken in an area where the trustees were, I believe, seriously underinformed. Yet Mary Patterson McPherson was singled out for a criticism that might have been leveled at all of us— being too busy or too uncritical or too leery of conflict to exercise, in our trusteeship, our own fields of expertise.[50]

The court stipulated that as soon as the conflict of interest was removed in regard to Dr. McPherson, she could again serve on the board. However, Dr.

Margaret Waggoner, president of Wilson College, was removed permanently as a trustee. Enumerating a number of failures that had occurred in the office of the president, the court, using statutory language, said, "The evidence establishes a gross abuse of discretion and authority on the part of Dr. Margaret Waggoner, President of Wilson College, and she shall be removed as a member of the Board of Trustees of Wilson College."[51]

Perhaps in too many instances, a college, or other charitable institution, gets into unnecessary trouble because the board of trustees places too much confidence in or delegates too much responsibility to its operating chief executive officer. Trustees should never become figureheads; they should be individuals of concern and dedication, who both desire and are willing to lend a helping hand to achieve goals. Further, trustees may consult the staff, but they should never replace their own judgment with staff consultations and recommendations because the essential function of trusteeship is to render disinterested judgments on the college's programs. Foremost, the trustee should be divorced from the day-to-day operation of the college or university. His or her judgments should be those of a generalist rather than a specialist, much as the president and the Congress of the United States are a check on the Pentagon and the military establishment.

The Judge Talks with the Press. In a rare instance Judge Keller granted the local press an interview to discuss the Wilson College case, noting that his decision was not an easy one. Journalist Dave Dunkle reported on Judge Keller's remarks from the interview, which helped clarify the rationale behind the judge's decision:

"I just felt she [Dr. Waggoner] had not properly discharged her duties as a trustee," Keller continued. "Based on the evidence presented, it was clearly impossible for Dr. Waggoner to continue as a member of the trustees. I had no authority to remove her as president and never considered doing so."

Keller noted that the by-laws of Wilson require that the college president be a member of the trustee, [sic] "but that could not override a court decision. They would have just had a vacancy on the board had they chosen to retain her as president. . . ."

He said that the present trustees, if they should ever decide to close the college, will still be required to prove the necessity of such an action.

"The burden of proof, of establishing the impossibility or impracticality of continuing as a college, will remain on the board," he said, adding that advance notice to the court and the Attorney General's office would be required.[52]

Judge Keller's words resoundingly remind trustees that there are legal limits to trustee power and that the court is willing to involve itself in the internal matters of a nonprofit institution when its trustees, stewards of property that has a public use, act against the public good. Moreover, the Wilson decision is instructive for colleges and universities in other states because Pennsylvania Nonprofit Corporation Law—like many other states—requires trustees to act with good faith and with the highest fidelity. Moreover, the statute, as interpreted by the courts, requires court approval before charitable property can be diverted to another charitable purpose from the original purpose for which the property was donated.

A determined response from a dedicated group of alumnae—whom some thought to be a group of maverick dissidents—refused to let Wilson die. Wilson became the "little college that could" after the obstacles were removed from its path of survival.

Dr. Harry Buck, professor of religious studies since 1959, "blamed the move to close on an administration that forgot it was the 1970s and ran the school like it was still the 1950s."[53] After Judge Keller's emphatic statement "Neither on the facts [n]or the law was the Board of Trustees justified in resolving on February 17, 1979 to close Wilson College as of June 30, 1979,"[54] Dr. Donald Bletz became acting president with the clarion call to rebuild. Under his leadership Wilson emerged into a new age. In a spirit of renewal the trustees chose Dr. Mary-Linda Sorber Merriam as Wilson's fourteenth president, and under her leadership Wilson began moving full steam ahead.

Perhaps there is a "singular appropriateness," as Judge Keller notes, "of Daniel Webster's famous statement in the Dartmouth College case: 'It is, sir, as I have said, a small college, and yet there are those who love it.' "[55]

"Like a Sardine Merging into the Belly of a Whale": Mannes College, New York, New York

The New York State Board of Regents. While the Wilson College trial was ongoing in Chambersburg, the New York State Board of Regents (hereafter, regents) was determining the fate of Mannes College of Music. The regents removed nine Mannes College trustees from office for "neglect of duty"[56] on 24 May 1979, one day before Judge Keller issued his decree to the Wilson board. The Mannes case presented a slightly different coloration in the trustee removal process in that a public body acting in an unusual instance of decisive intervention determined whether a private college should continue in operation.

The regents in the Mannes case acted under the state's Education Law. This law authorizes the removal of a college trustee for "misconduct, incapacity, neglect of duty, or where it appears to the satisfaction of the regents that the [college] corporation has failed or refuses to carry into effect its educational purposes."[57] Created in 1784 the Regents of the University of the State of New York is the oldest agency regulating all education in New York. Its authority extends over public and private institutions classified as educational in the state, including the provision that it has sole authority to incorporate any university, college, library, museum, and other entities that can convince the regents that its "approved purposes are, in whole or in part, of educational or cultural value deemed worthy of recognition and encouragement."[58]

Controversy at Mannes. Located in New York City and occupying four brownstone buildings, Mannes College of Music, established in 1916 by David and

Clara Damrosch Mannes, lists many well-known musicians among its graduates, including Julius Rudel, Murray Perahia, and Frederica von Stade.

The controversy that erupted in January 1979 and ultimately led to the removal of nine trustees in May of that same year began when the boards of Mannes College and the Manhattan School of Music, the largest conservatory in the country, contemplated a merger. The aim of the merger was to ease financial difficulties in both schools, although Mannes had survived a series of fiscal crises in its recent past.

Threatened with heavy deficits in 1975, Mannes raised $183,000—chiefly from an appeal to foundations and private donors—to head off a shutdown. Shortly thereafter the board appointed as president Miss Rise Stevens, the former Metropolitan Opera singer, who, after three years, resigned in a dispute with the board. The board then appointed Mr. Jack Watson as acting president. During his tenure the pot came to a rolling boil.

A bitter controversy surrounded the contemplated merger, with both students and faculty opposed to the plan. Those familiar with the merger plan said that the terms of the consolidation largely benefited the Manhattan School. The faculty not only demanded that the board desist from all future merger talks but went so far as to adopt a resolution of no confidence, asking the board of Mannes to resign. "The resolution stated," reported the *New York Times*, "that the 14–member board had demonstrated 'consistent inability to meet the financial needs of this institution [Mannes],' that it had 'ignored the professional opinions of the faculty,' and disregarded the needs of the students."[59]

Before the merger the students circulated a petition demanding that the trustees oppose the plan, which was euphemistically referred to as a "unification" of the two institutions. The merger was to take place with the stipulations that "the Manhattan curriculum remain unchanged, that no Manhattan teacher could be discharged, that the consolidated institutions accept no more than 10 or 15 Mannes teachers and that the new name of the school begin with 'Manhattan.' "[60] Mannes had about 160 teachers on its faculty at the time, although many were employed on a part-time basis. Further, the newly constituted eighteen-member board would include only seven members from the Mannes board. Clearly, the Manhattan trustees would be in the majority on the new board.

Two concerned, dissenting Mannes board members, Craig D. Burrell and Miss Marya Mannes, poet and critic and a daughter of the founder, first filed suit in the state supreme court asking that the majority trustees be "made to show cause why they should not be restrained from 'acting in any way to promote or effect the merger' until the issues in the dispute could be resolved."[61]

Despite the force of opposition, the merger resolution sailed through the boards on a conditional vote pending approval by the New Ycrk State Board of Regents.

In the complaint to the court, the petitioners charged that the fiscal picture of Mannes had been misrepresented by the board to pave the way for the merger. The *New York Times* reported:

"No attention was given to the fact," he [Mr. Burrell] said, "that in the years 1975, 1976, and 1977 there had been no deficit and that the prospects in 1978 had appeared to be so favorable that in July 1978 a mortgage on the school property had been paid off, although no demand for payment had been made by the lender."[62]

To expedite the case the New York County State Supreme Court issued a show cause order, a legal proceeding that speeds up the beginning of litigation by requiring the adverse party to respond more quickly than ordinarily under a complaint. (The trial court in New York State is called the supreme court, whereas the state's highest court is styled the Court of Appeals.) One day before the hearing was to occur in the supreme court, the Mannes board decided to call off the merger plan on the basis that the proposal did not offer optimal educational opportunities to students and faculty. Despite this decision, dissension, cleavages, and divisiveness snarled the trustees' activities.

Filing a petition with the regents, the two dissenting trustees, along with a group representing the faculty, requested that eleven members of the fourteen-member Mannes board be removed for willfully engaging in the dismemberment of Mannes. The regents in the meantime authorized Chancellor Theodore M. Black to investigate the circumstances surrounding the merger, leading to the creation of a three-member regents committee to inquire into the situation. Subsequently the committee, after a formal hearing, reported its "reluctant but unanimous and inescapable conclusion that the Mannes College board of trustees has, during the past year, demonstrated with respect to certain critical matters a collective neglect of duty which is appalling."[63]

The Regents Remove the Board of Trustees. The full board of regents, supporting its inquiry committee, voted to remove nine members of the Mannes board and appointed new ones. Included in the removal order were the two dissenting trustees, because their actions were indistinguishable from other members on critical matters, the committee said.

Among the "critical issues" cited in the findings of the regents committee were the following:

- That the trustees permitted the acting president, Mr. Watson, in substance, to eliminate one major department of the college by laying off faculty members and to decimate a second department with no reasoned consideration or formal authorization by the trustees and no consultation with the faculty.

- That the board, despite Mr. Watson's firm intent to resign as of the end of June, 1979, had neither made an appointment nor had a serious search under way for a new president.

- That the trustees had permitted the administration to distribute a catalog for the academic year 1979–80 not only listing among the faculty for the forthcoming academic year individuals who had been terminated but also offering the courses taught by the laid-off faculty.[64]

Concerning the acting president's involvement, the Mannes trustees unequivocally conceded at the regents hearing that the Mannes board had neither "approved nor disapproved" presidential decisions. About this the regents' report states that "inaction by the trustees clearly constitutes an abdication of their individual and collective responsibilities."[65]

Although the regents committee recommended the removal of nine trustees, the committee found the merger actions neither improper nor necessarily inappropriate. "While the way in which some of the respondent trustees dealt with the merger possibility was inept and was insensitive to the legitimate concerns of both faculty and students," the regents said, "the actions in question do not reach the level of misconduct, incapacity, or neglect of duty."[66] Thus, the board of trustees of Mannes were removed not for the merger plans but for other actions that demonstrated a "collective neglect of duty" as determined by the regents.

The board of regents appointed new trustees. They in turn promptly appointed a new administration headed by Mr. Charles H. Kaufman, a spokesperson for the faculty who had criticized the reason—which was financial in nature—given for the merger by the old board. "There was no way it could have survived," said the college's new president. "The trustees were attempting to bury the school. They were doing everything they could to get rid of it."[67] Mr. Kaufman at one point in the controversy had eloquently referred to the merger of Mannes with the Manhattan School as "a merger, yes—like a sardine merging into the belly of a whale."[68]

Bitter Pinch of Pain: Grace Institute, New York, New York

Exercising Corporate Powers. A trustee can be removed by the court or by the board itself for proper cause. In New York the law is settled that a corporation possesses the inherent power to remove a member, officer, or director for cause. This is true even though the charter or bylaws do not provide for trustee removal. Acting under corporate law, the board of trustees of Grace Institute removed a life member and trustee for engaging in behavior the board believed to constitute "disloyalty." The case made it all the way to the Court of Appeals of New York, which supported the board of trustees.

Grace Institute was founded by William P. Grace and Michael P. Grace. Incorporated by an act of the New York Legislature in 1897, the institute serves "the purpose of furnishing women and girls instruction in trades and occupations and in branches of domestic arts and science."[69] Three named members of the Grace family and their successors were constituted body corporate; all the powers and privileges of the corporation were to be exercised by the trustees, which consisted of the three life members and a variable number of other individuals selected by the life members. At the time of the litigation, there were nine trustees.

Michael P. Grace II, a successor to one of the original life members, had begun several legal actions against the institute—actions in which he was uniformly unsuccessful. The board of trustees, primarily as a result of the lawsuits started by Michael Grace, drew up charges against him and held a hearing, in which he was represented by counsel but refused to testify. Thereafter the board removed him as life member and trustee of the institute on the grounds that his "conduct was so inimical to the corporate interests as to require his removal."[70] In 1966, Michael Grace began a court action against the board. After reviewing each action and the entire record of the case, the Court of Appeals reached the conclusion that the evidence clearly supported the findings of the trustees—that is, that Michael Grace "had embarked on a course of conduct designed to involve the Institute in endless and costly litigation and that the suits were undertaken for the purpose of harassing the Institute and its members."[71]

Counterpoint. Mr. Grace contended that only the legislature could remove him since "only the Legislature has the power to change the rights and privileges specifically granted by the act of incorporation."[72] But the court said that Michael Grace obviously misinterpreted the nature of the rights and privileges accorded to him because "the Legislature surely could not have intended that a life member retain his position regardless of the manner in which he acted and regardless of the manner in which he abused his trust."[73] A trustee cannot, of course, be removed as long as she or he abides by the conditions of the trust, that is, so long as she or he faithfully serves the charitable organization. But the court confirmed that once one "breaches that condition and engages in activities that obstruct and interfere with the operation of the corporation and the purposes for which the Legislature created it, he may be removed."[74]

The Court of Appeals held that corporate law and not trust law would govern in the case. The same result could have been achieved under trust law because a trustee can be removed either by a court or a person authorized by the trust to do so.[75]

A Side Issue. Because both parties requested the Court of Appeals to consider whether Corinne Grace, Michael's wife, could become a life member and trustee, the court decided to state its view for the guidance of the lower court, in the interest of avoiding future appellate litigation. Corinne Grace could, the court said, take Michael Grace's position as life member and trustee; however, "if Corinne chooses to emulate the conduct of her spouse, then the corporation may remove her from office and, if necessary, petition the Legislature to amend the incorporating act so as to eliminate the position of life member—a position hardly essential to the effective operation of the corporation."[76]

The Never-Never Land of Self-hiring: Wayne County Community College, Detroit, Michigan

Turmoil at WCCC. Trustee replacement and restructuring of boards to this point in our discussion have centered primarily on removal by the courts, by the regents of New York, and by the board of trustees itself. The story is somewhat different in the case of governmental colleges and universities, since statutory

law governs, and the legislature has the authority to alter or dissolve any body
that it creates to act as an agency in the administration of civil government. A
college or university is such an agency. The recent incident involving charges
of mismanagement by the trustees of the Wayne County Community College
(WCCC), Detroit, serves as an example.

As a tax-supported institution, WCCC receives about 50 percent of its funding
from the state and the rest from county and local taxes and tuition. WCCC
opened its doors in 1969 to provide low-cost, quality education to the citizens
of Wayne County. In recent years, however, the college and its trustees have
been plagued by charges of mismanagement, unstable leadership, nepotism,
cronyism, political firefights, questionable use of money, and hiring teachers
with faulty credentials. When the North Central Association of Colleges and
Schools, one of the country's six regional accrediting agencies, placed the five-
campus school on probation, the waters became even more roiled. Without North
Central accreditation, students at the school would be unable to transfer credits
to most other colleges.

The presidential purges—four different presidents in four years—political
squabbling, and administrative blunders gridlocked the college into a suicidal
self-interest power struggle. The situation became intolerable as the press heightened the school's troubles in banner headlines and detailed, racy reporting both
of the ongoing political internecine war at the college and especially of its board
of trustees. One stormy board meeting ended with microphone throwing and
table overturning.[77] Some observers blamed a bad press for the troubles of
WCCC. But the *Detroit Free Press* wrote, "A dump truck full of flowery press
releases could not, for example, erase the spectacle of the toppled tables and
obscene gestures that have marked some of the public meetings of the board of
trustees."[78]

Suffering from a general lack of public credibility, the college's enrollment
nose-dived, almost as rapidly as it had expanded a decade earlier. WCCC became
a beleaguered institution in disarray. Dr. Phillip Runkel, state superintendent of
public instruction, decried, "It's a damn shame for students and taxpayers."[79]
Governor James J. Blanchard signed into law Public Act 258 of the Public Acts
of 1983, designating the superintendent of public instruction as the monitor of
WCCC with broad powers. Effective control of WCCC was turned over to Dr.
Runkel on 5 January 1984. The WCCC board, through its questionable practices,
lost control of the entity entrusted to its care.

Never in Michigan's history of higher education had the state moved to strip
a board of trustees of its lawful powers, but never, it was argued, had a college
undergone turmoil such as that at WCCC.

Calling the turmoil at WCCC disgraceful, Mayor Coleman A. Young blamed
the turbulent situation on self-serving conduct by trustees. He identified the root
of the problem at WCCC as a lack of a policy barring board members from
holding paid staff positions. The mayor, who was not alone in his criticism of
the self-hiring policy, was bolstered by other people. " 'The institution is rife

with nepotism and patronage,' said Richard Simmons, WCCC president in 1981 and 1982. 'I found it to be an unconscionable situation. People are constantly hired because of their friends, not their abilities.' ''[80]

The Legislature Acts. Before the enactment of reform legislation, a special committee created by a House resolution to study WCCC prepared a document titled "Report of the Special Committee to Study Wayne County Community College" (hereafter, *Report*). The *Report*, which served as a catalyst for Public Act 258, suggested a sense of urgency about the educational process at WCCC because the college, beset with many problems, had reached a point bordering on the inability to manage its own affairs.

The Special Committee studied a number of issues, targeting the following as areas of major concern:

- The charge that large purchases are made without competitive bids such as that pointed out by the Auditor General where the College granted a multi-million dollar computer service contract as a sole source contract.

- Numerous comments have been made both publicly and privately regarding the proper role of the Board as a whole and of individual Board of Trustee members and their alleged interference in the administration of the college.

- Ethical questions of conduct in the following areas: business dealings by Board members with college employees; negotiations; business activities and speaking engagements for honoraria on the part of college administrators.

- Unwillingness of college officials to release information to the news media and public.[81]

The Letter of Transmittal accompanying the *Report* states that the actions of the college's board of trustees indicate that

it takes lightly the responsibilities of attending to the leadership of the college. The balance of self-interest against community-interest is inappropriate for meeting the responsibilities for which the Trustees were elected. The long- and short-range fiscal, administrative, political, and educational implications of frequent changes of administrative leadership are not at all in the best interests of the college or the community.[82]

Acting under statutory powers granted by Public Act 258, Dr. Runkel proceeded to direct the WCCC board of trustees to implement immediately several recommendations of the Special Committee's *Report*. He also instructed the board as follows: "As monitor I am requesting that the board take no actions to alter the administrative organizational structure or enter into individual contracts or agreements for a period of 90 days without my review relative to emergency needs."[83]

From the beginning of his monitorship, Superintendent Runkel stressed the need "to bring respect and credibility to this institution which has such tremendous potential."[84] He called on everyone to work together to create a new image.

The Accrediting Association Issues Its Report. The *Detroit Free Press* reported on the North Central Association's preliminary report. North Central's report reinforced the criticism that had been aimed at the board of WCCC by making the critical observation, "The individual board members must understand that their function is to help the college and not help themselves by vying for positions in the college administration for themselves or their relatives."[85]

Deeply concerned about the governance problem at WCCC, the North Central Association's preliminary report of April 1984 cogently states:

> Board members admit freely that they have engaged in nepotism or that they have sought appointments to top administrative positions in the college. . . . Some individual members are more concerned with specific projects or interests of their own than with the overall direction of the college. . . .
>
> The board at WCCC should stop interfering with the administration of the college. . . . The college has suffered from a board that has little or no sense of its role [and has disposed of college presidents] if they attempt in any way to get control of the institution.[86]

In October 1984 the North Central accreditation team, chaired by Dr. Wallace B. Appleson, president of Harry S. Truman College in Chicago, in the customary exit interview "complimented the College for a strong faculty, modern facilities, state-of-the-art equipment and good programs, but he said that Wayne County Community College's Board of Trustees and administration have 'operated in a culture that condoned irregularities simply because they have happened before.' "[87] Accreditation at the college was continued; however, the team recommended that the college be placed on probation.

Agenda: New Image. With the growing realization that a meddling board of trustees was responsible for many of WCCC's problems, Dr. Runkel successfully argued for a bill that would restructure the board. In a bold political move, the Michigan legislature passed legislation that increased the board from seven to nine members, forced the incumbent trustees to face reelection—despite the fact that their terms were not up—and reduced trustees' terms of office from six years to four years. " 'I think it's a good bill, because it will hold the board accountable to the voters every four years,' Runkel said. . . . 'If we're going to straighten out that institution, the first place we have to start is with its governance.' "[88]

Even though the legislature has the power to alter, change, or dissolve an agency of government created to administer civil government, the action was a drastic move for the legislature because it involved removing elected public officials. The situation was serious enough that the legislature made the bold move with an almost unanimous vote.

The look of the board dramatically changed as a result of the new law and the elections it mandated. On 1 January 1985 only three former board members won reelection, but the majority of the new board members took office in a spirit of reform. A rebuilt WCCC board made a fresh start with the aim of creating a new image for WCCC and its board as a high-priority item on its agenda. Several new board members indicated they would be seeking a top-notch educational administrator who would bring stability and respectability to a college that had had neither in the past four years. After a national search conducted by the Association of Governing Boards of Colleges and Universities, Dr. Ronald Temple was appointed president of WCCC. He was instructed by the board to bring only policy issues to meetings, not day-to-day administrative problems, which were his to solve.

As a final note about the possible wrongdoings in the WCCC situation, so widely written about in the press, these issues were handled quietly by the attorney general's office, Dr. Runkel's staff, and members of the legislature. Thus, behind-the-scenes negotiations saved WCCC from a long and costly court action, which would have cost WCCC dearly in its thrust to build a new image. By the fall of 1985 the enrollment decline from 22,000 to 11,000 had stabilized, with approximately 11,000 students enrolled in classes.

According to reportage in the *Detroit Free Press*, "Roy Levy Williams, Chrysler Corp. community relations manager and chairman of a citizens advisory committee appointed by Runkel, said he is confident the new board can create a new image for the college."[89] The Williams committee played a pivotal role in bringing order out of chaos during the transition from the old to the newly elected board. With a fresh start perhaps WCCC will again become a pioneering community college.

CONSTITUTIONAL MANDATES AND INDEPENDENT COLLEGES

The courts have consistently distinguished the portion of American life that is "private" (individual action), and not circumscribed by constitutional mandates, from aspects that are clearly "public" (state action). This has been true despite the presence of such involvements with government through state and federal funding, state accreditation, or state regulation and supervision. Such activities are insufficient to bring an otherwise independent or private institution within the state action doctrine.[90] State action arises under the Fourteenth Amendment when the activity complained of is believed to be so entwined with the state that it is the state that is acting.

Private institutions often claim they are not instrumentalities of the state; that is, they are not agencies of state government and their actions do not constitute a state function. It thus follows that the Fourteenth Amendment, which applies the Bill of Rights to the several states, does not apply the Bill of Rights on the same basis to the independent (or private) areas because their actions are not that of the state. Rather, they engage in independent (or private) action and are thus outside this application of the Fourteenth Amendment.

Derek Bok, president of Harvard College, admonishes, "Although private universities are probably not subject to the Bill of Rights, no one could defend having one set of rules for faculty members in state universities and another and more limited set for scholars employed by private institutions.''[91] As social policy changes, it is highly likely that charities retaining a distinctive legal public character, although privately managed, will need to comport more with the Fourteenth Amendment, based on the performance of state action. The Girard College case that follows suggests that the dripping faucet of state action may be beginning to wear the legal sandstone barrier down to equitable size.

A History of Fiercest Quarrels: Girard College, Philadelphia, Pennsylvania

The Original Sin. The history of Girard College is remarkable to the point of being legend. From its creation, the Girard trust has been embroiled in litigation to determine its validity as a charitable trust as well as to uphold its specific provisions. In the course of its existence, it also has undergone trustee replacement in order to fulfill restrictions placed by Mr. Girard in his famous will that permitted only "poor male white orphan children" to be eligible for admission to Girard College.[92] It is almost unbelievable that one small college could be the focal point of a legion of major decisional law.

Stephen Girard, a famous merchant prince of the early nineteenth century, died in 1831. He left the major portion of his estate in trust to the city of Philadelphia for the establishment of Girard College for the education and maintenance of "poor white male orphans" between six and ten years of age.

The Girard trust, like Ben Franklin's will, had been considered for more than a century and a quarter as *"fixed, firm, and as unmovable as a rock."*[93] As time was to tell, however, U.S. Supreme Court decisions with enough force at the fulcrum "of justice for all" would remove the Girard "white" rock. One cannot completely understand the Girard College case without considering the historical background of the Girard trust, which has become time-honored in Pennsylvania.

Mr. Girard's heirs attempted to overthrow his will, basing their claim on the 1819 U.S. Supreme Court *Hart*[94] decision, which held that charitable trusts were invalid in a state such as Pennsylvania in which the Statute of Elizabeth—a law inherited from England—was not in force. This English statute was significant because it provided the machinery for enforcing charitable trusts. But in *Vidal v. Girard's Executors*[95] the Supreme Court in 1844 reversed the holding in *Hart* that charitable trusts were invalid. The Girard will led to the Supreme Court decision perhaps establishing the basic principles of the law of charitable trusts in this country.

The court had no problem in deciding that Mr. Girard's wish for a school for orphan children was a charitable purpose. The real challenge, however, lay in the fact that Pennsylvania had *not* adopted the Statute of Elizabeth.[96] Because of the importance of the issue and the able individuals who served as lawyers, *Vidal* drew a lot of public attention and aroused a great deal of concern. Mr. Horace Binney, a noted Philadelphia lawyer, represented the Girard executors, and Mr. Daniel Webster was on the heirs' side. Samuel Adams reported in his diary that Mr. Webster was to receive $25,000 if he were successful in having the will put aside.[97]

Mr. Binney persuaded the Court to uphold the trust. His careful historical research showed that charitable trusts were enforced in England by the courts of chancery long before 1601, when the Statute of Elizabeth was enacted. Recognition and enforcement of charitable trusts thus antedated the 1601 statute.[98] Although the statute had not been adopted in Pennsylvania, he argued that this was irrelevant because charitable trusts were part of the common law of that state, and the common law of England was in force in that state. The U.S. Supreme Court held that the Girard trust was valid, thereby sustaining the legality of the establishment of Girard College as well as once again recognizing the charitable trust as part of the American charitable scene.[99]

Vidal produced a triumph for charitable trusts in the most altruistic and constructive sense of that term. The influence of *Vidal* was immense and far-reaching, although its immediate effect was to further the philanthropic objectives of Stephen Girard's wish for the establishment of Girard College as a testamentary trust.

The Girard Trust and Social Policy. With changing social conditions, values, and standards over the years, buttressed by profound U.S. Supreme Court decisions, constitutional amendments, and new laws, the Girard trust found itself deeply embroiled in one of the most hard-fought social issues of the mid–1950s: racial integration. The trustees of Girard College were obligated, as a matter of law, to follow the mandate of the trust instrument until they received instructions from a court to do otherwise. However, the denial of admission to two black applicants after the landmark 1954 U.S. Supreme Court civil rights decision, *Brown v. Board of Education,*[100] was certain to invite a long legal quarrel. And it did.

Brown, a celebrated decision, declared that the 1896 *Plessy*[101] rule of "separate but equal" was no longer valid, destroying completely the constitutional foundation on which legalized segregation rested. Relying on *Brown*, the U.S. Supreme Court finally held the Girard trust to be invalid on constitutional grounds, but only after a lengthy legal battle.

The contentious and protracted legal squabble that involved Girard College in charges of racial discrimination can be roughly summarized as follows. When the two boys, William Ashe Foust, age 8, and Robert Felder, age 7—both nonwhite—were denied admission, suit was instituted against the trustees of Girard College. The children desiring admission argued that the white restriction was against the public policy of Pennsylvania and the United States and that the court should remove the white restriction through the doctrine of *cy pres*, which permits the court to alter a trust that has failed in its purpose. (The power of *cy pres* belongs to the courts, not legislatures.) They also contended that the operation of the Girard trust by the Board of Directors of City Trusts (hereafter, City trustees) was state action, despite the fact that Girard College was an independent college. They argued that Stephen Girard had so entwined the state in the affairs of the college that the trustees' actions were indistinguishable from those of the state.

The Orphan's Court of Philadelphia County held that it could not apply the doctrine of *cy pres* because there was no lack of qualified white applicants and, therefore, no failure of purpose of trust. Second, the lower court held that the white restriction did not violate the Equal Protection Clause of the Fourteenth Amendment to the U.S. Constitution, as the children maintained, because the trustees were not a governmental body, that is, an agency of state government. The court further said that no right or privilege was more valued than the transfer of property at death by will, and the power to enforce wills was one power reserved to the several states under the U.S. Constitution.

The Pennsylvania Supreme Court affirmed the orphan's court decision. The U.S. Supreme Court, however, reversed the judgment of the Pennsylvania court, declaring: "The Board which operates Girard College is an *agency* of the State of Pennsylvania. Therefore, even though the Board was acting as a trustee, its refusal to admit Foust and Felder to the college because they were Negroes was discrimination by the State. Such discrimination is forbidden by the Fourteenth Amendment (emphasis added)."[102]

Agency, as used above, means that the trustees were an instrumentality of the Commonwealth of Pennsylvania. When the trustees were acting, they were doing so on behalf of the state. In an effort to absolve the state of any unconstitutional involvement in the matter, the board of trustees was quickly restructured.

On receiving the case from the U.S. Supreme Court, the Pennsylvania Supreme Court sent it to the orphan's court. This court promptly removed the City trustees and installed new "private" trustees styled "Trustees of the Estate of Stephen Girard," whose sole function was to administer Girard College in terms of the will.[103] On the face of it, the action by the orphan's court was not unconstitutional per se, because the court was duty bound to supervise Mr. Girard's testamentary affairs. But the court could not associate or implicate itself in the discriminatory purpose of the white restriction.[104]

It is important to note that the City trustees did not appeal their ouster, and that the new set of "private" trustees continued to enforce the racial restriction. The appeals court noted that all of the fervent activity and its motivation—restructuring the board—was conspicuous.

About the change in trustees, Professor Austin Wakeman Scott astutely observes, "It would seem that, quite apart from the question of public policy, the state court might properly have applied the cy pres doctrine and held that it would conform more nearly to his intention to remove the restriction rather than to remove the trustee."[105]

Finally, in 1968, the United States Court of Appeals for the Third Circuit held that Girard College must admit any "poor male orphan" who qualified for admission notwithstanding that the former trustees had been removed as trustee and new "private" trustees assumed office because such substitution of trustees by the court was unconstitutional. When the orphan's court substituted trustees, it was, by its action, engaging in state action (the court being an agency of government). In short, the court's decision "resulted in the institutionalization of Girard College as a governmentally sanctioned center of racial bias."[106]

There is no blanket rule for state action; the courts decide case by case on the merits involved. The U.S. Supreme Court refused to hear an appeal. The fierce battle over the white restriction was finally over.

"There Is a Time for All Things." Cervantes once observed, "A private sin is not so prejudicial in the world as a public indecency." The court of appeals pulled Girard College kicking and screaming into the twentieth century: the abhorrent racial restriction, and its public indecency, had finally been removed.

One can perhaps understand why the trustees did not immediately see the importance of their decision to disqualify children because of race. However, it is reasonable to question why, after the U.S. Supreme Court decision in 1957, the trustees did not act to remove the offending provisions in the trust instrument by seeking court instructions for ridding the instrument of the white restriction. It would have been wise for them to have done so at the time of the children's applications, which invited responsible trustee action. At least on moral grounds such a courageous act would have exonerated the City trustees.

The Girard trust brings to light the symbiotic relationship of the legal and the moral.[107] Racial discrimination is now against public policy (which is not morality). What is legal is the maximum one can get away with under the law, whereas what is moral comes from a different standard. The argument can be advanced that the trustees were doing their job by simply obeying the instructions in the gift instrument. But this argument is weak for two reasons. First, the trustees were a proper party in the long, costly legal travail through both the state and federal courts. Second, effective trusteeship entails more than narrow administrative plodding; it also calls for judgment, common sense, business acumen, and statesmanship—all exercised for the community's interest.

A donor may impose duties on a trustee that are possible to fulfill and legal at the time the gift instrument becomes effective. On the other hand, if at some future time a duty, as the one in Girard's will, becomes impossible to accomplish or requires the trustee to perform acts that are illegal or inconsistent with public policy, the impeding duty will need to be altered or erased. For the City trustees to have moved with averment—simply by considering statesmanlike qualities in an early attempt to find a solution to the problem—the trustees could have been seen as forward-looking fiduciaries.

INFRINGEMENT OF FIRST AMENDMENT RIGHTS

Freedom of the press became the rallying call on college campuses in the late 1960s, with student journalists producing a spate of cases on the law and the student press under First Amendment claims. The decisions often favored students, overruling unreasonable school policies that interfered with students' free expression rights. Greater freedom, in general, was accorded to colleges than to high schools, in the belief that college students were older and that the tradition of free expression was better established in institutions of higher learning than in secondary schools. The case that follows extended that right to a faculty adviser of a student newspaper who wrote an editorial accusing a board of trustees' chairman of a conflict of interest in the award of an institutional contract.

College Professor on Tenterhooks: Brookdale Community College, Lincroft, New Jersey

Fire Away and Then Forget about It—Maybe. In 1974 Ms. Patricia Endress, an assistant professor of journalism and a student newspaper adviser at Brookdale Community College, wrote an editorial that "accused the chairman of the board of trustees of a conflict of interest in allegedly making 'a deal' whereby his nephew's company received a contract from the college for the furnishing of audio-visual equipment."[108]

An outraged and embarrassed college president undertook an investigation of the matter, in which other officers of the college participated. As a result, the president, unbeknownst to Professor Endress, presented a recommendation to the board on 27 June 1974 that her contract be terminated just three days before she was to gain tenure. This came as a complete shock to Professor Endress because on the same day that the editorial appeared, the president mailed to Professor Endress her contract and congratulated her on attaining tenure. More-over, her work had received laudatory reviews, especially her notable success in raising the quality of the newspaper, which had received its first award from the Associated Collegiate Press with marks of distinction in coverage and content.

Professor Endress sought reinstatement in the Superior Court of New Jersey to her position as well as compensatory and punitive damages against the president and all the members of the board in their official and individual capacities. Ms. Endress alleged, among other things, impairment of her First Amendment rights and arbitrary termination of her contract.

At the trial she testified that she favored an investigative reporting approach and that she encouraged her students to use such an approach in their reporting. "While student copy was submitted to her, she had no censorship role and exercised no editorial veto. The student editors were fully responsible for that which was published."[109]

Professors, Journalism, and Standards. In recommending her dismissal to the board, the president alleged that Professor Endress "had violated her duties and responsibilities as a journalism teacher and advisor to the newspaper by ordering the publication of the article and editorial."[110] He also alleged that she had caused the publication of "libelous matter contrary to accepted journalistic standards."[111]

The trial court held in favor of Professor Endress, finding that her dismissal was not the result of dissatisfaction with her services but rather of the incorrect feeling that she had libeled the chairman of the board. The fact that Professor Endress was the faculty adviser did not exclude her from protection under the

First Amendment. It was never open to question, nor was it at the time of these events, that activities connected with the publication of the student newspaper fell within the protection of the First Amendment.

Professor Endress was awarded $80,000 in compensatory and punitive damages and $10,000 lawyers' fees against the college president and trustees. She also was awarded back salary of $14,121 as well as all pension and retirement benefits at an annual salary rate of $19,121. Disregarding pension benefits, the trial court awarded a total settlement of $104,000. The court ordered a contract for the following year that had the same force and effect as if it had been issued during the previous year.

Example Setting. Compensatory damages make up for out-of-pocket expenses and for other general or special damages, such as pain and suffering and emotional and mental distress, and humiliation. A court may also assign punitive damages "to punish the wrongdoer for a willful act and to vindicate the rights of a party in substitution for personal revenge, thus safeguarding the public peace."[112] Punitive damages are in the nature of a criminal fine or penalty and are awarded where the action was aggravated. In the Endress case, they were awarded because the action taken against Professor Endress was deemed to be degrading. The purpose of awarding punitive damages is to deter future wrongful acts—example-setting. When one's face is spat in, damages should include more than the cost of a washcloth and towel; they should also include redress for feelings of shame and degradation.

Trustee Vulnerability. The lower court held that the president and board had discharged Professor Endress solely because she had exercised her constitutional right of freedom of the press, association, and speech. The New Jersey Superior Court, Appeals Division, concurred[113] and would not disturb the trial court, holding that there was not just cause to dismiss Professor Endress from employment or to rescind her contract for the following year.

The appeals court upheld the back-pay award of $14,121 but modified both the compensatory and punitive damages awarded by the trial court. The appellate court reduced compensatory damages from $10,000 to $2,500 against the college president and board members. It also reduced the punitive award against the president from $10,000 to $2,500 and dismissed the $10,000 punitive awards against each member of the board of trustees.[114]

The trustees were not immune from civil rights action brought by Professor Endress because members of the board of trustees of Brookdale Community College should have known that her dismissal as faculty adviser to the student newspaper on the grounds of the editorial she had written would violate her First Amendment rights. Thus, the board of trustees was liable for its decision, and compensatory damages were awarded because of a deprivation of federal rights.

Professor Endress, a top-notch journalism teacher, fell temporarily under an unwarranted cloud of administrative suspicion.

She suffered the shame and mental anguish of being summarily terminated without any opportunity to give her side of the controversy [declared Judge Merritt Lane, the trial judge.] She experienced problems when she tried to get a job from Middlesex Community College. I am sure this suit will remain with her regardless of what the verdict of this Court may be.[115]

But if the president and board figured they could bluster their way through this bending of constitutional rules, they were mistaken. A board may make a decision, but that does not mean it is a good decision. Thus, it is important for the courts to have the power of review—the final say—over board decisions that vitiate the public good.

The Endress case lays open the vulnerability of personal liability exposure, especially when individuals in high office engage in what President Calvin Coolidge once called the "malady of self-delusion." Regardless of one's authority, one would be wise to heed Judge Lane's emphatic statement that "punitive damages are absolutely necessary to impress upon the people who are in authority and other people in authority that an employee's constitutional rights may not be infringed."[116] When such rights are infringed, there is a price to be paid for overzealous acts in excess of the exercise of trustees' enfranchisement.

Subsequent to the trial court's decision, the New Jersey State Division of Criminal Justice opened an investigation of Brookdale's financial records. The division found "no evidence of wrongdoing" in procedures for awarding contracts.[117] Even though the chairman of the board of trustees was exonerated of any wrong in the awarding of contracts, the Justice Department's statement had no bearing on the appeals court decision of compensatory and punitive damages for abridgement of constitutional rights; this was a separate issue.

SUMMARY

Boards of trustees *are* their colleges and universities. Boards have the duty to see that charitable property under their control is not diverted from the public purposes for which it was entrusted to their care. Moreover, courts have frequently intruded into the affairs of colleges and universities for a variety of reasons. Litigation has mushroomed, involving boards that failed to pay attention to the management of their schools.

In the Wilson College case a Pennsylvania trial judge ruled that the trustees of the college, before trying to close the school, had been misled by its president, had permitted mismanagement of the college, especially in the area of admissions, and had failed to bring their expertise to the board. The judge refused to allow the closing, noting the necessity for prior judicial approval before a board could terminate a school in its current form. Further, the judge removed two of the trustees for patent conflict of interest, failure to exercise recognized expertise, and gross abuse of discretion and authority.

In the Mannes College case the New York State Board of Regents removed the majority of a board of trustees that had come to its attention because of an aborted plan to merge the school with another, which in itself was permissible under New York education law. It removed them for, among other reasons, permitting the school's acting president to cut back departments without the authorization of the trustees or consultation with the faculty, failing to look for a permanent president, and permitting the distribution of an inaccurate description of the school—all of which constituted a collective neglect of duty.

In the Grace Institute case the New York Court of Appeals, applying corporate law, held that a board of trustees acted properly in removing a life member of the board believed by the board to have engaged in activities that obstructed and interfered with the operation of the organization and the purpose for which the legislature had created it.

In the Wayne County Community College case, the Michigan legislature acted to remove control of a governmentally created college from its board of trustees and to restructure the creation of future boards, because of the board's questionable practices. The WCCC case shows that whatever a legislature creates to administer civil government, it has the power to alter and change.

In the Girard College case lengthy litigation finally resulted in a federal court's finding that state action, sufficient to apply the Fourteenth Amendment prohibition against racial discrimination, had arisen from an inferior state court's restructuring of a board of trustees so the new board could continue to apply a racially restricted will clause. The federal court prohibited the continued application of the racial restriction, despite the fact that Girard College was an independent institution created by a testamentary trust and received no direct governmental financial support. The trustees could have avoided the long and costly battle by exercising good judgment and common sense, by seeking instructions from a proper court, which they had not only the right but duty to do.

In the Brookdale Community College case, the Appellate Division of the New Jersey Superior Court held members of a board of trustees and its president personally liable for damages in a civil rights action because they should have known that their treatment of a faculty member involved with the student newspaper would violate her First Amendment rights.

Trustees are fiduciaries and as such are common-law trustees, which makes them officers of the court. Insofar as courts are a part of civil government, eleemosynary trustees are officers of the state. Trustees are fully accountable—mainly through a public official to the courts—to the public they serve. And they can be removed by the courts, usually for gross mismanagement or misbehavior, in order to prevent further harm to the charity and the public interest.

5

MUSEUMS

We need something to give us a greater solidarity—to put a soul into our community—to make us love this place above all others. This art alone can do.

Lorado Taft, "Address," *Dedication of the Ferguson Fountain of the Great Lakes*, 1913

THE PUBLIC NATURE OF CHARITIES

Reshaped by eighteenth-century social and political reform movements, the history of art and the museum world assumed a different coloration. It was out of the ashes of the French Revolution that the modern art museum, with its chronological telling of history through works of art, was born.[1]

Before the French Revolution, access to the princely collections—some of which would eventually help form art museums—was severely restricted. The French Revolution produced for the people a great moment of triumph in the history of art museums. On 10 August 1793—one year to the day after the overthrow of the French monarchy—the revolutionists declared the right of all citizens to see magnificent art collections that previously had been the pleasure of only the privileged. The revolutionists opened the Louvre to everyone[2]—the butcher, the baker, and the candlestick maker.

The overthrow of the French monarchy also eventually caused the Smithsonian Institution to receive one of its finest objects—the Hope Diamond. It is believed that Marie Antoinette on occasion wore the sparkling blue treasure, reputedly stolen from the eye of an idol in the Far East.

Following the tradition established by the French that museums remain public, but employing trust law derived from England, museums in this country have been organized as charities. Much like the French, the courts here have declared that museums be public and open to everyone.

A nonprofit museum, under the law, is accountable to the public, even though it is not an agency of government administered by public (governmental) authority. The nonprofit museum retains a distinct public character, despite its private managerial prerogatives. The public nature of a charity was reaffirmed by the Pennsylvania Supreme Court in connection with the Barnes Foundation when the Court said, "An essential element of a public charity is the right of public visitation for the correction of abuses and the enforcement of the founder's will.[3]

Opening Things Up: The Barnes Foundation, Merion Station, Pennsylvania

Argyrol and the Barnes Foundation. Dr. Albert C. Barnes, who had amassed a considerable fortune through the discovery of a chemical compound trademarked Argyrol—which he kept secret and exploited commercially—created the Barnes Foundation to manage, among other things, his magnificent art collection. Located in Montgomery County (near Philadelphia), Pennsylvania, and numbering more than a thousand paintings, the collection contains not only the works of the masters, but also masterful works by the masters. Included are Renoir, Cézanne, Manet, Degas, Seurat, Rousseau, Picasso, Matisse, Soutine, Modigliani, Glackens, and Rouault. The old masters are represented as well, including Giorgione, Titian, Tintoretto, Paolo Veronese, El Greco, Claude le Lorrain Chardin, Daumier, Delacroix, Courbet, and Corot. The monetary value of the collection is estimated to exceed $100 million.[4]

It was Dr. Barnes's desire that his art gallery be open to the public on an orderly basis. The notion that his magnificent art collection was to be open to all—to people from all walks of life—after the death of his wife and himself, can perhaps be explained by his adventuresome mind. The court reported how he offered his art collection and arboretum: "The plain people, that is, men and women who gain their livelihood by daily toil in shops, factories, schools, stores and similar places, shall have free access to the art gallery and the arboretum upon those days when the gallery and arboretum are to be open to the public."[5]

The Chosen Few. Regretfully, the trustees—apparently not fully understanding Dr. Barnes's desire that the public should benefit from his gift—closed the museum to the public and blatantly admitted doing so in their 1960 brief to the court.[6] An earlier suit, begun by a citizen and editorial writer for the *Philadelphia Inquirer*, failed because the attorney general of Pennsylvania needed to bring suit; a citizen and newspaper reporter was not a proper party plantiff under Pennsylvania law.[7] The attorney general of Pennsylvania brought suit to have the museum opened to the public.

Despite the fact that the Barnes Foundation had been declared a charity, "its officers and trustees . . . consistently refused to the public admission to its art gallery," declared the Supreme Court of Pennsylvania. "This is not what Dr. Barnes contemplated and it certainly is not what the tax authorities intended."[8] Making the art gallery available to a selected restricted few had in effect made the foundation a private cultural preserve, neither serving the common good nor carrying out Dr. Barnes's desire. The court said that the test of a charity can be found in its "extensiveness," stating that "if the general benefits of a charity are subject to private preferences or conditions by which a large proportion of the general public will probably be excluded, it is a private charity."[9]

Making Charity Work. The Barnes Foundation, a previously adjudicated charity, was opened to the public by the court, although the court was punctilious in recognizing the trustees' managerial authority to provide appropriate control. They could determine when and how the public was to have access to the art gallery, but the public was not to be completely shut out.

This incident provided the Pennsylvania Supreme Court with the opportune moment to reaffirm its position with regard to charities:

> It would be an inadequate form of government which would allow organizations to declare themselves charitable trusts without requiring them to submit to supervision and inspection. Without such supervision and control, trustees of alleged public charities could engage in business for profit. It is because of the temptation which such lack of supervision would offer, that a Congressional committee observed: "Foundations should not only operate in a goldfish bowl, they should operate with glass pockets."[10]

Much as the French revolutionists opened the Louvre, the Pennsylvania Supreme Court opened one of the great art galleries to the public, as the donor had instructed. It was, after all, Dr. Barnes's wish. Perhaps the Barnes trustees failed to grasp either the historical significance of museums to be public or the importance of the gift instrument under which the charitable property was conveyed. The ultimate truth, however, is that the courts will, when the public good demands it, bring trustees in line with their fiduciary obligations under the law.

A Legacy from the Past: The Hill-Stead Museum, Farmington, Connecticut

Hill-Stead, a neocolonial structure and a house museum of medium size, remains open today as a popular attraction to the public. Like the Wilson College case, the court mandated the trustees of the Hill-Stead Museum in Farmington, Connecticut, to reopen the museum after having voted to close it. After the closure decision, the attorney general of Connecticut, as the representative of the public in testamentary trusts for the public interest and acting under his statutory and common-law powers, began legal action against the trustees to keep the museum open.[11]

The trustees, although acting for no personal advantage, were nevertheless adjudged by the court to have committed a breach of trust for failing to act according to the trust instrument. The lower court found in favor of the attorney general and the Supreme Court of Connecticut concurred.

Events Creating Hill-Stead. The Hill-Stead Museum was the private residence of Mrs. Theodate Pope Riddle and her parents, who built it around the turn of the century. Hill-Stead is historically significant in that it represents the finest type of residential architecture in vogue at that time. In *The American Scene*, Henry James was moved to describe Hill-Stead as " 'a great new house on a hill' that was 'apparently conceived—and with great felicity—on the lines of a magnified Mount Vernon.' "[12]

Four months before her death in 1946, Mrs. Riddle prepared a fifty-page will directing that her home and its contents were to be maintained just as she left them—nothing to be added and nothing to be let out. In the event of some catastrophe, such as fire, Hill-Stead was not to be rebuilt.

Mrs. Riddle came from Cleveland, Ohio, where her father, Alfred Pope, made his fortune in the malleable iron business. Wishing for his daughter Theodate to be exposed to eastern society so she could perhaps more ably handle Cleveland's high society, Mr. Pope sent his daughter to Miss Porter's School in Farmington. Theodate, relishing the East, began persuading her parents that they should cease trying to convince her to follow in their footsteps in Cleveland's high society and instead build a home based on plans she had designed.

Finally convinced of their daughter's steadfast determination to remain in the East, although not of her abilities in architecture, which was Theodate's first love, the Popes decided to build Hill-Stead. Mr. Pope hired Mr. Stanford White, the architect of the era, to plan Hill-Stead. Mr. White's architectural fee of $50,000 was reduced to $25,000 because of Theodate's assistance. She was later to become a licensed architect (one of the first women architects in the country), having been tutored by members of the Art Department at Princeton University, then an all-male university. Later she was to be elected to the American Institute of Architects.

Construction on Hill-Stead began in 1889 and was completed in 1901, when Mr. and Mrs. Pope and Theodate moved in. After Mr. Pope died in 1913, Mrs. Pope and Theodate continued living there. Theodate later married Mr. John Riddle, who was at one time ambassador to the Court of St. Petersburg and later to Argentina. Mr. Riddle died in 1941 and Theodate died five years later.

Hill-Stead as a Memorial. Hill-Stead contains the very best from every era, country, and art that money could buy at the time: pre-Columbian statues, contemporary bronzes, the finest porcelain, Chippendale furniture, a custom-made Steinway, and an outstanding collection of impressionist art. Mr. Pope was one of the first Americans to collect impressionist art at a time when most impressionist painters were still being laughed at in their own country.

"The collection is of undoubted quality," writes *House and Garden*'s Roderick Cameron; "however when visiting Hill-Stead today it is actually the house itself that impresses one the most."[13] Hill-Stead is as much alive and fresh as when it was built more than eighty years ago. Although no one has lived in the house for more than forty years, it strikes the visitor as being not only quite American (despite the fact that it is filled with many objects from abroad) but also timely. Mr. Pope financed Hill-Stead and is credited with acquiring the impressionist art—the objects that principally convinced Theodate to make Hill-Stead into a museum for the public's enjoyment.

Quite different from other homes and "cottages" built by the wealthy in this beaux-arts classicism period, such as those in Newport, Rhode Island, and the Hudson River valley, Hill-Stead reflects the personalities of the individuals who constructed it. It is deeply etched with Theodate's fine taste, forged in part by her strong determination to have a full meaningful life, not just a shallow social life—the expectation of so many women during her time. Theodate developed herself during a time when women were not expected to realize their fullest professional or personal potential.

Theodate Pope Riddle was deeply attached to the home she helped design. She treated it with the greatest of care and respect, regarding its treasures as a memorial to her parents. Her wish was to be buried in the garden, but the authorities would not allow it. The curator said, laughing: "I assure you, had she been at her own funeral, she most certainly *would* have been buried in the garden."[14] Mrs. Riddle was an independent, intelligent, and freethinking individual. She even joined the Socialist party, much to the credit of her spirit of independence and her father's dismay.

In her fifty-page will Mrs. Riddle provided that her trustees could close the museum if "in their absolute discretion" they found that there was insufficient public interest in the museum.[15] It is on this point that the imbroglio over the museum's closure started.

In 1951 the trustees, acting under this provision in the will, decided to close the museum—not based on the standard established by Mrs. Riddle but at the request of the Pope-Brooke Foundation, a corporation that managed the Avon Old Farms School (hereafter, school). The foundation wished for the assets realized from the closing of the museum to be gifted over for the operation of the school, which Mrs. Riddle had handsomely supported during her life for about $7 million. The school, like Hill-Stead, was a memorial to Mrs. Riddle's parents.[16]

The Trustees' Vote. The foundation approached the trustees of the museum, stating that the financial condition of the school was precarious and that in their judgment it was more important to save the school than the museum. Of the trustees who voted in the affirmative to close the museum, each assumed a different posture in rendering his or her decision. No trustee voted on the principle that there was not sufficient interest in the museum to keep it open. "Public interest was not even a topic of discussion at the meeting" of the trustees to discuss closure.[17]

Some trustees tried to place themselves in the position of Mrs. Riddle, if she were alive, to determine what she would have done. "The question is of course not what did the testatrix [Mrs. Riddle] mean to say, but what did she mean by what she did say."[18] Another trustee based his decision on the school's financial needs. Another favored the school over the museum. Clearly, the trustees placed their own preferences over that of the donor.

Had the trustees' decision been implemented, it would have terminated the trust, permanently closed Hill-Stead, scattered its contents, frustrated Mrs. Riddle's beneficent conception of an art center for that section of Connecticut, destroyed the museum's educational and artistic value to the general public, and worked an irreparable injury for which there was no adequate remedy in law.[19]

The trustees of the Hill-Stead Museum did not act in terms of their own personal advantage. The trustees of both charitable institutions, the museum and school, were "honorable ladies and gentlemen. None of them was actuated by a personally selfish motive."[20] Even though they believed that they were acting in good faith, the court determined the trustees had exceeded the bounds of their authority, resulting in a breach of trust. Thus, the court interceded to keep the museum open.

Water Finding Its Own Level. The key issue in the Hill-Stead case was not purely that the trustees' decision would have closed the museum. Nor was it the fact that the museum was an institution in which Mrs. Riddle had "faith and which she had handsomely endowed to ensure its perpetuation."[21] Rather, the issue was one of "abuse of discretion." Ruling on the trustees' vote to close the museum, the court concluded that for the trustees to close the museum for the reasons given, the trustees had "abused their discretion."[22]

There was no question that Mrs. Riddle granted discretion to her trustees, but she also set up a stringent standard—that is, sufficient public interest in the museum—by which to measure that discretion. The court made it abundantly clear to the trustees that they had failed to apply the standard of public interest in reaching the closure decision and that "they took unto themselves a power not granted by the will."[23] The trustees of the Hill-Stead Museum were trustees of that museum and no other entity. Regardless of how altruistic the trustees' intentions were in assisting another charitable project, they owed a duty of loyalty to the trust. "Trustees have no powers," the court declared, "not expressly or impliedly conferred on them by the terms of the trust. . . . Their obligation to obey the instructions of the donor of the trust is the cornerstone upon which all other duties rest"[24] (citation omitted).

"To the extent," declared the Connecticut Supreme Court, "to which the trustees had discretion, the court will not attempt to control their exercise of it as long as they have not abused it. . . . But the law will not tolerate its abuse, however great the creator of the trust intended the grant of discretion to be"[25] (citations omitted). The donor may enlarge the trustees' authority through such adjectives as "absolute," but the trustee is not given unlimited discretion. Neither does such language "necessarily remove the trustees from judicial supervision."[26]

Trustees have a duty to adhere to the directions in donative instruments unless and until a court of proper jurisdiction instructs otherwise. The court will enforce the wishes of the donor unless the instructions are either illegal or against public policy. When in doubt about the provisions contained in a trust instrument, the wise trustee will petition the court. In some jurisdictions it is extremely important for the trustees to follow correct procedure. Once the court interdicts, it retains control, so it is wise for trustees to be appropriately informed about the relevant law in force.

Banishing B. F. Ferguson's Memorial Ghost: Chicago Art Institute, Chicago, Illinois

Pride in One's Hometown. It may be that "even the most precise, explicit standards in a charitable trust document can be circumvented by a trustee or administrator determined to alter the use of the trust,"[27] as the case of the B. F. Ferguson Monument Fund so monumentally shows.

On his death in 1905 Mr. Benjamin F. Ferguson, an old and respected businessman, left almost all of his estate in trust to be used permanently for the erection of statuary and artistic monuments in the city of Chicago. Naming the Northern Trust Company as trustee and the Chicago Art Institute as subtrustee, his will reads:

My said Trustee after paying the bequests hereinabove mentioned and establishing or realizing and keeping intact a permanent trust fund of not less that $1,000,000.00 shall annually thereafter or oftener, if required, pay the entire net income arising therefrom (after deducting its compensation as Trustee herein mentioned) to The Art Institute of Chicago, to be known as the B. F. Ferguson Monument Fund and entirely and exclusively used and expended by it under the direction of its Board of Trustees in the erection and maintenance of enduring *statuary* and monuments, in the whole or in part of stone, granite, or bronze, in the parks, along the boulevards, or in other public places within the City of Chicago, Illinois, commemorating worthy men or women of America, or important events in American History. The plans or designs for such *statuary* or monuments and the location of the same shall be determined by the Board of Trustees of such Institute.[28]

Two longtime friends of Ben Ferguson were instrumental in securing this unusual and magnificent bequest for the people of Illinois: Daniel Burnham, the Chicago city planner, and Charles Hutchinson, president of the Art Institute Board. Mr. Burnham convinced Mr. Ferguson of the great value of his generous gift, and Mr. Hutchinson assured him that the institute would administer his fund in a way to provide the people of Illinois with the best statuary available.

In 1905 the *Chicago Tribune* headlined, "Will of B. F. Ferguson Assures City Place Among World's Cities Beautiful," and then reported:

By the will . . . Chicago is given the opportunity to become a center for sculpture. . . . No other city in the world has such a fund available as that left by Mr. Ferguson, and officials of the Art Institute, artists, and devotees of municipal art freely predicted that the bequest would in another generation make Chicago the richest city in the world in sculpture and the Mecca of artists.[29]

At the time of the announcement, William French, director of the Art Institute, proudly declared: "The city's future in art is now assured, and it is great. . . . It is a long step toward making Chicago the 'city beautiful.' "[30] Mr. Hutchinson, who wanted to have only quality works erected every two or three years, diligently and faithfully oversaw the Ferguson Fund affairs until his death in 1924.

At the dedication exercises for the first statue, titled *Fountain of the Great Lakes*, sculptured by Chicago's own Lorado Taft and financed by the fund, Mr. Taft said, "I remember what a thrill I felt when the significance of his unprecedented benefaction first dawned upon me."[31]

Charles Hutchinson, president of the board of trustees of the Art Institute, also spoke at the dedication exercises proclaiming, "This is but one of many monuments which will in time be erected and add greatly to the beauty of our city."[32]

The Ambiguous Phrase. Mr. Ferguson's farsightedness included some precautions. He had willed the Art Institute an annuity of $1,000 a year for its own use. A later complaint by Wesley Greene, a citizen, resident and taxpayer of the City of Chicago, contended that this was a device used by Mr. Ferguson because he "anticipated the possible temptation of the vast sum of money that would be administered" by the Art Institute and that by so providing for it, "there would be no violation or deviation of the clear and unmistakable language" of his will.[33]

Funds for the public purpose of beautifying Chicago's streets, boulevards, and public ways were to open opportunity for what some believed to be a worthier use of Mr. Ferguson's generous charitable bequest. In the early 1930s the Art Institute, feeling the pressure for more space for its burgeoning collection—but hurting for funds because of the Great Depression—began to cast about for new sources of money. More and more they looked to the rich Ferguson Fund to solve their growing, pressing financial exigencies.

In 1933 the trustees of the Art Institute made their move on the Ferguson Fund by filing a complaint in the Cook County Circuit Court because they found the phrase *enduring monuments* ambiguous and difficult to understand. They asked the court to construe the word *monument* in the will to determine if it would include a memorial building for the Art Institute. The court decided that the word *monument* did include a memorial building and that "the trustees of the Art Institute, in the exercise of their discretion under the will as construed, may use the moneys of the fund in the erection and maintenance of statuary and memorial buildings or other forms of monuments."[34]

A subsequent complaint to the court alleged "that there [had] been a lexicon revolution relative to the word 'monument', which when defined by the word 'statuary' could and did mean a physical building of bricks and mortar."[35]

The Finest Hour. Attorney Luis Kutner described the manner in which the 1933 court construing occurred.

On May 22, 1933, at 10:02 a.m., the Art Institute filed a Complaint in the Circuit Court of Cook County, requesting the court to construe the language of sub-paragraph 5(e) of the B. F. Ferguson will so that the word "monument" might include a building; specifically, an addition to the Art Institute. This suit was filed quietly and without previous publicity. At 10:04 a.m., on the same day, the Attorney General's Answer was filed, making only a nominal defense and conceding all the points raised by the Art Institute.

Minutes later, at 10:17, a seventeen-page decree was entered declaring that the word "monument" in the Benjamin Ferguson will could indeed include a building, and that the Art Institute could use the accumulated and future income of the Ferguson Fund for the construction and maintenance of an addition to the Institute. It was subsequently discovered that the Art Institute's Complaint, the Attorney General's Answer, and the court's decree were all typed on the same typewriter, all bore the same watermark, and the Attorney General's Answer was enclosed in the reversed blue backing of the Art Institute's counsel. Moreover, although the decree referred to "the proof, oral, documentary and written, taken and filed in said cause," in fact no witnesses were heard *and no transcription of any proceedings appears in the court files.*[36]

In less than one hour the income from a great charitable trust for the erection of statuary was commissioned for bricks and mortar at the Chicago Art Institute, despite the wishes of the donor. The long shadow cast by what the complaint to the court alleged to be a "hoax" was later to raise the ire of a number of individuals and organizations who gradually came to realize what really had happened.[37]

Fooled with Hope. Writing in *FOCUS/Midwest*, Elinor Richey of Chicago tells about Mr. Ferguson's contact with the Art Institute in order to insure that his wishes would be clearly understood:

Newton H. Carter, then Art Institute secretary, told the *Chicago Tribune* that prior to his death Mr. Ferguson had "called on the officers of the Institute with his attorney" and explained his bequest to them. "Mr. Ferguson said he had traveled in Europe constantly and was struck by the impressiveness of art works in the parks and along the boulevards. He said he regretted that Chicago should be so far behind other municipalities and wished the money expended with a view to filling the void."[38]

As an apparent justification for the adaptive reuse of the great fund, the chairman of the Ferguson Fund for over thirty years declared that "Chicago is 'amply provided' with sculpture and 'progressive cities' don't erect it any more."[39] It may be observed, however, that many forward-looking cities have not only invested heavily in statuary and monuments since the creation of the Ferguson Fund in 1905 but also continue to do so.

The long-deferred construction project finally became financially possible when, in 1955, the B. F. Ferguson Memorial Fund grew from its accumulating income to $1,600,000. A small hitch, however, developed in the Art Institute's plan. Its trustees decided that rather than construction of exhibition and display space, at this time the need was greater for a new administrative wing. Such a change, the scrupulously careful trustees believed, called for the reaffirmation of the court's 1933 decision granting them the right to use of the Ferguson Fund for construction.

The critics of the institute's plan were prepared and waiting, immediately plunging the matter into a legal struggle. The Art Institute's suit to gain approval for its plan was challenged by the National Sculpture Society, but the court ruled that the society could not intervene in the suit. Thereafter, Wesley Greene brought a taxpayers' suit to enforce the Ferguson trust; however, the court stated that it failed to see the basis of the taxpayers' suit and ruled that only the attorney general could bring suit to enforce a charitable trust in Illinois. Further, the court observed that the Greene suit bordered on maintenance; that is, turning the remedial process of justice into a weapon for oppression.[40]

Carefully delimiting the allegation with reference to the attorney general of Illinois at the time of the 1933 court decision, the Greene suit alleged that even though the attorney general was "a man of great integrity, honesty and esteem," he nevertheless relied upon the "combined prestige" of the Art Institute of Chicago and the Northern Trust Company of Chicago, allowing them "to dominate and dictate the entire proceedings which were bottomed and conceived in fraud." The court found, however, that there was insufficient "allegation of facts to show fraud in the actions of the attorney general of the State of Illinois."[41]

Greene's suit foundered for the same reason the earlier case had done so: it was well-settled law in the state of Illinois that "as the protector of public charitable trusts," the attorney general was the sole representative of the people, with exclusive power to initiate litigation against a charitable entity. Thus, Greene's taxpayers' suit was dismissed, and the altered use of the Ferguson Fund was accomplished—with full judicial sanction.

A Sense of Public Duty. Attorney Kutner reports that after dismissing the suit, Superior Court Judge Abraham Marovitz told the Art Institute's counsel: "I have read the entire case of 1933 and all the papers and articles relating to the matter, as well as Mr. Ferguson's will made in 1904 and probated in 1905, and I cannot agree that Ferguson intended for the income from his money to be used to erect an administration building."[42]

Thereafter, Judge Marovitz also met with Mr. Kutner and the Corporation Counsel of the City of Chicago to discuss the issue of the Ferguson Fund, reaching the conclusion that the Illinois Trust Law was in need of drastic overhaul. Kutner reported that "Judge Marovitz urged passage of a law which would permit a taxpayer to challenge the use of charitable trust funds."[43]

After exhausting all legal avenues, the public interest groups—and other individuals desiring to restore the B. F. Ferguson Monument Fund—appealed to the new attorney general, William Clark. He lent a sympathetic ear.

Attorney General Clark contacted the directors of the Art Institute, informing them that even though he could do little about the change in the fund, he was unhappy about how they as fiduciaries had handled the Ferguson Fund. In his state of disquietude, Attorney General Clark threatened "to open a general, critical investigation of the Art Institute's finances unless the Ferguson Fund was restored" and administered according to the donor's intended wishes. Fearful of the adverse public criticism that would result from such an attorney general's inquiry, the trustees of the Art Institute, not totally insensitive to the implications of the attorney general's request, "agreed to use all the accumulated and future income of the Ferguson Fund for the erection of statuary in parks of Chicago," as Mr. Ferguson had wished. Thus, quiet, "behind-the-scenes pressure" by a dedicated attorney general brought positive results, which years of contentious litigation in the Illinois courts had been unable to achieve.[44]

It should be noted, however, that among the monuments credited to the Ferguson Fund was "39,000 square feet of space returned to gallery use by the B. F. Ferguson Memorial Building at the Art Institute of Chicago."[45] Since this space was added to the Art Institute, several new statues have been erected in Chicago with the Ferguson Fund, including Henry Moore's *Sundial*.

The facts seem to indicate only one conclusion: Ben Ferguson intended his money to be used for the creation of statues and works of art throughout the city of Chicago, not for the construction and maintenance of an administrative wing for the Art Institute. The National Sculpture Society of New York made an important positive and enlightening point when it told the court "that the diversion of the fund may have the effect of making testators [donors] unwilling or reluctant to make bequests or set up trusts for or to charitable and educational institutions for fear that such bequests and trusts will not be used in the manner intended by the testators."[46] Such affirmation of the importance of integrity for cultural institutions should serve as a chilling reminder concerning the worth of gifts and bequests and also the value of goodwill and trust when it comes to fund-raising.

The Whole Moral Law. The Ferguson incident illustrates the magnitude of duty of loyalty in administering trust funds. Austin Scott writes about Professor Josiah Royce's concern for loyalty, "In loyalty, when loyalty is properly defined, is the fulfillment of the whole moral law."[47] The measure of dim light that can be cast on the charitable scene by trustees who maneuver in the tight little world of money, power, and politics has a salutary effect on all—the good and the not-so-good. As Mr. Kutner warns, "The trustees must not be permitted to so construe the trust instrument so as to thwart the settlor's intent and to use the trust to serve their own vested interests."[48]

Although the people of Illinois are the beneficiaries of the Ferguson estate, Mr. Ferguson had the right to determine how the public was to benefit from his bequest. Both law and custom afford any donor the right to determine in what manner his or her bequests may contribute to the betterment of society. This privilege is inherent in our democratic process, and it is incumbent on the court to enforce it.

DEACCESSIONING

With the widely publicized criticisms of the Metropolitan Museum's deaccessioning of several modern paintings, including Henri Rousseau's *Tropics* in the early 1970s, it might have been reasonable to assume that a popular misconception about trusteeship could at last be put to rest. In effect, the misconception was the belief that there were no generally accepted standards by which to measure trustee conduct. At least one might conclude this in the area of deaccessioning, the process of withdrawing an object from a museum's collection for sale or exchange. Deaccessioning per se is not illegal or unethical, but the failure to use proper methods both in the process of deaccessioning and the subsequent use of funds derived from it can be.

After New York Attorney General Louis J. Lefkowitz concluded his inquiry into the Metropolitan Museum's deaccessioning procedures, he found no technical grounds for legal action; however, he was deeply concerned with the lack of guidelines. At his insistence, the Metropolitan created guidelines.

Attorney General Lefkowitz then formulated deaccessioning guidelines for all museums in New York, published them, and held a public hearing on the matter at the World Trade Center in New York. In his opening remarks at the Attorney General's Conference of Museum Representatives, Mr. Lefkowitz delivered a conciliatory but firm address explaining that it was not tax exemption that gave his office power to oversee the activities of charitable organizations.

Mr. Lefkowitz reaffirmed the long-standing common-law principle of the attorney general's role in charitable affairs. He said:

I mean that my office has been given by law, long antedating the independence of our country, the high duty of representing the people for whose benefit you hold charitable and educational assets and to ensure that their interest in those assets is not adversely affected. It is for this reason, and not because you are tax exempt or because you may get some small help from public funds, that my office is concerned with your activities.[49]

It is of interest to note that one individual who testified at the conference was Dr. Frederick Dockstader, director of the Museum of the American Indian. Art museum critic Karl Meyer quotes Dr. Dockstader at the Attorney General's Conference as follows:

I feel that with the deaccession and problems developed out of the Metropolitan situation there does have to be some looking into the preservation and integrity of collections. However, I must admit that I am quite seriously frightened by the amount of paperwork which this could develop. I daily come into a snowball hill of paper which I am never able to keep up with. . . . I honestly feel we should try to establish a standard of procedure which the Attorney General would be able to act upon wisely, and I do not question his right to do so. . . . On the other hand, I recognize that not all of my colleagues wear the same halo I do. Once in a while we slip from grace.[50]

Dr. Dockstader did not wear his halo too well, for he slipped from grace in the fracas described in the next case.

Putting a House in Order: Museum of the American Indian, New York, New York

Selling a Collection. In his wonderful little essay entitled "Habit," William James says, "With mere good intentions, hell is proverbially paved."[51] There are perchance few times in which the basic truth of this aphorism is as roundly displayed as in the well-appointed trustee meeting room. Illustrative of how trustee plaster sets is the incident involving the Museum of the American Indian (Heye Foundation) of New York City.

Charged with a violation of their public responsibility due to a failure to modify outmoded practices, the trustees of this museum gradually yielded under intense legal pressure from the state attorney general of New York. At issue was the necessity for trustees to change their old ways of doing business, while saving what many believed to be the museum's unique, invaluable, and irreplaceable collection from further harm owing to alleged breaches of trust by the museum's trustees.

As a charitable trust, the museum's purpose includes the collection of anthropological objects related to the aboriginal people of the Americas and the study of their languages, literature, history, art, and life. The museum and its unusual collection is the result of the interest of George G. Heye, an engineer who accumulated great wealth through investments in Standard Oil and who took a keen interest in Indian artifacts while building a bridge in Arizona. Mr. Heye personally oversaw all the operations of the museum from its creation as a charitable trust in 1916 until his death in 1958.

Through a figurehead board of trustees mainly made up of friends who would be sure not to interfere with his running of the museum, Mr. Heye bought, sold, and traded as he pleased with little concern either for documentation or whether the public visited the museum.[52]

Reputed to have the nation's largest and most comprehensive collection of the country's art and artifacts pertaining to Indian art, culture, and history, the museum collects objects related to American Indians from the Arctic to the Tierra del Fuego. The collection has an estimated 4.5 million objects, including common as well as uncommon ones, such as arrowheads, totem poles, tomahawks, houseposts, beaded necklaces, leather moccasins, peace pipes, handcrafted clay sculptures, and pre-Columbian golden statuary.

It would be difficult to assess the collection's value, since its worth is determined by its uniqueness and research potential. During the deaccessioning fracas, Dr. William Sturtevant, curator of ethnology at the Smithsonian, said, "There is no such thing as a duplicate."[53] Being somewhat different from Western art, in which value is determined by spectacular pieces, the art of primitive (or preindustrial) cultures carries significance for both its aesthetics and what it has to say about its creators.

A chief value of primitive art lies in the ethnographic information it provides for comparison, since it can reveal significant data about earlier cultures. Thus, twenty tomahawks tell more about a culture than does one or two, which perhaps questions the notion that a balanced collection is best for this type of museum. Some critics strongly believe that trading in order to achieve balance leads to a degradation, not an advancement, of the collection.

This position has reasonable intellectual merits because an ethnologist using artifacts in problem solving needs to have as many similar items as possible, unlike an amateurish dilettante, who has only a casual and random fascination in interesting, but disparate, objects. "Thus, to many scholars," observes the *New York Times*, "selling privately any work from a primitive group is like selling a baby for adoption on the black market. Vital documents get lost, catalogue numbers are removed, the object's roots, its history, its vital statistics disappear."[54]

War Drums. The brouhaha over deaccessioning began in 1974 when a dealer offered one museum trustee an item from the museum's collection, which had previously been on exhibit at the Walker Art Center's Indian masterworks show. Curious and surprised at the solicitation, the trustee asked the museum for its deaccession information only to find that the item was still listed as part of the museum's inventory. *The New York Times* gave this account:

> Three different dealers were offering through photograph a set of carved Kwakiutl houseposts belonging to the Heye. The asking price: $130,000. Among those who were solicited was Edmund Carpenter, a Heye trustee and noted anthropologist. He turned them down. But a few weeks later he received a letter from Dr. Dockstader declaring that a dealer had offered $55,000 for the group. Perhaps the museum could get more, suggested Dr. Dockstader. What were the trustees' views?
>
> "I was outraged," says Dr. Carpenter, "Imagine asking me to approve a sale for $55,000 when I knew a dealer was selling—and possibly had already sold—the work for $130,000. And how did they get those photographs?"[55]

Commenting on the situation, Leonard DuBoff, the noted legal art scholar, said, "Further inquiry led to the discovery that deaccessioning was almost entirely handled by the director, Dr. Dockstader, without comparative valuations, committee approval or consultation with the trustees."[56] Dr. Dockstader freely admitted, " 'On some trades I've been gypped, . . . and on others I've come out ahead.' "[57]

After his inquiry into the museum's deaccessioning practices, Dr. Carpenter proceeded to move on what he believed to be an unorthodox procedure for deaccessioning, moving at a trustee meeting that all deaccessions should go to other museums or to public sale with full disclosure of records and documentation. The motion failed to get a second. " 'I'm sick of being told museums must deaccession,' said Dr. Carpenter [afterward]. 'Of course, they must. But in this instance that's an excuse to mask surreptitious deals on the commercial market. You can't play games with an ethnological collection.' "[58]

Carpenter gave the board a chance to begin righting a ship that had been swamped by the tidal wave of trustee inertia, indifference, impassivity. Rebuffed by his fellow trustees, Carpenter took his complaint to the office of the state attorney general, who began an investigation into several of the museum's activities. As a member of the board of trustees, Dr. Carpenter had a legal right to act outside the board (as an entity), since he had reasonable belief that the trustees of the museum had committed a breach of trust. (In some states it is a matter of statutory law that a board member may bring suit against fellow trustees for alleged breach of trust.) He charged the other trustees and the administration with "mismanaging the museum's collection of 4.5 million pieces, along with sloppy and inaccurate record-keeping and conflicts of interest."[59]

Several breaches of fiduciary duty were allegedly committed by the trustees: "Self-dealing, waste and its concealment, delegation of discretionary duties, failure to maintain accurate records, falsification of annual reports and falsification of valuation of gifts for tax purposes."[60]

After the attorney general's office had been informed, it petitioned the court to make an inventory of the museum's collection, to place a restraint on disposition of items within the collection, and to remove the director and most of the trustees for the "surreptitious and wasteful" way in which artifacts from the museum's collection were either sold or given away. The petition for removal in itself represented a highly unusual legal procedure because trustees are usually given the benefit of the doubt as public-spirited citizens who volunteer their time and often are chief benefactors of the charity.

Straightening Things Out. Before a trial occurred the defendant trustees agreed to a stipulation, requiring them to comply with certain conditions. Some are

- that a stipulation be sought from the attorney general, subject to approval by the Court of any further deaccessioning transactions;

- that an inventory be undertaken of the entire collection under the supervisory powers of the attorney general, although the inventory was to be accomplished at the museum's expense;

- that the director be relieved of all administrative duties and powers;

- that a new administrator be employed with ministerial duties that do not include the authority to acquire or dispose of items from the collection—this being the sole province of the trustees;

- that the trustees will obtain the consent of the attorney general before a new administrator receives appointment; and

- that the attorney general shall have the right to review any proposed nomination to the board of trustees and the consent of the attorney general shall be obtained prior to the appointment of any new trustee.[61]

Through alleged breach of trust, the trustees lost legal managerial control of the museum that had been entrusted to their care, and their subsequent actions were carefully scrutinized by the attorney general—the people's representative—through the ultimate authority: the court. Before the upheaval the board consisted of eleven trustees. A number of them resigned during the judicial inquiry. As of this writing, under a restructured board, there are twenty-three trustees with staggered and measured terms, including for the first time a number of Native Americans. Dr. Roland W. Force, director of the museum, says: " 'Perhaps our most important new policy is that we have defined Native Americans'—the preferred term for Indian—'as a constituency of the museum, and are attempting to respond to their needs and aspirations.' ''[62]

Continuing Trials and Tribulations. Despite the fact that the board of trustees of the Museum of the American Indian was restructured by the court, it is not fully on the road to recovery. At its current location in New York City at 155th Street and Broadway, the museum draws too few visitors and has inadequate storage space for its fragile collection, which must be protected from decay. The trustees, therefore, began to cast about for a new home. Merger plans were discussed with the American Museum of Natural History, but fear of loss of autonomy quickly derailed this plan.

Next, H. Ross Perot, the Texas executive who had made a fortune in computers, entered the scene, complicating matters further. He offered to invest $70 million in the museum if it were to move to Dallas, Texas.

However, New York State Attorney General Robert Abrams had learned of this possible arrangement through private citizens. He told the museum's trustees that they managed a charitable trust and that under the terms of the trust instrument they needed New York County Supreme Court approval to make such a move and that he had every intention of taking appropriate action to enforce their fiduciary obligations under the law.[63]

What is astonishing is that even after direct court intervention, resulting in the restructuring of the board, apparently the trustees were not aware that they were administering property belonging to the people of New York and that the contemplated change required court approval. Also, the New York Board of Regents, which holds legal responsibility for charitable trusts, such as the Museum of the American Indian, would need to grant approval before the museum could move from New York.[64]

Since the attorney general's advisory warning, the trustees have gone into court seeking a "bill of instructions," that is, an initial pleading by petitioner in equity. The disposition of the museum is up in the air. Although the court may take a dim view of the museum's move to Texas, it may sanction it, especially if the trustees can make a case that they are unable to fulfill their legal responsibilities in New York.

Certainly, if museum trustees do not assiduously follow good museum management practices, they can expect legislatures to enact laws to bring their actions more in line with the public good. Perhaps such legislation will be as stringent as that faced by European museum managers, who are extremely envious of the American freedom.

Deaccessioning Art at the Fogg Museum: Harvard University, Cambridge, Massachusetts

The case law in the area of deaccessioning is scant, and it may be unwise for museums to test too many times the question at law, since a museum's public image could be seriously impugned. This is not a trivial matter because charitable institutions depend on both the goodwill of the public and its beneficence through gifts, gifts in kind, and so on.

Corporate America spends millions on public relations—its public image. Why? Public relations is the important process of aligning institutional policies, ideas, services, and actions to the public, or a class of it, whose confidence the charity needs and wants for the explicit purpose of gaining understanding, acceptance, and support. Abraham Lincoln captured the essence of public relations when he said, "With public sentiment nothing can fail, without it nothing can succeed."

Trouble at the Fogg Art Museum. The planned deaccessioning of art objects in 1982 at Harvard's Fogg Art Museum, reputed to house the greatest university art collection in the world with more than 80,000 items, tested fully the tenability of Mr. Lincoln's statement. The Fogg sorely needed an addition. The addition eventually became a separate building called the Arthur M. Sackler Museum, joining the Fogg and Busch Reisinger museums to form the Art Museums of Harvard University.

Trouble began for the planned addition to the Fogg Museum when bids came in $1.5 million over the Fogg's projected costs. With high hopes for the new structure, the museum managed to raise the additional funds. However, because of the developing financial exigencies within the university's operating budget, Harvard's fiscal managers became concerned with the cost of maintaining the new museum. They insisted on the creation of a special fund to meet projected operating costs for the new building, despite the fact that such a goal was generally considered unrealistic for nonprofit institutions. A plan to deaccession art objects grew out of the need to establish a stabilization fund of $3 million to relieve the anticipated pressure on operating expenses for the new museum.[65]

The plan for deaccessioning art forced the Association of Art Museum Directors (AAMD) to issue a simple, but strongly worded, resolution condemning Harvard's contemplated move. The association was made up of approximately 150 directors of the largest art museums in the United States and Canada.

Passed unanimously at the association's midwinter meeting, the resolution appears in full text as follows:

DEACCESSIONING POLICY

RESOLVED, That the President of the Association of Art Museum Directors be directed to communicate to Derek Bok, President of Harvard University, that the members of this Association are deeply troubled by reports that the Harvard Corporation has approved the concept of the sale of works of art in the collection of the Fogg Art Museum to guarantee or otherwise underwrite operating expenses either directly or indirectly. Further, the membership of the Association of Art Museum Directors directs the President of the Association to express in the strongest possible terms that the sale of the collection in this manner is contrary to accepted principles of our profession as stated in paragraph 27 of *Professional Practices in Art Museums*, 1981, as follows:

"The deaccession and disposal of a work of art from a museum's collection requires particularly rigorous examination. Deaccessioning should be related to policy rather than to the exigencies of the moment, and funds obtained through disposal must be used to replenish the collection."

Such an action would constitute a breach of principle inconsistent with Harvard University's historic position of leadership within the profession. This action would also set a dangerous precedent for others charged with the responsibility for collections and represents a grave disservice to the art museum community.[66]

The Harvard Corporation, shortly after AAMD's resolution, announced that the project for the addition to the Fogg Museum would be canceled, enraging the museum's supporters who had made a painstaking five-year effort to raise the funds for the desperately needed building project. In rationalizing its decision not to sign the contract and move forward with the construction, President Bok "explained that the Fogg is currently searching for a new director to replace Seymour Slive, who is retiring in the fall, and it would have been impossible to attract a top person in the field if it ignored the call of the museum directors to drop the deaccessioning plan."[67]

Governance at Harvard. It is necessary here, with a few rapid strokes, to explain the system of governance at Harvard. The governing organization for Harvard University consists of the Corporation and the Board of Overseers. The Corporation consists of the president and treasurer, *ex-officiis*, and five Fellows, who are self-perpetuating, although appointment is with the consent of the Board of Overseers. The Corporation manages the financial affairs of the university without the need of consent for specific transactions by the Board of Overseers. Thus, the Corporation—a body of seven—has wide authority in university financial affairs.

The Board of Overseers consists of the president, treasurer, *ex-officiis*, and thirty alumni-elected individuals who serve for six-year overlapping terms. The board, among other things, reviews academic matters and the departments of the university through some sixty visiting committees whose membership includes overseers and others.[68]

The Museum's Visiting Committee Reacts. A thirty-four–member Visiting Committee oversees the Harvard Art Museums. Friends of the Fogg and its Visiting Committee, many of whom hold their position on the committee by virtue of their power, wealth, and prominence, were quick to make known their disappointment (publicly and privately) about the last-minute cancelation.

Their response was bitter, often heated, and at times perhaps exceeded the bounds of propriety. Once people are angered, it becomes easy to whip a community of supporters to a fine froth—even individuals who tend to abhor the public limelight. One museum employee concisely summarized the issue: "It was a bunch of art historians against a bunch of bankers, and the bankers won."[69] To many people, the issue was too great to let the Harvard Corporation walk flat-footedly away from the problem, for the friends of the Fogg strongly felt that those responsible knew what was right and what was wrong. The friends could question without fear, and so tested the inner dimensions of the Harvard Corporation's authority and power.

At the time that the corporation canceled the project, $21 million had been raised. But it is fundamental that a charitable institution may not raise money for one purpose and then use it for another. Almost $11 million specifically designated for this purpose would have had to have been returned to unhappy donors.

The *New York Times* reported, " 'I am through with Harvard—I would not give them another red cent,' Ruth Carter Johnson, a committee member and chairman of the Amon Carter Museum in Fort Worth, said to The Harvard Crimson."[70]

Ralph Colin, a long-standing member of the Visiting Committee as well as a collector and donor to the project, sent a blistering personal letter to President Bok. He charged that

either you are unaware of the Fogg's role and importance, as are the other five members of the [Harvard] Corporation, or being aware, you are unwilling to go to bat and if necessary lay your job as President on the line to accomplish what needed to be accomplished. You may therefore take your choice as to whether "ignorance" or "ignominy" more aptly describes the basis of your behavior.[71]

Mr. Colin also wrote that he believed that the project had been canceled because of "the corporation's fear of repeating its mistakes in the recent building of a generator for the medical facilities." The generator referred to is the Medical Area Total Energy Plant (MATEP), which was originally estimated to cost $50 million,[72] but was completed for $371 million.[73]

The Debt Issue. During the tumult *Boston Globe*'s Robert Levey asked the burning question "How could Harvard University, with its massive $1.6 billion endowment, [currently $3.6 billion] be so financially strained that it would cancel construction of a much-needed art museum addition just because it was $3.3 million short of the $24.8 million goal that was set to build and operate the place?"[74] To deal with this question, the Harvard financial picture at the time of the planning for the Fogg addition must be carefully considered. Harvard had already been burned pretty badly with cost overruns on MATEP, which at the time were being financed out of the university's budget, which was also feeling the draw of the high operating costs for two of its newer building projects, the Holyoke Center and the Loeb Drama Center.[75]

Harvard's operational budget was, like the overloaded clothesline, stretched to the breaking point because of its commitment from the general operating budget for the construction of the MATEP. Harvard sought and received relief from its financial exigencies connected with the power plant by selling tax-exempt bonds through the Massachusetts Health and Educational Facilities Authority (MHEFA).

According to Harvard's *Financial Report,*

the costs of MATEP, including capitalized interest during the construction period, have been financed through the issuance of $371 million of tax-exempt MHEFA bonds. These borrowings financed the plant at the lowest possible interest cost and restored the General Operating Account's liquidity, which had been reduced by its internal advances for the plant's construction.[76]

Changing One's Mind. The central issue in the Harvard controversy was the plan for the highly questionable deaccessioning of art objects to establish a "stabilization fund" that would earn high-yield interest rates to pay in part for the new museum's operating expenses. Harvard assured everyone that only the interest would be used to pay for projected deficits.

Under intense public pressure the powers-that-be at Harvard changed their minds. Happily for everyone concerned, the uproar was put to sleep by the Visiting Committee, which raised another $3 million. And to everyone's delight the project was completed with no deaccessioned art footing any of the bill. It was, after all, a matter of bankers' power versus art historians' power, and they both won.

Scaring off Donors. Clearly, the Harvard Corporation got into hot water when it contemplated what some people judged to be an unethical and unprofessional deaccessioning of art to fund operating costs for a new building. The Fogg deaccessioning incident was not one of litigation but of public relations. "Just by mentioning, though later abandoning, a deaccessioning plan at the Fogg," reported the *Boston Globe*, "Harvard has probably scared off some potential donors of art. . . . And serious doubt has been cast on Harvard's basic commitment to supporting the fine arts."[77]

The highly questionable plan to deaccession art objects was stopped not by legal action but by a professional association's code of ethics solidly bolstered by a determined insistence to enforce that code. One can assume that the governing authorities were perhaps fearful that an unhappy donor of deaccessioned material might go to the attorney general of Massachusetts with the AAMD's statement in hand, alleging that the Harvard Corporation was acting irresponsibly and unethically and against the public interest.

When the AAMD issued its resolution, the Harvard Corporation gave a knee-jerk reaction to cancel. The Fogg incident illustrates that charitable trustees are not free agents; they are stewards of charitable property, and there are principles to be upheld in this regard.

What the Sam Hill! The Maryhill Museum, Goldendale, Washington

The adrenalin in small town weeklies, like large city newspapers, runs high when it comes to alleged cultural abuse. Before the Washington attorney general filed suit in Klickitat County Court against the museum's trustees for alleged breaches of fiduciary duties, the local press heightened emotions through banner headlines, focusing on mismanagement, nonmanagement, and self-dealing. The Northwest from Portland, Oregon, to Seattle, Washington, was in a stir, which set into motion an irreversible chain of investigations, lawsuits, resignations— all of which were finally laid to rest by restructuring the museum's board of trustees.

The Maryhill Museum of Fine Arts in Goldendale, Washington, was formed in 1923 by Sam Hill, the road builder. In 1926 Queen Marie of Rumania dedicated Maryhill in its bucolic setting. The museum, a steel and concrete structure patterned after Le Petit Trianon at Versailles, was named after Mary Hill, Sam Hill's daughter.

Maryhill as a Cattle Ranch. Located on the Columbia River 110 miles from any metropolitan center, Maryhill as a small museum has its share of souvenirs, memorabilia, curios, and trifles. What makes Maryhill exceptional, perhaps distinguishing it from its sister institutions of comparable size, is that it contains a fine collection of Alaskan, Eskimo, and Native American artifacts as well as two collections of Auguste Rodin's works and drawings. One Rodin collection is a group of fifty-three plasters, terra-cottas, and bronzes that the artist used for reference and study in his Paris studio—it is a collection of "Rodin's Rodins." The other is the largest collection of authentic Rodin drawings outside the Musée Rodin in Paris.[78]

The Maryhill Museum also owns and operates a 6500-acre wheat and cattle ranch on which it is located. When Sam Hill created his museum, he determined that it would be governed by a seven-member self-perpetuating board of trustees, each of whom would serve until death or resignation. As is often the case with personally created museums, the original trustees of Maryhill were friends and relatives of Mr. Hill, and the operation of the museum became a family affair, despite the public beneficial interest. One trustee, Hazel Dolph Clark, recommended that a relative of hers be retained as a carpenter to build cabinets and to prepare generally for the building's public opening. The carpenter, Mr. Clifford Dolph, must have duly impressed the trustees, for they made him the permanent director, a position he held for thirty-five years.[79]

As the original trustees disappeared from the scene, the makeup of the board changed with the appointment of businesspeople, lawyers, doctors from both southern Washington and northern Oregon. They focused their attention almost exclusively on the 6500-acre ranch and the museum's portfolio—and admittedly so, as reflected in one trustee's comment that Maryhill was "just a cattle ranch that accidently owned a museum." Thus, the trustees left the administration of the museum to Mr. Dolph with minimal supervision.[80]

Mr. Dolph apparently bought and traded from the collection as he saw fit, changing the thrust of the museum's collection in the process. He indulged his own tastes by buying rare and unique chess sets. All of this was accomplished, according to Robert Campbell, who was Mr. Dolph's successor, without the careful supervision and approval of the trustees—something required of individuals operating in a fiduciary relation to a museum. After Mr. Dolph's retirement Robert Campbell ordered an inventory of the collection, only to find the disappearance and deterioration of the museum's holdings, most noticeably in the primitive arts collection. An independent professional appraiser "estimated the value of the missing artifacts to be in the range of $200,000."[81]

Restructuring the Board of Trustees. Armed with the inventory report, which provided strong evidence of a number of irregularities, Mrs. Mary Stevenson of White Salmon, who was a member of the Washington Arts Commission and who had been appointed to the museum's art committee by Mr. Campbell, contacted the attorney general's office in 1975 to discuss problems at the museum. As a result of this conference, the attorney general agreed to conduct an investigation, which subsequently became stalled for lack of adequate staff to handle the investigation. To overcome this problem, a citizens committee was formed to advise the attorney general's office. This committee ultimately recommended that the board of trustees be restructured and that the bylaws and articles of incorporation be rewritten principally to ensure that new procedures would be adopted for the selection of trustees and for the length of their terms of office.

As an alternative to a possible lawsuit for the trustees' alleged breaches of fiduciary duties, the attorney general proposed the idea of an eight-member advisory committee to join with the museum's board of trustees to rewrite the bylaws and articles of incorporation leading to the desired administrative reform.

The trustees, while maintaining that the threatened suit was groundless, felt that even a groundless suit would damage the museum and thus decided to work with the attorney general to settle the potential litigation. Accordingly, they amended their bylaws to permit the advisory committee. However, controversy soon erupted when the attorney general appointed to the advisory committee five members the trustees found objectionable. According to Mr. John S. Moore, attorney for the trustees, the advisory committee at the first meeting between the two groups attempted "to throw out four of the five trustees. This was contrary to the promise to the trustees from Defendant Slade Gorton that the Advisory Committee and the trustees '[would] work *together* in improving this valuable resource.' "[82]

Bickering continued. The trustees refused to adopt the new articles of incorporation. Captain A. Leppaluoto, chairman of the museum's board of trustees, commented on the joint meeting between the trustees and the advisory committee: "It was a well-oiled and a fast train ride."[83] When it came to the showdown of who was going to run things, the board of trustees or the interim committee appointed by the Washington attorney general, real conflict developed. Unable to resolve their differences, the litigants headed for court. The case was settled by a stipulation that contained a new set of bylaws and articles of incorporation jointly created by the interested parties.[84]

Filing Lawsuits. The trustees were first to file suit. They claimed there had been "a material breach of the compromise agreement to settle the alleged potential claims against trustees of Maryhill Museum."[85] The attorney general then filed a complaint requesting an accounting, surcharges, removal of trustees, and appointment of new trustees.[86]

Of particular interest is the first paragraph of the attorney general's complaint, which reads: "This action is brought by SLADE GORTON, attorney general [later U.S. senator from Washington State] pursuant to his common law and statutory duties . . . to enforce charitable trusts in the State of Washington."[87] The attorney general of Washington state, under the law, represents the beneficiaries (the public) of charitable trusts such as Maryhill Museum, despite the fact that the Maryhill Museum of Fine Arts is a nonprofit corporation. A charitable organization may be organized as a trust or corporation, but in the eyes of the law, it is a charitable trust.

The Washington attorney general charged breach of trust in a number of categories:

• a petty cash bank account was kept in the director's name during his tenure in office, never accounting to the board for the disposition of any monies deposited in the account;

• the director sold assets of the museum without the permission of the trustees;

• the trustees should have asked for an accounting of the director's transactions in the exchange of museum property;

• for several decades the trustees failed to conduct an annual audit by a qualified accountant of the financial transactions of the museum;

• the trustees failed to observe the standards of museum trustees generally;

• there were self-dealing transactions leading to a serious breach of trust; and

• the trustees failed to observe the prudent person rule.[88]

The prudent person rule, which forms the basic standard of trust law, was first expressed in 1830 by Justice Samuel Putman of Massachusetts, when he stated that a trustee "shall . . . observe how men of prudence, discretion and intelligence manage their own affairs, not in regard to speculation, but in regard to the permanent disposition of their funds, considering the probable income, as well as the probable safety of the capital to be invested" (citing, *Harvard College v. Amory,* 26 Mass. [9 Pick.] 446, 461 [1830]).

The old board and the new board jointly adopted the new agreed-on bylaws and articles of incorporation when they took office. Noteworthy is that four members of the former board were retained on the new nine-member board, although the trustees now serve staggered, limited terms, rather than holding office for life. This new convention is more in line with current thinking about board membership. As a result of alleged trustee mismanagement and nonmanagement—resulting in the interdiction of the attorney general's office, investigations, and lawsuits—the board of trustees at Maryhill Museum was restructured. The new staggered and limited terms guarantee trustee turnover in the future. A group of determined individuals, working with the attorney general, brought change to the Maryhill Museum.

A Museum-Piece Lawsuit: The George F. Harding Museum, Chicago, Illinois

The Harding Museum case is emerging as a museum piece itself. A series of reverses, setbacks, financial intrigue, and long court entanglements have piqued everyone's curiosity. The case rises from alleged serious trustee abuse, including the secretive removal of precious art objects from Chicago for sale in New York. The alleged violations in this case embody many principles already discussed and strongly suggest serious breaches of trust. Legal experts and other observers expect the case to be far-reaching in establishing guidelines for administering nonprofit, tax-exempt institutions such as Harding.

At this writing, the Harding Museum case is still in litigation, as it has been since 1976. The material presented herein is based mainly on the Illinois attorney general's pleadings and *Chicago Tribune* reportage. At this time the matter is still before Judge Albert Green, and the defendants have been proved guilty of nothing. Before touching on some of the legal points, some background on the museum is necessary.

The Harding Museum Is Created. George F. Harding—a powerful political figure, financier, and large Chicago landowner—assembled the remarkable Harding Collection, which contains some 2500 objects, including paintings by Rubens, Goya, and Remington, perhaps America's best-known western artist. Especially strong are collections of knights' armor and weapons as well as the early firearms that made knights' armor obsolete. The estimated value of the collection is from $25 to $30 million.

In 1930 Mr. Harding incorporated his collection in what is believed to have been a move to keep the collection intact, out of probate court, and exempt from federal taxes. When Mr. Harding died, he bequeathed not only his famous collection to the people of Illinois but also a substantial part of his $4.1 million estate (exclusive of the value of the museum) to support the Harding Collection.

Given to the public for its appreciation and enjoyment, the Harding Museum, an Illinois nonprofit corporation, is an adjudicated charitable trust.[89] In 1939, with the announcement of Mr. Harding's generous gift to the public, Arthur J. Murphy, attorney for Mr. Harding and a director and officer of the museum, proclaimed: ''Mr. Harding's collection is a gift to the public. . . . It will be open just as the Field Museum is, and thus Chicago has acquired a cultural institution that is outstanding in this country.''[90]

Originally located in a simulated castle on Lake Park Avenue, the Harding Museum—then a popular attraction to everyone, including schoolchildren—fell to urban renewal in 1964. The collection was then transferred to the top floors of a fifteen-story building on East Randolph Street. Former chief of security for the museum, George Otlewis, ''testified that it was closed from 1964 to 1970 so the collection could be 'catalogued.' Afterwards, viewing was limited to small supervised groups so visitors would not steal or damage anything."[91] But the attorney general's complaint alleges that the trustees, "intentionally and in disregard of their duty, have failed to properly display" the museum's art and artifacts to the public for its "viewing and appreciation."[92] It was Mr. Harding's wish that the museum benefit the public at large, and if it can be proved that the trustees did not properly display the items to the public, then this constitutes a violation of the trustees' fiduciary duty, since it is contrary to Mr. Harding's wish.

This Is My "Baby." The attorney general began a civil suit against the Harding Museum trustees for mismanagement of charitable assets. The matters that the attorney general complained of were the effects of these actions on the public welfare and interest. Alleging several breaches of trust, the attorney general argued that the officers and directors of the Harding Museum were "acting in a fiduciary capacity with relation to the . . . George F. Harding Museum . . . and as such [were] common law trustees."[93] In short, trustees are officers of the court. It makes no difference, therefore, that they are trustees of a corporation; their legal position is relatively the same as if they were unincorporated trustees.

In the beginning of the run-in, Herman M. Silverstein, chairman of the Harding Museum board, told the *Chicago Tribune*, "We've got to be careful who we let in—every time we get our name in the paper, we get people who just want to see our guns. And they're trying to figure out how to get them. Somebody will get hurt." Mr. Silverstein also told the *Tribune* that the museum was his "baby" and stated that "he [had] spent his life fretting and worrying over the museum's future."[94]

Saving One's Skin. The property on East Randolph Street, which had been purchased for about $1.5 million with Harding Museum money, was sold in 1981 for $6.25 million, forcing the collection to be warehoused, with the public again being denied viewing privileges. The attorney general charged that the purchase of the buildings on East Randolph Street was a violation of the trustees' duty to *diversify* the museum's assets and that the gain on the sale of the property in 1981 realized "an unreasonably low rate of return from such a speculative investment."[95]

A trustee is required to diversify among various classes of investments as well as within any one class. Even though the courts have not specified a maximum percentage, the cases together "indicate that courts acknowledging and enforcing the duty of diversification will treat the investment of greater than twenty to twenty-five percent of the trust assets in one form as prima facie evidence of breach of duty."[96]

Illinois law requires that directors of nonprofit organizations "shall consider the long and short term needs of the institution" in investment matters. "The real estate investments failed to provide for the short-term annual needs of the Museum when balanced against any long-term speculative gain in the future."[97] Further, during this period of speculative investment, the museum registered annual debts of $200,000 to $300,000, totaling more than $4.5 million from 1964 to 1980.[98] Because of the alleged mismanagement by the trustees, "the Museum was placed in a desperate financial position."[99]

Finally, in 1982, in a move (editorialized by the *Chicago Tribune*) allegedly to lighten the unceasing legal thrust being exerted on the Harding trustees by the attorney general, the collection was gifted over to the Art Institute of Chicago.[100] Although the collection has been permanently transferred to the Art Institute, the Harding Museum still exists as a legal entity. The lawsuit is still pending, with its trustees facing some serious charges involving alleged abuses of museum property.

Getting to the Top.

The trustee violates his duty to the beneficiary, [notes the *Restatement (Second) of Trusts*] not only where he sells trust property to himself individually, but also where he uses the trust property for his own purposes. Thus, he cannot properly use trust money in his business, or lend trust money to himself, or lease to himself land which he holds in trust.[101]

One alleged offense centers on self-dealing, which is a violation of the fiduciary's duty of loyalty. The attorney general alleges that one trustee, Herman M. Silverstein, misused charitable assets for personal gain. In 1967 Mr. Silverstein, through a letter dated 20 January 1967, urged the board of trustees to transfer $250,000, realized from the sale of museum securities, to Mr. Silverstein, who in turn used the money to buy shares of stock in Mid-America National Bank. These he placed in his own name. The purpose was to enable Mr. Silverstein to buy controlling interest in the Mid-America National Bank of Chicago, with the declared intention of becoming chairman of the board and president of the bank. The plan worked; he became both chairman and president of the bank. The attorney general alleges that using museum assets to help Mr. Silverstein "acquire control of the Mid-America National Bank is an act of self-dealing."[102] He also maintains that Mr. Silverstein had "unjustly enriched" himself by gaining control of Mid-America National Bank through the $250,000 transaction as well as by enjoying the "salary and other emoluments" as both chairman of the board and president of the bank.[103]

The attorney general also alleges that the trustees engaged in self-dealing when they displayed sixteenth- and seventeenth-century Turkish knives in the Mid-America National Bank's window in August 1967, as shown in a *Chicago Tribune* photograph. At the time of the display, defendant trustees owned a substantial amount of bank stock; thus, the attorney general alleges that the trustees were using trust property for their own benefit.[104] This incident is analogous to the instance in which a trust is created of an English estate that carries valuable sporting privileges, for example. The trustee cannot enjoy the privilege of shooting game, but the trustee does have the obligation to lease the privilege for the benefit of the trust estate.[105]

The attorney general's pleadings further allege that the trustees misused and abused their positions of trust through self-dealing, because the trustees, who held ownership in the bank through stock, made loans to the museum on which more than $201,989 was paid in interest. The attorney general charges that the bank, as a disqualified entity, could not loan money to the museum because the museum trustees "own over 35% of bank stock outright or in trust."[106]

Paying Bills on Time. Such skill and care in managing trust property require trustees to pay taxes in a timely manner to avoid penalties. A trustee may be surcharged for assigned penalties arising from nonpayment of taxes. The attorney general alleges that the trustees are "guilty of financial waste" because they "have subjected trust property to a potential liability of $110,218.52 in interest and penalities on late payment of 1967 real estate taxes."[107]

"You Don't Know What You Are Doing." As discussed, standard museum management practice coupled with legal requirements mandates that funds raised from deaccessioned art and other objects must be used for the purchase of similar objects—not for the general administration of the museum. The attorney general alleges that the trustees sold valuable museum property for the "purpose of raising monies to offset the intentionally and imprudently incurred annual financial deficits."[108]

Until stopped by court order, the trustees of the Harding Museum sold parts of the collection. It is alleged that the moneys were not segregated into an account for purchase of other art objects. The sale of the art and artifacts caused a furor in Chicago, with cultural organizations such as the Chicago Symphony Orchestra joining the upraised voices asking that the rare musical instruments be kept in Chicago. At the time of the sale of antique musical instruments from the collection (including a renowned double virginal built in 1623 by Hans Ruger the Younger of Antwerp, bringing a record $65,000 from an unnamed German museum), the attorney general alleged that the sale was a "breach of the museum's charter" and that the "museum officials misused its assets for their own purposes in a fraud on the museum and the public."[109]

The secret sale of Eugène Delacroix's *L' Arabe au tombeau,* an oil on canvas signed and dated in 1838, brought the full wrath of the press down on the trustees. Delacroix was the leader of the romantic art movement in France in the early nineteenth century, and his masterpiece commanded $130,000. Herman Silverstein told the *Chicago Tribune*—which had taken exception to both the sale of the Delacroix and the secrecy surrounding it—that "these stories about the museum are ruining the museum. You don't know what you are doing."[110]

Other items sold by the museum, according to the Final Pre-Trial Order, included precious art objects at Hanzel Galleries in 1973, bringing $172,413.60 in cash proceeds; rugs and oriental carpets at Christie's in 1976 for $88,949.89; a mummy in 1975 for $5,000; and walking canes in 1972 for $14,850.[111]

Before other art objects could be sold at the prestigious New York auction house of Sotheby Parke Bernet, which had offers of more than $1 million, the court issued an injunction stopping the sale. The museum trustees claimed they were selling the art objects on the advice of a consultant, because it was their intent to concentrate on the armor and subjects related to the armor.[112] Given this reason, one wonders why the Delacroix painting was sold. It depicted an Arabian knight kneeling in front of his stallion. Did the Delacroix not represent one artist's interpretation of the medievalists?

The attorney general alleges that "the proceeds of the sales of many valuable artifacts of the George F. Harding Museum were deposited in the general operating funds of a 'museum' which discouraged public viewing." The attorney general asserts that the sales were "improper" for two reasons: (1) the use of the proceeds from the sale to support the general museum is a violation of general museum management and (2) the primary duty of the trustee is to preserve and protect trust property. The trustees never petitioned the court for instructions; therefore, they exceeded their authority in dismantling the collection.[113]

The Remedy. The attorney general is requesting that the court remove the trustees; that the trustees be liable for the interest expenses that occurred during their administration; that the trustees return all salaries, benefits, and perquisites they received as officers and directors from the time of their first breach of trust to the present; that they be barred from ever holding another position of trust directly or indirectly related to charitable assets and from acting as trustees, fiduciaries, advisory board members, directors or officers of any charitable trust, foundation, or charity in the state of Illinois; and finally that the assets of the museum be placed in a constructive trust.[114] (A *constructive trust* is one imposed by the operation of law or the court to prevent the unjust enrichment of trustees [the legal owners] who hold property in trust for the beneficial use of another. This it does by disallowing the trustees the legal right to acquire or retain property through wrongdoing, such as actual or constructive fraud, unconscionable conduct, or abuse of confidence.)

The Harding trustees have been advising the Chicago Art Institute on the Harding Collection. This, among other things, has prompted the attorney general to request the court to bar the individuals from holding another position of trust in Illinois.

"All of Society Is Involved in the Case." "This is one of the most difficult cases I've had to decide in my career on the bench," [115] declared circuit court judge Donald A. Covelli. It also has been one of the longest litigated cases of its kind, compelling Attorney General Tyrone C. Fahner to appear personally in court to help his assistants with the case by telling the current judge, Albert Green, "I feel I have been abused and the court has been abused. . . . There's been foot dragging for years."[116]

Not only did a cloud of secrecy envelop the museum's collection over the years but the trustees also claimed a secrecy for its records, instructing their accountants to tell the court that a legal privilege of secrecy existed between an accountant and his or her client. Judge Green ruled that the Harding trustees "had no right to a privilege of secrecy because the museum is a public charity. 'All of society' is involved in the case, he said."[117]

An editorial in the *Chicago Tribune* underscored Judge Green's point when it warned that trustees were not the owners of the property they administered and that trustees could not indiscriminately dispose of assets without considering the public interest. The *Tribune* also stated that the situation at the Harding Museum was serious enough to justify the attorney general's involvement.[118]

The attorney general maintains that through their actions the trustees damaged both the museum and the beneficiary: the public. We will have to await the court's decision to determine the full impact of this case. If followed through to its logical legal conclusion, however, the Harding Museum case will result in a clear judicial restatement of the fiduciary duties of common-law trustees.

ART AND INTERNATIONAL LAW

The "Boston Raphael" Incident and the Chicago Connection: The Boston Museum of Fine Arts, Boston, Massachusetts

In 1977 during the Harding Museum hubbub, the "Boston Raphael" incident surfaced again—this time in Cook County Circuit Court in Chicago. As part of the ongoing legal proceeding, the court ordered the Harding trustees to appraise the condition of the $25-million collection. The trustees' attorneys recommended to the court an outside appraiser, Perry T. Rathbone, who was a director of Christie's USA, a London-based art auction house. Assistant Attorney General Donald Mulack, the prosecutor, objected to Mr. Rathbone's appointment, charging that he had been director of the Boston Museum of Fine Arts (BMFA) at the time that museum was embroiled in a worldwide art scandal.[119]

The Harding Museum trustees were quick to denounce Mulack's charges as "totally irresponsible," because Mr. Rathbone had been proved guilty of nothing.[120] Mulack, however, maintained that Rathbone had resigned his post in Boston after the scandal involving the BMFA's acquisition of a previously unknown small Raphael painting titled *Portrait of a Young Girl*, allegedly taken from Italy without an export license.

The Raphael—although doubts were expressed about its authenticity in the *London Times*—was part of the BMFA's debut on the occasion of its centennial, forming an important part of that celebration before its rightful ownership was settled publicly. "The painting was imported into the United States in violation of both Italian and American laws by the museum's director, Perry T. Rathbone, and a senior curator, Hanns Swarzenski, with the concurrence of key museum trustees."[121]

Art and the Law. Under Italian law all works of art that are considered to be an important part of its national heritage are prohibited from export unless the government grants permission. Any painting by Raphael, one of the greatest of the sixteenth-century High Renaissance masters, is regarded as part of Italy's national legacy. The Italian government, as a result of its investigation, alleged that no such authorization was given for sale of the Raphael and that the painting was obtained through "undoubtedly clandestine" means, spirited from Italy, and then brought to the United States through irregular channels.[122]

The plot thickened when it was learned that the painting allegedly was brought into this country in a museum staff member's suitcase, without a customs declaration.[123] A painting, under U.S. Customs laws, may be imported into the United States duty free, but it must be declared. Disobeying the law in such matters is a criminal offense, subjecting the work of art to forfeiture or the importer to prosecution by the United States government. Administrative procedures exist, however, for the return of seized merchandise on the payment of a fine.

The *Boston Globe* reported Mr. Rathbone's reaction to the revelation of the incident as follows:

"Pure supposition on the part of that fellow in Rome," was Rathbone's reply. "How can he make such a claim when the painting was entirely unknown, uncatalogued, unlisted, unillustrated and unpublished up 'til now?

"This is merely a supposition on his part that the way the picture left Italy was 'undoubtedly clandestine'. He's trying to attract attention to himself. He's simply leaping to conclusions. It happens all the time when something unknown appears. It's almost routine for the country of ultimate origin to claim it was taken from there.

"We gave our word not to identify the former owner. We simply said the painting came from an old European collection, which you'd naturally expect anyhow. But that does not imply it was acquired in Europe. It could have come from this country," Rathbone said, adding the picture "is here to stay."[124]

Several years later, during the Harding fracas, Mr. Rathbone was to tell the *Chicago Tribune*'s William Currie in a telephone interview that "he knew the painting had been taken from Italy without permission but 'stolen art is sold in the art community all the time.' "[125]

Legal proceedings were initiated not only in Italian courts but in American courts as well. Italian authorities began pressing criminal charges against BMFA officials who visited Genoa "in the summer of 1969 and illegally bought the disputed painting from a local art dealer."[126]

During the uproar Italian authorities declared they would invoke all existing treaties and conventions in which Italy and the United States had agreed to extend legal assistance to each other in order to retrieve the painting, deemed to be part of their national heritage. The incident involved high government officials in both countries.

A federal grand jury heard charges concerning the alleged illegal importation; however, its deliberations were kept secret. The United States government began a civil case for forfeiture of the painting to the United States government on grounds it was brought into this country illegally. When a U.S. attorney and customs agents originally presented museum officials with legal papers for the forfeiture of the painting, it was to have been removed to a local bank vault. However, because of fears that the harshness of the New England winter might damage the painting, it was impounded in a museum safe under the U.S. Customs' seal until it was returned to Italy.

The Cure. The Raphael portrait of his small, dark-haired, dark-eyed subject was finally consigned to the Italian government under an agreement signed between Mr. Rodolfo Siviero, head of the Italian Commission for the Recovery of Works of Art, and Mr. George Seybolt, president of the BMFA's board of trustees. The agreement stipulated that the painting came to the BMFA through "irregular channels . . . without the knowledge of those responsible as members of the board of trustees."[127] (Presumably the phrase "responsible as members of the board" refers to the Acquisitions Committee.)

Following the public exposure of the alleged wrongdoing, both the curator of decorative arts, Hanns Swarzenski, and the director, Perry T. Rathbone, resigned. What Thomas Hoving once referred to as the "chase"—the acquisition of that rare and unusual object to establish a reputation—apparently can chase a director from office.

The painting was imported "with the concurrence of key museum trustees. . . . (There were no resignations by members of the board.)"[128] Thereafter the trustees issued guidelines reaffirming that works of art were to be purchased through regular channels.

The dispute was resolved only when the Italian masterpiece was seized by U.S. Customs officials, the BMFA's trustees consigned the painting to the Italian government, and the BMFA trustees paid a $5,000 fine for violation of U.S. customs' regulations.[129] "The return of the painting and the payment of the fine for allegedly smuggling the painting in, Mulack said in his affadavit, acknowledged that the laws of Italy had been violated by the museum while Rathbone was its director."[130] Mr. Mulack charged that Rathbone had been involved in the controversial incident from the beginning. Judge George Schaller of the Cook County Circuit Court agreed with Mr. Mulack that Mr. Rathbone's appointment "would have the adverse effect of tarnishing these proceedings," and therefore Mr. Rathbone would be dropped from further consideration.[131]

Hypothetically Speaking. Beyond the decision of the Cook County Circuit Court, the "Boston Raphael" incident packs a walloping lesson for trustees. Let's assume that the federal courts had found individual BMFA board members guilty of a criminal offense. Assuming there was a conviction, the attorney general of Massachusetts could have begun a proceeding in state court for the individual trustee's removal from office. Even a museum of august probity— and the BMFA is such a museum—is not above the law. Boards of trustees are fully accountable at law for their agents. Ignorance of either managers' actions or the law is inexcusable and defenseless because it is the trustees' duty to administer the charitable enterprise with reasonable care and skill and to supervise its staff properly.

SUMMARY

Museums in this country have been organized as charities, and courts have declared that they are public and open to everyone. A nonprofit museum is accountable to the public even though it is not an agency of government. It retains a distinctly public character despite its private managerial prerogatives.

In the Barnes Foundation case the Pennsylvania Court ordered the trustees of a charity to open its museum to the public as the founder had intended. The court noted that by declaring itself a charitable trust or public charity, the foundation had submitted to supervision and inspection.

In the Hill-Stead Museum case the Supreme Court of Connecticut held that trustees have a duty to adhere to the directions in donative instruments unless and until a court of proper jurisdiction instructs otherwise. The court will enforce the wishes of the donor unless the instructions are either illegal, impossible to fulfill, or against public policy. Thus, the trustees could not close a museum in order to give the assets realized to a school. Even though they had acted in good faith, they had exceeded the bounds of their authority in the donor's will, which specified closing only if there were insufficient public interest in the museum. They had abused their discretion which, while great, was not and could not be unlimited.

In the Ferguson Monument Fund case, the Illinois attorney general exercised the persuasive powers of his office to convince museum trustees to use a fund as the donor had intended, to erect sculptures and monuments, rather than as they wished. Both law and custom give the donor the right to determine how the public is to benefit from a bequest.

Deaccessioning per se is not illegal or unethical, but the failure to use proper methods both in the process of deaccessioning and the subsequent use of funds derived from it can be.

In the Museum of the American Indian case, the New York attorney general stepped in as a result of complaints about how the museum's artifacts were being disposed. Before trial the defendant trustees signed a stipulation that gave the attorney general a great deal of direct involvement in the running of the museum. In a later development the trustees began to look for a new home for the museum, including areas outside New York. The New York attorney general once again intervened to inform the trustees that they needed New York court approval for any such move.

In the Fogg Art Museum incident, a strongly worded resolution of the Association of Art Museum Directors condemning the planned deaccessioning of art by Harvard's Fogg Art Museum caused Harvard to announce cancelation of a major museum project, owing to a stated lack of funds. The resolution noted that "deaccessioning should be related to policy rather than to the exigencies of the moment." The project later was revived, but the incident illustrated that charitable trustees are not free agents but are stewards of charitable property.

In the Maryhill Museum case, the Washington State attorney general intervened after allegations of mismanagement, nonmanagement, and self-dealing were directed at the museum's trustees. The trustees agreed to work with the attorney general to settle potential litigation and amend their bylaws to allow for an advisory committee. After some bickering, the case was settled by a stipulation that contained a new set of bylaws and articles of incorporation jointly created by the interested parties.

In the Harding Museum case the Illinois attorney general began a civil suit as a result of alleged trustee mismanagement of charitable assets. The attorney general's allegations included failure to display the museum's art and artifacts properly to the public, failure to diversify the invested assets of the museum, self-dealing or a violation of the fiduciary's duty of loyalty, intentionally and imprudently incurring unnecessary interest and expenses on real estate taxes, and selling assets to offset debt and pay for administrative expenses. The case is not yet settled.

In the "Boston Raphael" incident Italian and American authorities combined to force the return to Italy of a Raphael painting that had been brought into this country illegally. Despite the knowledge of several key trustees, there were no resignations or indictments. However, boards of trustees are fully accountable at law for their agents, and it is the duty of the trustees to administer the charitable enterprise with reasonable care and skill and to supervise its staff properly.

6

SCHOOL AND PUBLIC LIBRARIES

The library is a mighty resource in the marketplace of ideas.
Right to Read Defense Committee of Chelsea, United States
District Court of Massachusetts, 1978

EARLY LIBRARIES

Ben Franklin and Library Development

In his *Autobiography* Benjamin Franklin talks about the importance of lending libraries to society: "These libraries have improved the general conversation of the Americans, made the common tradesmen and farmers as intelligent as most gentlemen from other countries, and perhaps have contributed in some degree to the stand so generally made throughout the colonies in defense of their privileges."[1]

A supporter of libraries throughout his lifetime, Dr. Franklin was not only one of the nation's first community librarians but also an ardent builder of library collections. He both founded the Library Company of Philadelphia and helped establish what might be considered the first public library in this country. How did this happen?

According to an exhibition catalog prepared by John A. Peters, a Franklin librarian, someone (although it is not documented who it was) approached Ben Franklin when he was minister to the French Court, suggesting that he donate a bell for a new meeting house. Mr. Franklin, being the wise man he was, recognized that "sense" was more important than "sound" in a country that had struggled so hard to achieve freedom from tyranny. He respectfully declined to donate a bell; instead he offered a library collection and asked his good friend the Reverend Dr. Price of England to select and forward the books.

Sense Being Preferable to Sound. The original letter to Price has been lost; a presumed original copy was found in France.[2] It reads as follows:

Passy, Mar. 18, 1785.

My dear Friend,

My nephew, Mr. Williams, will have the honour of delivering you this line. It is to request from you a List of a few good Books to the Value of about Twenty-five Pounds, such as are most proper to inculcate Principles of sound Religion and just Government. A new Town in the State of Massachusetts, having done me the honour of naming itself after me, and proposing to build a Steeple to their Meeting House if I would give them a Bell, I have advis'd the sparing themselves the Expense of a Steeple at present, and that they would accept of Books instead of a Bell, Sense being preferable to Sound. These are therefore intended as the Commencement of a little Parochial Library, for the Use of a Society of intelligent respectable Farmers, such as our Country People generally consist of. Besides your own Works I would only mention, on the Recommendation of my Sister, Stennet's Discourses on personal Religion, which may be one Book of the Number, if you know it and approve of it.——With the highest Esteem and Respect, I am ever, my dear Friend,

Yours most affectionately

Rev. Dr. Price   B. Franklin[3]

The First Public Library. Originally consisting of 116 volumes, the town and parish library still exists, currently housed in the Franklin Public Library in Franklin, Massachusetts. The receipt of the library was a memorable event, but not without some controversy over who had the right to use the books. Soon after the collection arrived, the debate raged in town meeting whether the entire town or only subscribers could read the books. For more than two years the controversy continued. Finally a town meeting voted to lend the books to all inhabitants of the town.[4] With the receipt of the Ben Franklin books and the subsequent town meeting vote, the Franklin Library can lay claim to being the first public library in the United States. This vote in 1790 by town meeting, the form of local government in New England, determines the matter.

For various reasons some historians deny Franklin the position of "first." Professor Jesse Shera, a library historian, says that such activity as occurred in Franklin was more a casual factor in the development of public libraries than the establishment of a library per se. Further, Shera says that the Franklin collection was housed in a hayloft for more than fifty years.[5] Third, a town meeting subsequently voted to require that all new books added to the original collection would be available only to library subscribers who paid six pence a year for library privileges.[6]

Despite all the arguments against regarding the Franklin library as the first public library, the facts remain that Benjamin Franklin gave a collection of books to the town named after him and that the town voted for the books to be available to all its citizens. This vote antedates the vote by town meeting in Peterborough, New Hampshire, to create a public library. However, the Peterborough public library, created in April 1833, can be credited with being one of the early town libraries in New England that continues in existence.[7]

Arsenals of a Democratic Society. As the nation grew and matured in its quest for democratic ideals, so did its libraries. It was believed that a democracy grew and thrived with an educated citizenry, and thus a knowledgeable public became a basic goal for the free public library movement. Gradually the library was to be transformed into one of the great arsenals of a democratic society, with governance passing from private elite status to a public instrumentality of American democracy. One argument advanced by the advocates of the free public library movement is that it would have been impossible for Gibbons's *The Rise and Fall of the Roman Empire* to have been written in this country because of the paucity of library materials.[8]

Like other charities, libraries grew out of the private sector. Most early colonial libraries (proprietary libraries) were organized as nonprofit corporations serving a special clientele—individuals of social standing and wealth. They were called public libraries but were really private, since one either had to own stock in them or pay annual subscription fees. They were of course strongly aristocratic in character, exuding an air of institutional superiority and reserve, which has carried through in some cases to this day.

The Boston Athenaeum is a good example of the early proprietary library and illustrates problems that can arise when trustees assume they are given sole power to manage the affairs of the institution and even the "ownership" of its property.

The Boston Athenaeum, Boston, Massachusetts

The Boston Athenaeum was established in 1807 through a special act of the Massachusetts legislature by a group of incorporators—intellectual literati—whose individual names appear in the act itself, and who owned one or more shares of the library's stock (certificates of membership).

The most affluent Bostonians of the early nineteenth century regarded themselves as citizens of the world, as highly educated and enlightened people who lived in the first literary city in the Union. Just as their portraitures mirrored the grace and refinement of their class, ownership of shares in the Boston Athenaeum portrayed the ideal image of a proper Bostonian, a resident of the Athens of America. Boston Athenaeum stock still exists today.

Like any public corporation, Athenaeum shares could be traded, bought, and sold freely. One could assume, however, that Boston Athenaeum shareholders would sell their shares only to people whose elitism was as beyond question as their own! In this sense, the obvious intentions and expectations of the shareholders were clear. The Boston Athenaeum was born a private club, composed of ladies and gentlemen who wanted assurance that in the dignified quietude of the institution in which they held one or more shares, they would be provided the kind of atmosphere and books appropriate to their class.

Books for the Common Person. In contrast, Athenaeum shareholders of the nineteenth century viewed a municipal public library as a "charitable" institution for the masses of people who needed to be introduced to books and who, of course, could not be expected to buy them. That Athenaeum shareholders wanted none of this for themselves goes without saying. The movement that created the Boston Public Library, nevertheless, was primarily a movement of intellectual idealism prompted by the teachings of the intellectual elite and typified by Horace Mann, who kept pounding into the public ear, "Give me books, and I'll empty your jails."

After the Boston Public Library came into existence in 1852 and its structure had been determined, its governance was nominally placed in a board of trustees under the theory that the people of Boston, for whose good it was intended, would not be capable of taking responsibility for its operation. Such responsibility was accordingly placed in a group of moneyed, self-proclaimed intellectual trustees.

Today the Boston Athenaeum and the Boston Public Library, despite differences in structure and underlying purpose, are charitable institutions serving the public good. The public retains beneficial ownership in these public benefit organizations, and their boards are fully accountable to the public as much as any charitable instrumentality created to serve the common good. The fact that stock is issued to the members of an association, where such certificates are merely receipts that enable the holder to vote, does not destroy the institution's charitable character.

The Boston Athenaeum trustees, who usually like to remain hidden from public view, surfaced into the public limelight when they did not adequately articulate the nature of their trusteeship. A howl developed in the press and beyond.

The Stuart Portraits. During the first years of the current decade, the Athenaeum, needing funds for both operation and acquisition, decided to sell the Gilbert Stuart portraits of George and Martha Washington, made famous through the years by our most common postage stamp. This sale was a matter of great public controversy. It was resolved only when it was decided that the portraits would be sold to the Smithsonian Institution's National Portrait Gallery, for a meaty $5 million, with the provision that they be exhibited in Boston one year in every five for a period of fifty years.[9]

During the ensuing fracas one Athenaeum trustee, apparently wishing to show a good Samaritan side, remarked, "A higher price would have been available in the public art market."[10] Indeed this was an extraordinary statement for a steward of charitable property. The threat of the sale of the paintings to a private person or even a foreign party, while astonishing, was for all intents and purposes empty trustee shouting, for such a sale surely would have been as impermissible as it was unimaginable.

The Commonwealth of Massachusetts, through its attorney general, did not enter into the controversy. However, had the trustees contemplated making the original sale to a private collector—most noticeably a foreign one—or even to a public municipal museum, undoubtedly the powers of the Massachusetts attorney general's office would have been invoked. And the sale would have been contested as being contrary to the public good.

"I think," the same trustee continued, "it is the institutions that are the local treasure, not particular objects."[11] The courts, to the contrary, have focused on particular objects in determining whether or not trustees' actions have impaired the public good.

The same trustee rhetorically queried, "Who is to decide which institutions are to have their property taken in the future and for what purpose?"[12] Charitable trustees are just that—trustees, stewards of charitable assets—and they must act in terms of the public good—the interest of the community at large.

PUBLIC AND PRIVATE INSTITUTIONS

From a legal standpoint there are public and private libraries, just as there are with other charitable endeavors. The former is publicly funded and governed; the latter relies mainly on private support and is operated by an independent (usually self-perpetuating) board. Even though each institution may receive and manage both public and private funds, that fact alone does not change its status as a public (governmental) or private (nongovernmental) entity.

The right of both public and private charitable institutions to coexist was solidified in the famous Dartmouth College case.[13] This case is historically significant as one of the great quarrels that helped shape the U.S. Constitution.[14] Ironically, the court's decision also provided the circumstances that led to the development of one of the oldest continuing publicly supported public libraries in the United States.

A Quarrel That Helped Shape the U.S. Constitution: Dartmouth College, Hanover, New Hampshire

The Right to Exist. In 1769, the tenth year of his reign, King George III of England granted Dartmouth College a royal charter. This established Dartmouth as a privately managed (nongovernmental) charitable corporation of learning to educate the Native Americans. In 1816 the New Hampshire legislature tried to assume control of Dartmouth by expanding its board of trustees. Without the consent of the corporation, the legislature passed a bill altering the charter in a material respect. Dartmouth College was to become Dartmouth University, a public (governmental) institution.[15]

In 1819 the U.S. Supreme Court held that the New Hampshire state legislature could not abrogate a contract under Article 1, Section 10, of the U.S. Constitution; the legislature's act impaired the obligation of the charter and thus was unconstitutional and void. Under its charter Dartmouth College was a private and not a public corporation. Furthermore, the court held that a corporation "established for purposes of general charity, or for education generally, does not *per se* make it a public corporation, liable to the control of the legislature."[16]

The significance of the U.S. Supreme Court decision is that it affirmed trustees' constitutional rights to maintain their independent status. The same constitutional protection applies to a private college that consents to being dissolved and subsequently converted into a state university.[17]

The U.S. Supreme Court Defines Corporation. The 1819 Dartmouth case also includes Chief Justice John Marshall's widely quoted definition of a corporation:

A corporation is an artificial being, invisible, intangible, and existing only in contemplation of law. Being the mere creature of law, it possesses only those properties which the charter of its creation confers upon it, either expressly, or as incidental to its very existence. These are such as are supposed best calculated to effect the object for which it was created. Among the most important are immortality, and, if the expression may be allowed, individuality; properties, by which a perpetual succession of many persons are considered as the same, and may act as a single individual. They enable a corporation to manage its own affairs, and to hold property without the perplexing intricacies, the hazardous and endless necessity, of perpetual conveyances for the purpose of transmitting it from hand to hand. It is chiefly for the purpose of clothing bodies of men, in succession, with these qualities and capacities, that corporations were invented, and are in use. By these means, a perpetual succession of individuals are [*sic*] capable of acting for the promotion of the particular object, like one immortal being.[18]

The Peterborough Library. The Dartmouth College case led directly to the forming of the Peterborough, New Hampshire, Public Library, which is one of the oldest continuing tax-supported public libraries. The history of the library is unusual. After the state of New Hampshire lost its appeal to the U.S. Supreme Court, the legislature, in a moment of pique, placed a tax on bank bonds with the explicit intention of using such revenue to create a state university. It was much too early in New Hampshire's development for such a dramatic move; therefore, the tax moneys had to be, as a matter of practicality, distributed to the various towns. The legislature directed that the money be spent on education.[19]

In 1833 the Town of Peterborough used its funds to create a library. This was an extraordinary move for a town to make at this time. In view of this, some historians credit the Peterborough Public Library as the first public library. Jesse Shera says that "the book collection of this first public library was similar to those of its social library contemporaries."[20]

In 1852, on the founding of the Boston Public Library (BPL), the modern public library movement received a real shot in the arm. Although public libraries, such as Peterborough, existed before the founding of the BPL, the creation of this library in a major metropolitan area—Boston was the third largest city at the time—was a hallmark for the public library movement. Boston became the first major tax-supported public library.[21]

The Dartmouth College case established the right for both private and public charitable institutions to operate in proximity to each other but as separate entities. By the same principle, within one institution private and public funds may coexist but must be kept as far apart as the cat and the canary.

As libraries became aware that private moneys were an insufficient source of funding, they turned to the rich public purse for broader support. The curious mix of private and public boards administering funds for the same library imprinted itself on the library landscape. Philadelphia (only one of many such cities) has two boards: a public and a private board consisting of the same individuals. The private board manages endowment, and the public board administers the Philadelphia Free Public Library and its ongoing programs. Many libraries and other charitable institutions have similar arrangements. Sometimes institutions have two separate boards consisting of different individuals. This situation can result in conflict, as happened in Waitsfield, Vermont.[22]

Who's in Control Here Anyway? The Joslin (Joslyn) Memorial Library, Waitsfield, Vermont

Power and Authority. In 1913 George A. Joslyn set up a trust for the Joslin Memorial Library in Waitsfield, Vermont, a small New England town. By leaving $5000 in trust to provide books for the library and repairs to the library building, Mr. Joslyn created a testamentary trust with a specific purpose, as opposed to a general charitable intent.[23]

Mr. Joslyn instructed that his private trustees were to manage the fund, but on request by the public trustees, they were to pay a sum not to exceed $400 from income or principal for books and building repairs, limited to a proportion of three-eighths for repairs and five-eighths for the purchase of books. Books for the library and repairs to the library building were the expressed, specific purpose of the trust.[24]

Conflict developed in the late seventies when the fund became sizable, far exceeding the $5000 original investment, owing "in large measure to the dereliction of the private trustees in not paying over funds to the public trustees when requested."[25] The private trustees petitioned the Washington County Superior Court to apply the *cy pres* doctrine, requesting an expansion of the charitable purposes of the trust. The court denied the request, finding that the specific conditions for application of the *cy pres* doctrine were not met, since the trust purpose was not illegal, impracticable, or impossible.

Objections Overruled. The public library trustees also petitioned the court for a declaration of rights and sought relief from several of the trustees' objections to the will, the first being the provision that they had to request the private board of trustees to pay over the annual sum to them. The trust instrument clearly provided for an annual payment out of the income or principal of "such sum, not exceeding $400.00 as may be from time to time requested by said trustees" for the purposes of the trust.[26] On appeal the Vermont Supreme Court held that "a request is essential to trigger the liability for the making of the annual payment, and this objection is without merit."[27]

The public trustees also objected to the provision that paying over unexpended balances was at the discretion of the private trustees. They claimed this violated the law giving the public trustees of a town library "full power to manage such public library and to receive, control and manage property which shall come into the hands of such town or village for the use and benefit of such library."[28]

The supreme court made it clear that the statute quoted above did not shield the public trustees from the authority of the testamentary trustees and that there were two boards involved whose roles and responsibilities did not overlap. The trust instrument imposed

an unconditional duty to pay over, upon request and in the stated proportions, the $400.00 annual payment. But . . . the deed employs the word "may" in connection with unexpended balances to be paid over in subsequent years. The trust deed manifests a clear intent to distinguish mandatory annual payment from the discretionary later payment over of unexpended balances.[29]

There was no contest because the statute gives the public trustees control over expenditures of money only after it comes into the hands of the town. On the other hand, nothing in the matter gives the private trustees any control over the expenditures of the money once it has been paid over to the town. Library management remains within the jurisdiction of the public trustees, and trust fund management remains controlled by the private trustees. The private trustees' authority in the matter of unexpended funds extends only to "whether or not the expenditures authorized by the public trustees shall be financed from the trust funds."[30]

The Vermont Supreme Court clearly differentiated the two boards' power and authority. It upheld the lower court's decision as well as amending it to the extent that regardless of how derived, all funds paid over to the public trustees through the trust agreement must adhere to the proportional restriction.

This case illustrates that the power of *cy pres* lies in the courts, and the court, when acting with the greatest of judicial integrity, will not abuse that power. The court conforms as much as possible to the testator's intention, applying the *cy pres* doctrine only when the trust is deemed illegal, impracticable, or impossible to enforce. The case also demonstrates the importance of segregating specific testamentary trust funds from the public budgetary money.

INTELLECTUAL FREEDOM AND CENSORSHIP

Intellectual freedom is part and parcel of the library profession. John Milton said in his *Areopagitica*: "A good Booke is the pretious life-blood of a master spirit, imbalm'd and treasur'd up on purpose to a life beyond life"[31] (as it appears in original). Yet the cancerous tumor of parochial censorship looms at every schoolhouse and library door.

A great contribution librarianship has made to the broader social order has been its firm bulwark against untoward censorship to provide wanted and needed books for the promotion of knowledge. The list of books the librarian has had to defend over the years goes on *ad infinitum*, including a few obvious examples: the Bible and Shakespeare.

In 1926 the noted controversialist H. L. Mencken found it necessary to appear on the Boston Common to defend the famed *American Mercury*. The Watch and Ward Society had banned the magazine because of a short story, titled "Hatract," about a prostitute. Showing up on the Boston Common with one hundred copies of the issue, H. L. Mencken began selling them, crying out like an old town crier. He was arrested but released hours later, with the case subsequently thrown out of court. It was a "choice of days" for this legendary newspaper reporter.

A Covenant

Library trustees and their agents enter a covenant to serve the public interest in terms of the printed word. When library trustees accept the keys of trusteeship, they accept a polished key—a public trust—for the printed word and for intellectual freedom. Once this irrevocable and binding covenant is broken, the lifeblood of the word is spilled on the canvas and the iron heel of mind control takes over.

Important as the issue of censorship is per se, more important to this discussion are the trustees' authority and power in matters relating to intellectual freedom and censorship. The next three cases consider the public library and school boards' responsibility, specifically the boards' power and authority in this critical area.

Are Library Directors Really Straw People? The Davis County Library, Farmington, Utah

Drawing up Charges. When self-seeking individuals deliberately gain control of a library board with the objective of directly influencing what materials are to be included in or removed from a library collection, a violation of the agreement between the board and the public occurs *ipso facto*. No public official worth his or her salt can be a single-issue candidate and yet serve the broader public welfare.

Such a violation occurred in Davis County, Utah, in 1979. Ms. Jeanne Layton, director of the Davis County Library System, suddenly faced a single-issue, hostile board when the inclusion of a particular book in the library collection was challenged. The challenge was mounted by one member, Mr. Morris F. Swapp, who also served as a county commissioner and was instrumental in having two new board members appointed who were allegedly sympathetic with his cause. No sooner had the new members taken office than they joined Mr. Swapp in a process to "decapitate" Ms. Jeanne Layton, presumably because she had failed to follow board member Swapp's order to remove a book. Ms. Layton scrupulously followed board policy in regard to the issue. It was not the first time the book had been challenged. However, the newly constituted board, which had a majority in favor of Swapp, drew up charges of insubordination, and on a three-to-two vote fired her.[32]

At the meeting in which the vote was taken, Ms. Layton answered each of the board's seven charges. About the charge of "excessive costs" in the processing of books, she said she was following board policy not to use state cataloging services. With regard to the charge that there was a limitation on bookmobile service, she said it was a matter of board policy not to provide bookmobile services within one mile of library buildings. The board also charged that there was a waste of tax dollars perpetrated by the purchase of books whose value to the community was not "optimum." Again she reiterated board policy.[33]

The incident received high media and public attention. Pete Giacoma of the American Library Association's *Intellectual Freedom Newsletter* wrote that "a cartoon published in the *Salt Lake City Tribune* of January 11, 1980, illustrates the personality clash. Jeanne Layton is pictured envisioning Commissioner Swapp as a torch-bearing puritan, while he imagines her as a smut-purveying child-corruption witch."[34]

It was alleged that members of the library board were members of the Citizens for True Freedom, a Utah organization claiming to defend the "right for morality." The group had, as a matter of course, attacked professional librarians.[35]

Jeanne Layton received support from the Utah Library Association, which passed a resolution censuring the library board for violations of intellectual freedom; from letters to the editors of local papers; from the *Salt Lake City Tribune*, which alleged that the board had engaged in "politics worthy of a banana republic despot"; and from friends of the library.[36]

Checks and Balances. Jeanne Layton did not take her firing lying down. She petitioned the federal district court in Salt Lake City for a preliminary injunction.[37]

Even though the underlying issue behind the dismissal of Ms. Layton was her failure to remove a book, the federal court made it explicitly clear that it was "*not* concerned with the First Amendment issue of the availability of books of one kind or another."[38] Instead the federal court said the issue before it was whether Ms. Layton had been deprived of a property right (continued employment) by the library board without procedural due process. Under the federal court order the Merit Council (a state agency) had to determine whether the library board followed proper procedure in Ms. Layton's dismissal and whether there was just cause for the decision.

The Merit Council ruled that the library board's compliance with procedural requirements was "minimal," although it was sufficient to satisfy merit regulations. On the other hand, the Merit Council said the library board "failed to establish that her termination was with cause."[39] After a review of her dismissal in federal court, which ordered the Merit Council to do its job, Ms. Layton regained her job. Subsequently, the library board lost its appeal of the case.[40]

Of primary importance is that the court placed a clear and unconditional restraint on board power, requiring adherence to legal and constitutional mandates. Boards, although given great discretion in the management of institutional affairs, cannot operate outside constitutional mandates. They are not free agents.

After the confrontation, Ms. Layton received the Robert B. Downs Award from the American Library Association for her courageous fight to keep her property interest (employment) and to bring the library trustees in line with their covenant with the public. The association also helped defray Ms. Layton's legal expenses, which exceeded $30,000, through its Freedom to Read Foundation.[41]

The Right to Read: Chelsea High School, Chelsea, Massachusetts

Launching a Protest. Censorship disputes occur both in public and school libraries, although the public schools are the more frequent battlegrounds. To a large measure, this is true because schools serve *in loco parentis*; that is, in place of a parent or guardian. Although public schools are rife with censorship issues, many never surface to public attention; but when they do, a community can be agitated to an untamed spume.

The picture of censorship and the public schools has been clouded by a series of conflicting court decisions. The current climate almost dictates that a trial occur before any challenged book may be removed from a school library. This is a costly legal procedure, not only in terms of the tens of thousands of dollars that can be expended by each side but also of the damage such public exposure can do to a librarian's professional career. It is a sobering thought.

In 1978 a legal battle of major proportions ensued in Chelsea, Massachusetts, when Andrew P. Quigley, chairman of the Chelsea School Committee (school board), launched a protest of the book *Male & Female, Under 18* (hereafter, *Male & Female*),[42] an anthology of writings by adolescents intended for adolescents and dealing with the visceral problems integral to growing up. He rested his argument on the holding in *Miller v. California*[43] that community standards and not national standards apply. The city of Chelsea became a political hotbed.

"The City to a Young Girl." It all started when a fourteen-year-old student of Chelsea High School borrowed the book *Male & Female* from the high school library. Her father read a poem entitled "The City to a Young Girl" (hereafter, *City* or "City"), written by a fifteen-year-old high school student, and then called the chairman of the School Committee to complain about the book.

School Committee Chairman Quigley went to the parent's home to obtain the book. He read the poem and decided that *Male & Female* should be withdrawn from the high school library "because of the 'filthy' and 'offensive' language in *City*. He made this determination without reading any other part of the anthology. The only person he consulted was the complaining parent."[44]

About the poem, the court said: "*City* is not a polite poem. Its language is tough, but not obscene. . . . The author is writing about her perception of city life in rough but relevant language that gives credibility to the development of a sensitive theme. *City*'s words may shock, but they communicate."[45]

Boston Globe's Jack Thomas captures the theme of the poem rather nicely. He writes, "The poem was written by a 15-year-old girl whose purpose was not to incite the lust of cigar-smoking members of the Chelsea School Committee, but rather to cry out against the sexual harassment she suffered while growing up in New York City.''[46]

Whose Sewer Fouls the Air? Chairman Quigley immediately scheduled an emergency meeting of the committee to consider the subject of "objectionable, salacious and obscene material being made available in books in the High School Library.''[47] In the meantime he wrote an article in the *Chelsea Record*, a newspaper he published.

It seems ironic that a journalist would kick up this issue, since reporters from colonial times have treated freedom of the press as a sacred democratic right. Yet a newspaper publisher seemingly embarked on a path of censorship.

Emphatically claiming that he was not a "prude" in such matters, Mr. Quigley editorialized about the objection of a parent to specific passages in a high school library book. Mr. Quigley added that it nearly made "me sick to my stomach" to know that it was possible for a high school student to obtain such a book from a high school library, "let alone one here in Chelsea." As part of his editorial Mr. Quigley warned the school administration that he was going to bring this matter to its attention so as to ensure that no such "filth" would again be available in the schools. Mr. Quigley continued that he wanted a thorough review to determine how it was possible for such "garbage" to make its way to library bookshelves where high school students could find it.[48]

Superintendent of Schools Vincent B. McGee became aware of the incident only by reading Mr. Quigley's article in the *Chelsea Record*. Many were distraught about the way in which Mr. Quigley handled the entire matter. (It may be noted that the only time a school board member exists as a board member is when she or he sits in the corpus of the school board itself; otherwise, the school board member is a private citizen. Good board members respect their commitment to their constituency by realizing that outside a board meeting their opinion is no more valuable than anyone else's.)

At the committee meeting, Mr. Quigley again "characterized the poem as 'objectionable' and 'outright obscene.' " He said it was "a 'serious mistake' to allow 'this filth on the library shelves,' and he wanted to 'make certain it doesn't happen again.' " Committeeman Anthony Tiro agreed: "The book is lewd and leaves nothing to the imagination. It's outright obnoxious."[49]

The *Boston Globe* editorialized:

The Chelsea Committee, as you might guess, is not the most sophisticated forum for a discussion of the subtleties of sexism and literature. In debate, the committee members make their points not by logic, but by raising their voices, as Anthony Tiro did the other night to exclaim, "Thank God our forefathers are not here to see this."[50]

Superintendent McGee cautioned the committee: "It was inappropriate to handle this complaint in an open school board meeting, and Quigley was 'setting in motion a chain of events that might lead to censorship.' "[51]

Chairman Quigley, unpersuaded, proceeded to denounce the book in his newspaper by writing another editorial, following the School Committee meeting. He again "characterized *City* as 'obviously obscene,' 'filthy' and 'vile and offensive garbage.' "[52]

The battle lines were drawn. A series of meetings took place involving various concerned parties. Finally the superintendent removed the book from the library with the School Committee's support.

The committee was also concerned with the process of how the book found its way into the school library. Wishing to get to the bottom of the matter, the committee called a meeting requesting Ms. Sonja Coleman, the high school librarian, to appear. Ms. Coleman defended the selection process used. She cited a number of sources, including documents from the American Association of School Librarians and the National Council of Teachers of English for support. Ms. Coleman defended the book and its use by students and faculty. But Quigley responded again that "*City* was 'low down dirty rotten filth, garbage, fit only for the sewer,' . . . and observed that, under local community standards in Chelsea, *City* was obscene."[53]

A Clash of Values. The committee was later to declare to Judge Joseph L. Tauro in federal court in Boston that *City* was not obscene and that it had been removed as a matter of course under state law, which grants the committee authority to operate the schools. Following their decision to remove the book and before going into court, the committee voted its reasons in a resolution prepared by counsel. It maintained that the reasons for removal were "formulated on the date of removal and were memorialized by a formal resolution of the Committee." The court, however, was not befooled by such obvious pageantry. It noted that the "resolution of the Committee was a self-serving document that rewrote history in an effort to meet the issues of this litigation. In simple terms, it was a pretext."[54]

At one point in the confrontation, the committee considered removing the librarian from her position. Under legal advice, however, it backed off from this senseless and perilous route.

It was the Right to Read Committee, a group of teachers and students, including the librarian, who filed a class action suit under Title 42, Section 1983 of the U.S. Code in the federal court. *The Right to Read Defense Committee* noted that Title 42 U.S.C., Section 1983 reads in relevant part, "Every person who, under color of any statute . . . of any State . . . subjects . . . any citizen of the United States . . . to the deprivation of any rights, privileges, or immunities secured by the Constitution and laws, shall be liable to the party injured in an action at law, suit in equity, or other proper proceeding of redress."

The suit claimed their constitutional rights had been abridged. The Right to Read Committee felt its position was in the interests of students and their right to know.

During the controversy the *Boston Globe* carried reports on the Chelsea case, concluding one article by printing the complete poem—not in verse form, but in regular newspaper column style with slashes between lines.[55] The incident lit up the switchboards at the *Boston Globe* and resulted in a barrage of letters to the editor, arousing many readers' interest.

It was, sadly enough, a clash of generational values fought out in a courtroom. Sociologist David Reisman in *The Lonely Crowd* described the dilemma magnificently when he talked about older generational values conflicting with newer, emerging societal values that developed during a period of openness and critical self-analysis.

Significant Court Findings. The committee maintained that it had an "absolute right to remove *City* from the shelves of the school library."[56] The court did not agree, noting that a school committee can determine what books will go into a library or even if a school is to have a library. Once a book is entered into a collection, however, the school committee does not have the same degree of discretion in its removal. Thus, "however absolute may be a school board's discretion in selecting books, there are boundaries to its authority to remove a book from a library."[57]

After careful consideration of the evidence, the court held that "the record leaves this court with no doubt that the reason the committee banned *Male & Female* was because it considered the theme and language of *City* to be offensive."[58] Further, not every removal of a book from a school is unconstitutional; however, when a book is removed, "because its theme and language are offensive to a school committee," the parties affected have a right to legal recourse.[59]

Although the committee claimed an "absolute right" to remove the book, the court held that "it had no such right, and compelling policy considerations argue against any public authority having such an unreviewable power of censorship."[60]

"The Marketplace of Ideas." Concerned with the fallout from this case, the court said that "the prospect of successive school committees 'sanitizing' the school library of views divergent from their own is alarming, whether they do it book by book or one page at a time." Judge Tauro reaffirmed the valuable First Amendment right when he said, "What is at stake here is the right to read and be exposed to controversial thoughts and language—a valuable right subject to First Amendment protection."[61]

Citing an earlier case, Judge Tauro focused the issue rather nicely: "In our system, students may not be regarded as closed-circuit recipients of only that which the State chooses to communicate. They may not be confined to the expression of those sentiments that are officially approved."[62] In the conclusion to his well-thought-out, skillfully written opinion, Judge Tauro provides a strong rationale for the school library in the educational process. He forcefully writes:

The library is "a mighty resource in the marketplace of ideas." There a student can literally explore the unknown, and discover areas of interest and thought not covered by the prescribed curriculum. The student who discovers the magic of the library is on the way to a life-long experience of self-education and enrichment. That student learns that a library is a place to test or expand upon ideas presented to him, in or out of the classroom.[63]

The Aftermath. As a result of valorous effort (because it is not easy to take on the establishment), the American Librarian Association awarded Sonja Coleman the John Phillip Immorth Memorial Award citation by the Intellectual Freedom Roundtable for "strong personal courage and integrity . . . in the vigorous defense of students' access to the poem, *The City to a Young Girl.*"[64]

Following this announcement, Mr. Quigley said: "What a real bunch of 'nuts'-'nitwits'-'idiots' and anything else we can think to call these type [*sic*] of people for honoring someone responsible for putting filthy words included in a poem in the high school library."[65]

Children Are People under the Constitution. The court, recognizing the awesome task school boards face, stated that local authorities are, and must continue to be, the principal policymakers in the public schools. Nevertheless, due to the limitations of the individuals who serve on such instrumentalities, school committees' actions must necessarily be judged within constitutional standards. When issues relating to schools lack constitutional proscriptions, the court is disinclined to interfere in the daily operation of the schools. School boards are ordinarily given great discretion by the courts under the assumption that they operate effectively under statutory and constitutional constraints in the discharge of their mission.

However, once the constitutional threshold has been transgressed, the courts recognize the rights of individuals to petition the court for redress of an infringement of constitutional rights. These rights apply to students as well because, as the court held in *Tinker v. Des Moines School District*, (hereafter *Tinker*)[66] children are people under the Constitution and retain rights as citizens. By barring the School Committee from banning the book, the lower court clearly placed a constitutional constraint on school board power.

School Board Policy on Library Books Runs Aground: Island Trees Union Free School District, No. 26., Long Island, New York

In 1982, after a decade of debate and a series of trials in the federal courts, the U.S. Supreme Court handed down *Board of Education, Island Trees Union Free School District No. 26, v. Pico* (hereafter, *Pico*).[67] The long-awaited decision had been expected to settle the issue of traditional school board authority to remove books versus the First Amendment rights of students. However, the issue was not decisively settled by the Court's plurality decision. A plurality decision is a minority decision given force by the majority's agreeing to the judicial result. A plurality decision carries less weight under *stare decisis* than does a majority opinion.

Pico produced seven opinions by the Court. Austin Broadhurst, counsel to the Massachusetts Association of School Committees (MASC), writes about the Pico case as follows:

Both the fragmented nature of the Court's holding and the narrow legal issue that the Court actually decided suggests that the broad language of the Court's opinion may be modified if subsequent cases involving the application of the First Amendment to public school libraries and curricula are accepted by the Supreme Court for decision.[68]

The principal issue in *Pico* was "whether the First Amendment imposes limitations upon the exercise by a local school board of its discretion to remove library books from high school and junior high school libraries."[69] A constitutional limitation was placed on school board powers when the Court held "that local school boards may not remove books from school library shelves simply because they dislike the ideas contained in those books and seek by their removal to 'prescribe what shall be orthodox in politics, nationalism, religion, or other matters of opinion.' "[70]

The Court's holding affects only the discretion of the school board to remove (not add) books from the school library because the plurality drew a clear distinction between the processes of selection and removal (which the dissenting justices found artificial). The plurality also carefully differentiated between the controlled environment of the classroom and textbooks and the informal nature of the school library. Textbooks are mandated reading, whereas school library books are voluntary, presumably ascribing a different role for the school library in the educational process.[71]

Background. The facts of the case arose out of a series of incidents that can be roughly summarized from the Court's opinion. Several members of the Island Trees school board attended a conference sponsored by Parents of New York United (PONYU), a politically conservative organization of parents concerned about education legislation in New York. At the conference, members of the school board obtained a list of books later described by various members of the board as "objectionable" and "improper fare for school students."[72]

In after-school hours, when no professional staff was present, members of the school board examined the school library card catalogs to determine which books from the list were available to students. They found that the high school library had nine of the books on the list and that the junior high school library listed one. In a subsequent meeting with the principals and the superintendent, the board gave an "unofficial direction" that all the books were to be removed from the library shelves and delivered to the board's offices so members of the board could read them. (It was later determined that the board removed the books without having read them.) The board characterized the books as " 'anti-American, anti-Christian, anti-Sem[i]tic, and just plain filthy,' and concluded that '[i]t is our duty, our moral obligation, to protect the children in our schools from this moral danger as surely as from physical and medical dangers.' "[73]

After the "unofficial direction" had been carried out, it became publicized, whereupon the board issued a press release defending its action. About the "unofficial direction," it should be noted that as a corpus the school board can act only by a vote.

The superintendent of schools objected to the board's informal direction, stating:

[W]e already have a policy . . . designed expressly to handle such problems. It calls for the Superintendent, upon receiving an objection to a book or books, to appoint a committee to study them and make recommendations. I feel it is a good policy—and it is board policy—and that it should be followed in this instance. Furthermore, I think it can be followed quietly and in such a way as to reduce, perhaps avoid, the public furor which has always attended such issues in the past.

The Board responded to the Superintendent's objection by repeating its directive "that *all copies* of the library books in question be removed from the libraries to the Board's office."[74]

Despite the existence of a policy, the board proceeded on an *ad hoc* basis. Finally, when enough public pressure built, created by the superintendent's insistence that the board follow its own policies, the board appointed a Book Review Committee (Committee) consisting of four members of the Island Tree schools' staff and four parents to review the books. Curiously, no librarian was included on the Committee. After the Committee made its report, the board substantially ignored the Committee's recommendations, deciding instead to return only one book to the library without restriction and another one to be made available with parental approval.

Outraged by the board's abuse of discretionary power, a group of students began action in federal court under Title 42, Section 1983, of the U.S. Code. They alleged that the board had "ordered the removal of the books from school libraries and proscribed their use in the curriculum because particular passages in the books offended their social, political and moral tastes and not because the books, taken as a whole, were lacking in educational value."[75]

The students claimed that the board's actions abridged their rights under the First Amendment. The board asked the federal district court for the Eastern District of New York to grant summary judgment in their favor, and the lower court did. The students appealed. The second circuit appeals court ruled in favor of the students, holding that the facts warranted a trial based on the students' allegations. The school board appealed to the U.S. Supreme Court, which granted *certiorari* (agreed to hear the case). In a plurality decision, the U.S. Supreme Court affirmed the appeals court decision that a trial had to occur.[76]

In more formal terms, even though the federal trial court granted the school board a summary judgment, under procedural law a summary judgment cannot be granted if there is a genuine issue surrounding any material fact. The U.S. Supreme Court decided there was a genuine issue of material fact presented by the case: whether the board exceeded constitutional limitations in exercising its discretionary powers to remove books from the school libraries.[77]

The U.S. Supreme Court held, in effect, that there had to be a trial on the facts before the books could be removed. At this point the Island Trees school board threw in the towel, voting four to three not to pursue the case any further and returning the books to the shelf.[78]

Some Legal Points. Again, the emphasis here is not on the merits of intellectual freedom per se; rather, the concern is with the constitutional limitations placed on school board power. The plurality decision of the Court carefully notes that it "has long recognized that local school boards have broad discretion in the management of school affairs." At the same time the Court also recognizes that the discretion of local school boards, which are instrumentalities of the state, "must be exercised in a manner that comports with the transcendent imperatives of the First Amendment."[79]

Enumerating the history of First Amendment issues in regard to students, the Court cited *West Virginia Board of Education v. Barnette*, in which it held that students could not be compelled to salute the flag. The Court quoted its earlier decision:

Boards of Education . . . have of course, important, delicate, and highly discretionary functions, but none that they may not perform within the limits of the Bill of Rights. That they are educating the young for citizenship is reason for scrupulous protection of Constitutional freedoms of the individual, if we are not to strangle the free mind at its source and teach youth to discount important principles of our government as mere platitudes.[80]

Later decisions followed this. In *Epperson v. Arkansas* the U.S. Supreme Court held that the state's anti-evolution statute violated the Establishment Clause of the Constitution and ruled that the federal courts were "to apply the First Amendment's mandate in our educational system where essential to safeguard the fundamental values of freedom of speech and inquiry."[81]

In *Tinker* the Court held that "a local school board had infringed the free speech rights of high school and junior high school students by suspending them from school for wearing black armbands in class as a protest against the Government's policy in Vietnam." Continuing the court said, "In sum, students do not 'shed their constitutional rights to freedom of speech or expression at the schoolhouse gate.' "[82]

The Right to Receive Information. First Amendment rights are available to students, and the Court reaffirmed that "the Constitution protects the right to receive information and ideas."[83] First Amendment rights given to students must be construed "in light of the special characteristics of the school environment." The school library, according to the Court, is one of those special environmental characteristics making it "especially appropriate for the recognition of the First Amendment rights of students."[84]

The Court noted that the school board has the right to determine the content of school libraries, but that its discretion could not be "exercised in a narrowly partisan or political manner. . . . Our Constitution does not permit the official suppression of *ideas*."[85]

Students retain the right to receive information, and a school board's motivation to remove books lodged on narrow political or moral beliefs can be challenged. "The extent to which books in libraries," according to MASC counsel Austin Broadhurst, "do or do not conform to general community values is not a constitutionally acceptable standard for a decision on whether to keep or remove them."[86] Also, note that the court distinguished between the acquisition of a book and its removal. The court acknowledged that a school board could enjoy great discretion in the acquisition of a book. On the other hand, once a book is acquired, a board's discretion becomes circumscribed in the event of removal. Since the issue in *Pico* was removal, the court considered only this. Further, a clear distinction was drawn between the curriculum, a mandated part of the school environment, and the school library as a voluntary option for students.

The Court recognized that the board did not follow its own administrative procedure for handling challenged materials. "This would be a very different case if the record demonstrated that the petitioners [board] had employed established, regular, and facially unbiased procedures for the review of controversial materials. But the actual record in the case before us suggests the exact opposite."[87] The board's procedures were extraordinary, and its "removal procedures were highly irregular and ad hoc—the antithesis of those procedures that might tend to ally suspicions regarding petitioners' motivations."[88]

In sum, the U.S. Supreme Court upheld the right of students to learn and inquire in a free environment unfettered by the usual authoritative school environment, which can be stifling to a young person's mind. School boards cannot ignore the U.S. Constitution. Most assuredly, the censorship battle goes on with no solution in sight, other than that each generation will need to work out its own set of values to solve the problem.

THE RISKY BUSINESS OF DEACCESSIONING ART IN A PUBLIC LIBRARY

Sharp Intervention: The Free Public Library, Paterson, New Jersey

The Finest Thing in Paterson. In 1982 a battle raged for months between the Paterson Free Public Library Board, the mayor, and the city council. It was a game of power versus force between the library board and the municipal government. Paterson, an aging industrial city located in the greater New York area, was beset with myriad financial problems created by severe federal cutbacks, a state tax cap, and an eroded local tax base. These strains worked a financial crisis to divide the city, pitting neighbor against neighbor, friend against friend, and library trustees in opposition to council members. Adversity gripped the city government in a power gridlock.

The hottest part of the political war came when the city council and the mayor laid siege to the art collection held in trust by the Free Public Library of Paterson. Order was finally restored to the community when Passaic County Superior Court Judge Peter Ciolino issued a permanent injunction forbidding the library trustees to sell its most valuable piece of artwork, William Merritt Chase's *In the Park*, as well as any other paintings held in trust.[89] (The law firm of Evans, Hand, Allabough & Amoresano handled the case for the Ad Hoc Committee against the sale of *In the Park* on a *pro bono publico* basis.)

Stirred to Anger. The proposed sale of the local treasure brought a howl of protest, stirring the community to anger. Were it to come onto the market, the painting would have been one of the finest Chase works to be sold in some time. Interest from as far away as Australia was expressed in the painting.

At first the library trustees failed to crumble under incredible pressure from the mayor to sell the Chase masterpiece. The *quid pro quo* was that the library budget might be better assured in the future, although there was no real guarantee of that. As Jerry M. Bello, president of the library board, remarked to the press, "I'd hate to have no money next year, and no paintings."[90] This was a very cogent comment; the political scene changes quite rapidly, almost moment to moment. Usually nothing is in writing, and personnel changes. The William Merritt Chase painting was held hostage in a local political war game.

The painting had been given to the library by Mrs. Garret A. Hobart in trust as a memorial to her husband, a native of Paterson who had served as vice president in the first McKinley administration. Had he lived (Mr. Hobart died of natural causes) and been invited to join the ticket again, he would have become president when Mr. McKinley was assassinated in 1901.

Libraries and the Visual Arts. The library had a fine collection of more than 100 paintings, with 68 regarded as significant. Most of the paintings had been given to the library when the prevailing belief was that libraries were not only for books but also for the promotion of knowledge through culture—a view espoused by the iconoclastic library leader, John Cotton Dana, director of the Newark Public Library. Integral to Mr. Dana's philosophy—and many copied his ideas—was that art should be closely allied with any library. While he was director of the Newark Public Library around the turn of the century, Mr. Dana founded a museum on the fourth floor of that library; at that time Newark did not have an art museum.

In 1913, when the Newark Museum created the position of director, it appointed Mr. Dana to that post, without salary. Mr. Dana contributed substantially to both the library and museum worlds, especially through his strong advocacy of the "populist" approach. Youth and libraries were of special concern to him. He believed, that "the library should be the most inviting, the most wholesome, the most elevating and the most popular place in the city for those who, without comfortable homes, wish to while away an hour or two. It should attract such visitors and it should hold them. This applies especially to young people."[91]

The Children Respond. The children in Paterson expressed these sentiments when the closing of the library was threatened. The *Record* reported:

Her brown eyes were full of sincerity, her expression was deadly serious. "We want our library to stay open," said Alda Mustafa, 15, as she warmed herself inside the South Paterson branch public library after 20 minutes of picketing outside School 9 with 36 classmates.

"If they close the library, we will have no place to go," said Miss Mustafa. "We have nothing to do after school. Here we have clubs, the poetry club, the knitting club. We have parties on holidays. We have one coming up on Valentine's Day."

Her classmates pressed close around her as she spoke. They shouted the merits of the library and showed off their signs. "Keep our Labary [sic] Open" was crayoned in purple on the 8-year-old's sign.[92]

The Paterson library board's insistence that the library was a cultural center was not without historical or contemporary significance. It took the children of Paterson to reaffirm this during a time of stress, when adults were seemingly unable to think clearly.

A Sea of Red Ink. Over the years the library board consistently encountered great pressure to sell the paintings, but in the face of public resistance, backed off from selling. The 1982 financial crisis was severe, with the city mandating 11 percent salary reductions and police and fire layoffs and eliminating many important services—all occurring in the face of an astronomical 28 percent tax increase. In the midst of this financial bedlam, it seemed, at least on the surface, that it was only a matter of "common sense" to sell the art objects to meet the budgetary crisis. The local press, surprisingly, advocated in an editorial that such a move was judicious and implored Judge Ciolino to rule in favor of selling the local treasure.[93] It was an amazing editorial.

The real skirmish came when the library's budget was slashed from $646,000 to $200,000—the minimum amount required in order to continue receiving state aid. The board had closed the branches for two weeks in May, which resulted in the budget's being increased to $375,000, although this increase came from the city council with strings; that is, the sale of the paintings was to make up the difference.

Even with the modest increase to $375,000, such a draconian reduction would necessarily wreak havoc on library services. Mr. Leo Fichtelberg, library director, outlined the worst-case scenario to the trustees. He said that if the mayor and city council did not change the proposed budget, the library would have to lay off twenty-two of its fifty employees, closing not only its seven branches but also the main library. The whole library system would be shut down. Dr. Helen Kehoe, head librarian at the main library, warned that the deed required that the building revert to the heirs if the city no longer used the gift.

"We discussed creating a fund," said Mr. Fichtelberg, "by selling some or all of the paintings, the interest from which could supplement the library's budget."[94] He also reported that he had discussed long-term financing, because the library, according to local budget officials, could no longer expect city funds other than the minimum required by the state in order to receive state aid.

The city council held the paintings hostage from the beginning of the budget dispute, maintaining that the library was only a place for books. City Councilman Thomas Rooney, Jr., the council's finance chairman, said: "If the paintings are sold, we will give all the money necessary to remain open. But the paintings must be sold immediately."[95]

On the other hand, the library board, an autonomous entity appointed by the mayor, maintained that the library was a center for culture. Jerry M. Bello, president of the library board, commented, "These paintings were given to our agency to be used by the City of Paterson forever."[96] Fichtelberg recalled: "When I first came here, these paintings were a pain to me. I'm a librarian, not a museum director."[97]

Withdrawal Pains. A tremendous public reaction did develop around the proposed closing. Mr. Robert Kushner said that "he owed his education to the library system. 'It's the poor man's universe.' "[98] The press editorialized: "A vigorous public library is one of a city's most valuable assets. It is justly known as the university for poor people."[99]

Throughout the conflict Howard Sterling, head of the fine arts committee and then director of the Greater Paterson Arts Council, stuck his neck out to save the artworks for Paterson. In a telephone interview he explained that in the 1920s Paterson lost a valuable art collection to other cities because Mr. Catholina Lambert, a wealthy industrialist who had been one of the world's great art collectors, tried to revive the silk industry. He placed his bet on the fact that the synthetics industry would not take off in the marketplace. Regretfully for art in Paterson, it did; and having used his famous art collection as collateral for the loans, Mr. Lambert had to sell his collection to pay the debt.

Mr. Sterling affirmed that he did not want to lose one of Paterson's last local art treasures. After all, these paintings, which were clearly in the public domain, belonged to the people—not to the trustees. From the beginning Mr. Sterling said that the Ad Hoc Committee he headed cautioned the library board that there would be serious legal obstacles to overcome if they were to sell even one painting; and if they tried to do so, he would institute suit against such a sale.

At the prodding of Mayor Frank X. Graves, the library board, however, voted to sell the Chase painting *In the Park*, but only if it were legal to do so. The mayor, as a member of the library board, cast his vote to sell. There was conflicting legal opinion: corporation council said it was within the board's authority to sell; but private council, retained by the board at Mr. Sterling's insistence, said the board could not sell the paintings without court approval.

Mr. Sterling said that correspondence in the Historical Society files, dating back to 1927 through 1932, clearly showed that Mrs. Hobart intended to create a memorial by leaving the paintings in trust. Mrs. Hobart's correspondence to the library board could not be located.[100] Mr. Sterling said that many individuals thought the library board wanted to sell the city's heritage, but he reminded the library board that "the painting was a gift given to the library. It was a trust given to you to maintain."[101]

Before the vote to sell, Mayor Graves spoke for one-half hour about the city's financial plight and the need for the painting to be sold to put the library back on its financial feet. " 'Closing the library would be like starving 50,000 minds for the next three months,' he said." The mayor challenged library board members by saying that if board members want to close libraries, they should put their resignations on the table. "How do you justify one painting against 50,000 minds?"[102] But Mr. Sterling countered that the painting was more important than keeping the library open for two months.[103]

The advocates of the sale missed one important point: the library board did not own the painting; they held it in trust for the people. The painting could be sold only after court approval and not before. There was sharp intervention by the court. In a restraining order Judge Peter Ciolino, Assignment Judge for the Superior Court of New Jersey, made it clear to the board of trustees that they did not own the paintings in the Hobart Collection. Judge Ciolino therefore "permanently enjoined" the board "from selling or otherwise disposing of the oil painting 'In the Park' or any of the other paintings comprising the 'Hobart Collection.' " He ordered the board to regain possession of the painting. And finally Judge Ciolino, with emphatic judicial dauntlessness declared that "the dedication by Mrs. Jennie T. Hobart was a memorial for Garret A. Hobart and that the Trustees hold the paintings comprising the Hobart Collection in trust for the purpose of such memorial and for the benefit of the residents of the City of Paterson."[104]

After the trustees voted to sell the painting, it was placed with Phillips Gallery of New York, which prepared a spectacular auction catalog featuring the Chase painting on the cover. After the restraining order came down, Phillips Gallery called for a $27,400 withdrawal fee, which took board Chairman Bello by complete surprise.[105] The gallery and the city finally settled, reputedly for less than this.

In the wake of the court order, the whole library system shut down on 20 December 1982, when it ran out of funds. It reopened in January 1983 with a renewed spirit to rebuild. As a final note, after the hubbub of the sale was over, the Metropolitan Museum asked to borrow the Chase painting for an exhibit, and it was gratefully loaned for that purpose.

The Paterson case had its effect on the broader community. Mr. Sterling said that a number of libraries that were hard pressed for funds under the tax cap had been considering the sale of valuable objects. This decision, however, has given trustees reason to pause and to rethink the nature of their public trust.

SUMMARY

Like other charities, public libraries grew out of the private sector. Most early colonial proprietary libraries were organized as nonprofit corporations, but they served a special clientele, individuals of social standing and wealth.

In the Boston Athenaeum controversy, public pressure contributed to the sale by the athenaeum of two valuable portraits to the Smithsonian rather than on the open market. Had the trustees attempted a sale on the open market, the Massachusetts attorney general could have intervened, and the sale could have been contested as being contrary to the public good.

There are public and private libraries just as there are other public and private charitable endeavors. The former are publicly funded and governed, whereas the latter rely mainly on private support and usually are operated by self-perpetuating boards. The right of both private and public charitable institutions to coexist was solidified by the U.S. Supreme Court in the Dartmouth College case. The case affirmed trustees' constitutional right to maintain their independent status and the right for both private and public charitable institutions to exist.

In the Joslyn case the Vermont Supreme Court exercised the usual judicial cautiousness in not applying *cy pres* and clearly differentiated the powers of public and private boards of trustees in handling matters relating to the same library.

Intellectual freedom is part and parcel of the library profession. The great contribution that librarianship has made to the broader social order has been a firm bulwark against untoward censorship. When library trustees accept the keys of trusteeship, they accept a public trust for the printed word and for intellectual freedom. It is important to consider trustees' authority and power in matters relating to intellectual freedom and censorship.

In the Davis County Utah Public Library case, a federal district court held that a library board had to follow appropriate procedural due process before dismissing a librarian and that there had to be just cause for the dismissal. The librarian had failed to follow a board's order to remove a specific book. The court placed a clear and unconditional restraint on board power, requiring adherence to legal and constitutional mandates.

In the Chelsea School Committee case, a federal district court held that while a school committee can determine what books will go into a library or even if a school is to have a library, the school committee does not have the same degree of discretion in the removal of books. Not every removal of a book from a school library is unconstitutional; but when a book is removed because its ''theme and language are offensive to a school committee,'' the parties affected have a right to legal recourse. School boards are ordinarily given great discretion by the courts under the assumption that they operate effectively under statutory and constitutional constraints in the discharge of their mission. However, once the constitutional threshold has been transgressed, the courts recognize the rights of individuals to petition the court for redress of an infringement of constitutional rights.

In the Island Trees case the U.S. Supreme Court, in a plurality decision, held that "local school boards may not remove books from school library shelves simply because they dislike the ideas contained in those books." The holding affects only the discretion of the school board to remove, not add, books from a school library. A genuine issue of material fact was presented by the case, and there had to be a trial on the facts before the books could be removed. Students retain the right to receive information, and the motivation of a school board to remove books lodged on narrow political or moral beliefs can be challenged.

In the Paterson Free Public Library case, a New Jersey Superior Court judge issued a permanent injunction forbidding library trustees to sell any of the library's valuable paintings held in trust, even though this meant the temporary closing of the financially beleaguered library. The library board did not own the paintings but held them in trust for the people. The paintings could not be sold, despite the trustees' vote to do so.

PRO BONO PUBLICO

While the human beings who are to obtain advantages from charitable trusts may be referred to as beneficiaries, the real beneficiary is the public and the human beings involved are merely the instrumentalities from whom the benefits flow.

In re Freshour's Estate, Supreme Court of Kansas, 1959

THE FINAL SAY

The reason so many of the court decisions included in this discussion carried such fierce shock waves was not so much that they were novel but that the myth that trustees have the final say—the ultimate authority—was so accepted. It is frequently stated that trustees sit on the top of the pyramid of power. They don't. The courts do. The board of trustees, although it may be appealed to by staff, is not the final court of appeal. Boards are only one link in the chain of command.

Clearly, as the various cases reveal, the courts have the final say. When trustees do not do their job or misbehave, the court will assume control and devise an appropriate remedy, including the removal of trustees from office.

Trustee Removal. One remedy available to the court for trustee misbehavior is removal from office. Since many trustees serve for power, influence, and prestige, removal is a tremendous blow to the individual's ego. Despite a belief in the collegiality of trusteeship, trustees will be removed, for the public's benefit, when they misbehave.

The power to remove a trustee for reasonable and just cause is one common-law incident of all charitable trusts. Generally, probate courts, by statute, and the equity court, in the exercise of its jurisdiction, possess the authority to remove trustees for cause. The attorney general or a co-trustee may initiate action for the removal of a trustee as provided by law.

The court gives careful consideration to a petition for removal and will not arbitrarily remove a trustee. A trustee will not be removed for a technical breach of trust or a breach of trust through mistakes. Ordinarily, there must be gross mismanagement or misbehavior for the court to remove the trustee. In general, common grounds for trustee removal focus on neglect, mismanagement, misfeasance, or other serious breaches of duty. Even though the court may remove a trustee for good cause, the petition for removal is addressed to the reasonable discretion of the court, and each case stands on its own merits. The public's interest is an important element in determining whether a trustee should be removed. Removal is usually done only to prevent further harm to the charity.

Other Remedies. In addition to trustee removal, some other remedies fashioned by courts to rectify wrongdoings have been to (1) reverse the trustees' decision, (2) deny the trustees continued legal managerial control of the charitable institution, (3) assess financial liability, and (4) assign compensatory and punitive damages. Once a court interjects its authority into the affairs of trustees, it retains jurisdiction over the charitable organization until the matter is judicially resolved. In some jurisdictions the court's involvement is permanent.

It must be quickly added that the courts do recognize the vitality of trusteeship, allowing trustees great discretion in the management of their respective institutions. But the court, on the other hand, will not tolerate abuses, breaches of trust, self-dealing, gross neglect of duty, conflicts of interest, and other wrongdoings, including *ultra vires* acts and abridgment of constitutional rights.

Ultimately what is "best" is a matter for the court to decide—not trustees. This is so because there must be an ultimate adjudicator—not necessarily what is morally right or wrong but what is judicially acceptable or unacceptable.

THE DYNAMICS OF CHANGE

As William James, the distinguished psychologist, so aptly observed a number of years ago, "Habit is the enormous flywheel of society."[1] Trustee habit, like flowing water, hollows out for itself a channel from the customary flow of events. Trustee routine, like water, runs in the same direction until an interceptor is introduced into the environment to change the habitual flow, permitting events to seek their own moral and legal levels.

That interceptor is change. Changes in the accountability patterns of trustees are becoming more pronounced as time passes. The courts are making it increasingly obvious that trustees do not have the ultimate authority and that the courts are willing to examine and correct trustee actions—even to punish or remove unworthy trustees. The public, including donors, is becoming more demonstrably irate over irresponsible trustee decisions and indifference. There is a gradual movement toward an age of accountability that must alter the flow of age-old trustee habits.

AGE OF ACCOUNTABILITY

As one digs more deeply into nonprofit charitable organizations, one begins to feel like the individual who explores the Russian stacking doll. Where does it end? In general, the cases presented in this book indicate that there is sufficient abuse to warrant renewed discussion of charitable trustee accountability.

The time-worn idea that trustees own their respective charitable entities must surrender to the realization that their ownership is only legal ownership—the right to manage property as a steward of assets held in trust for the public. As stewards, trustees serve as the guardians and managers of America's richest treasures: the museums, libraries, universities, hospitals, and other institutions designated exclusively for the public good. The benefits of these invaluable treasures flow to the American people, sometimes directly (as in a museum that is open to the public) and sometimes indirectly through conduits (the students who attend a college, for example, through whom the benefits of education flow to society).

As public awareness of these beneficial interests increases and as competition for charitable donations grows more keen, the public image of a charitable institution becomes pivotal. Donors and other interested individuals with special interests tend to be more than a little annoyed when they witness their beneficence diverted to other purposes; when their donations earmarked for one purpose are used for another; or when the expressed wishes of a donor are misconstrued, misinterpreted, or disregarded. Poor decisions not only negatively affect public support and beneficience for a charitable institution but also can incite public pressure to force trustees back into line with the public good.

Why don't we hear about these types of incidents more often? A major road-block in the journey toward comprehensive accountability still exists—public inaccessibility to trustees' meetings and information. Nongovernmental charities still escape close public scrutiny because they are generally not subject to open meeting laws. Thus, the trustees can function in secrecy, with little or no accountability to the public on a day-to-day basis.

Some legal scholars argue for a more unified law of charities. On the other hand, some claim there is a sufficient body of law, although it varies from jurisdiction to jurisdiction, to regulate nonprofit organizations. Even though there may be new legislation, the problem seems to lie more in enforcement. The question thus becomes this: How can the right of public visitation be more effectively implemented so as to correct abuses and to enforce the founder's will?

Stonewalling public accountability could produce a metamorphosis in the application of the open meeting laws. Only a few short years ago, governmental fiduciaries at all levels were taken by surprise when the advent of widespread open meeting laws opened up their agencies and boards to the public. These laws, despite their shortcomings, have been generally effective in the governmental sector. It may be that they offer the potential of being equally effective in the nongovernmental, nonprofit (public benefit) area as well.

Applying the open meeting laws to public benefit charities would, with minimal expense to the state, effect more accountability. The public, through the press and other interested parties, would have an opportunity to find out what is going on and to comment on it. Abuse, should there be any, could be identified and reported to the attorney general who in turn could investigate the situation and take appropriate action if warranted.

Beyond the public's beneficial interest in charities, the public also invests heavily in nonprofit entities by indirectly subsidizing them with exemption from local, state, and federal taxation; by allowing tax deductions for donations to them; and by giving federal, state, and local aid. To date, the courts in the main have held that these factors are not determinative in bringing charitable organizations under the state action doctrine or to force nongovernmental charities to open their meetings to the public. There seems, however, to be little that could stop the various state legislatures from applying the open meeting laws. Such legislative enactments would not turn the charitable entity into a governmental agency. It would only bring more accountability while minimizing supervision costs to the state. The people have a right to just supervision and accountability at a reasonable cost.

The authority granted any board of trustees, public or private, ultimately lies with the public, to whom a board is in the last resort responsible and accountable. Trustees of privately managed charities may not like the possibility of being subjected to public scrutiny, but the advantages to be gained from such supervision far outweigh any inconvenience that may be caused by having open meetings.

ENFRANCHISEMENT

Another barrier to accountability, perhaps a more fundamental one, is the existence of widespread misconceptions about the enfranchisement of charitable trustees, that is, the privileges granted by government to nonprofit trustees to operate eleemosynary organizations for the public good. Once there is clearer trustee thinking about the responsibilities of the nature of a public trust that comes with well-grounded common-law principles, the road may be cleared for closer adherence to the beneficial interest of the public. This will surely lead to better-informed decisions on the part of trustees and, it is hoped, less abuse.

The essence of the enfranchisement of a charitable trustee—whether it be a charitable trust or corporation, publicly or privately managed—is fiduciary, involving a confidence, or trust. Even though there may be specific laws regarding a particular type of charitable institution, for example, a hospital, the fiduciary principle creates a commonality among various charitable entities.

Specifically, the charitable trustee owes a fiduciary duty to the public, which reposes confidence in the trustee to manage the charitable entity for the public. This dictates a standard of behavior far and above the everyday world.

The fiduciary principle gives rise to the trustees' duties and determines the underlying structure for the trustees' powers. Trustees enjoy great latitude in discharging their fiduciary duties. But as fiduciaries, they have not been given unlimited discretion in terms of what they see as best for the public interest.

There are definite sources (and inherent limitations) for the trustee's duties, including the charter, the terms of the trust instrument, and certain well-settled rules of law that apply to all trustees.

Charter. Each charitable organization derives its existence from a charter or gift instrument that outlines the specific charitable purposes of that organization. Thus, board members in their fiduciary capacity have obligations not only to the public at large but also to the charitable organization's purpose as granted in the charter. Simply stated, trustees' basic responsibility is to set policy for the allocation of resources, both human and monetary, to achieve the objectives of the institution as expressed either implicitly or explicitly in its charter. Should trustees act beyond the scope of their chartered authority, the nonprofit corporation or individual trustees may be held liable for *ultra vires* acts.

Donative Instrument. Not only must prudent trustees remain faithful to the specific purposes for which the charitable organization is chartered, but trustees also owe a duty to the donor. Both law and custom afford any donor the right to determine in what manner his or her bequests may contribute to the betterment of society. Upon accepting a trust, the charitable trustee is under a duty to administer it according to the purposes and expressed terms of the trust instrument. Such adherence to the donor's wishes is mandatory until or unless a court of proper jurisdiction instructs otherwise. Accordingly, charitable contributions in general must be used only for the purpose for which they were received in trust.

Regulatory Authority. Yet another constraint placed on trustees is regulatory authority. Decisions of private independent boards of trustees are subject to governmental authority through three sources of law: (1) common law (court-made law from individual case decisions), (2) statutory law (written law originating in legislatures) and (3) administrative rules and regulations (mandates emanating from the executive side of government).

The board of trustees acts as a single body, which is legally empowered to administer all aspects of the institution. Although day-to-day management duties may be delegated to others, the board of trustees is legally responsible, and fully accountable at law, for its agents. Ignorance of either managers' actions or the law is not a defense because it is the duty of the trustee to administer the charitable enterprise with reasonable care and skill, and with selfless loyalty to the institution.

WHO GOVERNS THE GOVERNORS?

In the final analysis the assets of a charitable organization—corporation or trust—belong to the state or the people. Trustees are thus to a large extent officers of the court or state and are fully accountable.

What happens if perchance trustees, either through ignorance or by design, were to abuse their fiduciary responsibilities or disregard the legal constraints placed upon them? Who brings them to task?

The logical answer, at first thought, would be that the beneficiaries should police their own trustees to protect trust assets. However, in the case of charitable trusts with unnamed beneficiaries, this becomes unwieldy and impractical. In general, the public is barred from bringing a suit against a charitable organization. This serves as a means of sheltering charitable organizations from unnecessary and excessive bombardment of suits resulting in costly legal fees and a beleaguered charity that would seriously deprive the public of its beneficial interest.

The traditional enforcer, by common law, is a representative of the public: the attorney general of the state or a county law officer. The powers of these offices generally extend equally to charitable corporations and to charitable trusts.

The attorney general is authorized to inquire into the status, activities, and functioning of charities. She or he holds a prerogative right not only to protect but also to enforce all charities, as well as to represent the interests of the community at large. She or he can and does bring suit against trustees for alleged abuse of their fiduciary obligations.

Considering the large number of charitable entities in any one state, imagine the immense responsibility (to say nothing of the power) placed in the hands of the attorney general. Some critics feel that this is too much responsibility for one person to handle effectively, partly because most offices of attorneys general literally have too few hands. The result is a minimum of effective legal regulation of charitable trustees. To remedy this situation there is a trend toward extending legal standing, the right to sue (proper party plantiff), to certain other parties—mainly individual charitable trustees who possess a special vantage point because of their deep knowledge of the affairs of the charitable enterprise they administer and other persons having sufficient special interest. As evinced in the cases described in this book, many jurisdictions have already moved in this direction either by statute or common law. Others may follow.

EMERGING TRENDS

A recent opinion survey based on interviews with business executives on nonprofit boards revealed three major problem areas: (1) time, (2) money, and (3) government involvement.[2] In addition, other immutable factors are creating new trends.

Litigation and Protection. Although trustees bemoan government involvement in their affairs, especially by the court, it is reasonable to assume that there will be more litigation in the future, if for no other reason than the fact that we live in a highly litigious society. Trustees need to become more astutely attuned to when and how to use the advice of competent counsel.[3] In addition they need to purchase insurance to protect themselves from third-party suits for which they can be held liable for the actions of the organization.[4]

The Businesslike Approach. Another trend that is emerging, according to a recent survey of the Association of Governing Boards of Colleges and Universities (AGB) is that more business people are joining college and university boards. They make up 40 percent of all board members, compared to 34 percent in 1977.[5] With the increase in costs of hospital insurance programs, corporations are deliberately placing more and more of their executives on hospital boards. Thus, it seems that corporate America is becoming ever more powerful in the nonprofit boardroom.

The danger here, of course, is that individuals coming from the profit-making sector may apply "the good businesslike" approach—the proprietary mentality. It should be emphatically repeated that "business" purposes have no place in a nonprofit boardroom or organization. Manufacturing and selling widgets is one thing, and running a nonprofit hospital or other charitable organization is another. Once a profit is turned, the nonprofit entity ceases to be a charity, and it should be stripped of its special privileges and status, such as tax exemption.

From the direction in which things have been moving in this country, more mixing of profit and nonprofit activities will likely occur. Over the past few years, regretfully, there has been a movement afoot in some states, including the larger ones, to allow mixing of profit and nonprofit activities. As a final thought on this matter, it is utterly repugnant for a civilized society, not only by ancient legal convention but by moral commitment, to allow entrepreneurs to make a profit from the sick, the indigent, or any other similarly situated person. It is morally reprehensible to abuse and debase human dignity and existence with dividend yield. The dividend wool has been pulled over the public's moral and charitable eyes. Recently the Catholic Health Association expelled a hospital for joining a profit-making chain in a move to mix profit and non-profit.[6] The association decided that it could not be for-profit and Catholic at the same time. What is desperately needed is more assertions of this sort.

Another trend is that more literature and assistance in the form of guidelines is increasingly available to help trustees. The appendix, for example, contains the recent guidelines issued by Attorney General Neil F. Hartigan of the state of Illinois.

Women and Trusteeships. A 1927 museum management text stated that "although women are capable as trustees they usually find work of the women's auxiliary to be more congenial."[7] It was not so long ago that boards met in local men's clubs.

Another interesting statistic that the *AGB Reports* supplied was the significant increase in the number of women serving on boards. They reported that 20 percent of college and university board members are women, representing a 15-percent increase from 1977.[8] This is a healthy and growing trend, moving humanity and shaping society beyond its parochial attitudes of former years.

There have been a number of pioneering women in trusteeship. For example, Mrs. John D. Rockefeller III serves as president of the board of the Museum of Modern Art, a leadership position she first assumed in 1959. A positive trend, more women are joining boards of trustees because they know they can be of service to the community.

TOWARD A VICTORY

Professor Cyril Houle once wrote: "A good board is a victory, not a gift."[9] Good boards and effective trusteeship do not just happen. Healthy trusteeships are as much a victory as is good health.

The primary condition of trusteeship—like life itself—is growth through experience and self-education. In a nutshell, what the good trustee has is a healthy respect for the law, a knowledge of the trusteeship principles, personal integrity, and a desire to do the best job possible.

No public trust today is more important than the trusteeship of America's charitable institutions. No civic service can be more rewarding. Many trustees are fulfilling their public trust by honoring it with the commitment that each has made to serve the common good. The victory that is won for good trusteeship is a victory *pro bono publico*.

APPENDIX

NEIL F. HARTIGAN

ATTORNEY GENERAL
STATE OF ILLINOIS

YOU—THE BOARD MEMBER
OF AN
ILLINOIS NOT-FOR-PROFIT ORGANIZATION

1. Be active.

You should attend meetings of the Board and Board committees on which you serve. You must have general knowledge and understanding of how the organization is functioning, and you must have particular knowledge and understanding about the purpose of the organization and the specific responsibilities assigned to you.

Absence from meetings and inactivity do not excuse you from legal responsibility.

2. Receive no material profit.

Board members only can receive reimbursement for reasonable expenses and costs incurred in carrying out their board responsibilities. Illinois law prohibits loans by the organization to its directors and officers. If a board member is also an employee, compensation can be paid but the employee-board member should not participate in setting his or her compensation.

3. Avoid conflicts of interest.

As a board member you owe a duty of loyalty to the organization which takes precedence over your personal interests.

Self-dealing. You should avoid transactions with the organization where you have a personal business interest beyond your interest as a board member. In the rare instance where it is in the best interests of the organization to deal with you, you should make a full disclosure to the board of all the circumstances involved in the transaction, be sure that the transaction is fair to the organization, refrain from voting on the transaction as a board member, and not be counted in determining the existence of a board quorum. This restriction applies also to your relatives, business associates and friends.

Organizational opportunities. In all matters of interest to the organization, you must put its interests ahead of your own. If an opportunity related to its purpose comes to you either as a board member or otherwise, you must make it available to the organization before you take it for yourself or another entity.

4. Exercise judgment in overseeing the organization's affairs.

As a board member you have a duty to care for the organization's affairs in good faith and with at least that degree of diligence, care, and skill which ordinarily prudent people would exercise under similar circumstances in like positions. Your good faith is not enough.

The board must act with knowledge and after adequate deliberation. The board must carefully set organizational policy and regularly oversee its administration by competent staff. To exercise its duty of care the board must:

Appoint and regularly review the chief administrative officer of the organization, and

Establish and monitor, without getting involved in day to day activities, basic organizational policies and procedures which

a. clarify and assure adherence to the purposes of the organization and monitor effectiveness in achieving results—a copy of the Charter, By-laws and tax exemption letter, if any, will help with this

b. assure a personnel program which provides competent staff

c. assure that staff compensation and professional consulting fees are reasonable

d. provide sound investment and management of organizational funds and assets not expended directly for charitable purposes, to yield a reasonable return without undue risk

e. protect the organization's property, including reasonable provision for safekeeping, replacement, and divestment procedures which will benefit the organization

f. require board review, adoption, and monitoring of the annual budget

g. ensure financial resources to conduct organizational activities

h. request regular financial information and, if appropriate, an annual independent audit of the organization's financial affairs

i. provide for competent legal counsel to assure compliance with applicable local, state and federal laws, including timely filing of reports

j. provide for regular meetings of the board and its committees with adequate reports on—and discussion of—organizational activities

k. maintain adequate minutes of board and committee meetings as well as other pertinent organizational records

l. provide for careful selection and orientation of new board members

5. Comply with applicable governmental regulations.

A number of local, state, and federal laws and regulations apply to not-for-profit organizations. The board is responsible for assuring that the organization complies with these requirements.

a. *Organizational Regulations*

Illinois not-for-profit organizations are organized either as not-for-profit corporations (Ill. Rev. Stat. 1985, Ch. 32) or as charitable trusts. Not-for-profit corporations must file reports with the Illinois Secretary of State's Office, and charitable trusts must file reports with the appropriate courts. The Secretary of State or the court is responsible for ensuring compliance with the laws under which the organization is created.

b. *Administration and Solicitation of Funds*

The Illinois Charitable Trust Act and the Illinois Act to Regulate Solicitation and Collection of Funds for Charitable Purposes generally apply to charitable not-for-profit organizations functioning in Illinois whose assets exceed $4,000 or who solicit more than $4,000 annually, and to all whose fundraising is not conducted exclusively by volunteers. Such organizations must register and then file annual reports with the Office of the Illinois Attorney General. The Attorney General is responsible for assuring that charitable funds are properly solicited and administered.

c. *Taxation*

Some not-for-profit organizations are eligible for tax exempt status. Each exemption from income, real estate, or sales tax requires a separate application. Most taxing authorities also require annual reports. Not-for-profit organizations are subject to all employer-employee taxes and regulations.

Contributions to some not-for-profit organizations are deductible by the donor from income taxation where specifically granted by the taxing authorities upon petition.

d. *General Regulations*

In conducting their operations, not-for-profit organizations are subject to most of the laws affecting individual and corporate conduct.

e. *Accountability*

The Illinois Attorney General has the responsibility to the public of assuring sound and legal operation of not-for-profit organizations. This includes bringing legal action against board members for failure to exercise their legal responsibilities. Board members can be held personally liable by third parties injured by actions of the organization. Directors and officers liability insurance is often available to cover some of these situations.

NOTES

Legal case references are given to sources that are most readily available. The legal specialist wishing companion citations will want to check with a law library.

1. AMERICA'S CHARITABLE ENTERPRISE

1. Orr Kelly and Barbara Quick, "Nonprofit Groups: Are They Worth Their Tax Breaks?" *U.S. News and World Report*, 31 January 1983, 38–40.

2. Adam Clymer, "Poll Finds Trust in Government Edging Back Up," *New York Times*, 15 July 1983.

3. W. K. Jordan, "The Development of Philanthropy in England in the Early Modern Era," *Proceedings of the American Philosophical Society* 105 (April 1961): 145.

4. Lynch v. Spilman, 431 P.2d 636, 642 (Cal. 1967).

5. Marion R. Fremont-Smith, *Foundations and Government* (New York: Russell Sage Foundation, 1965), 13.

6. Jackson v. Phillips, 96 Mass. (14 Allen) 539, 556 (1867).

7. Dexter v. Harvard College, 57 N.E 371 (Mass. 1900).

8. President and Fellow of Harvard College, *The Story of Harvard: A Short History* (Cambridge, Mass.: The University Information Center, 1975), 2.

9. Arnaud C. Marts, *The Generosity of Americans: Its Source—Its Achievement* (Englewood Cliffs, N.J.: Prentice-Hall, 1966), 180.

10. Alexis de Tocqueville, *Democracy in America*, ed. Phillips Bradley, 2 vols. (New York: Knopf, 1945), 2:106.

11. *The Nonprofit Organization Handbook* (New York: McGraw, 1980), xv.

12. "A Museum on Holocaust," *Boston Globe*, 1 May 1984.

13. Harold Faber, "Where Hudson River School Began," *New York Times*, 15 July 1983.

14. Fay S. Joyce, "Coast Millionaire to Open Art Museum in SoHo," *New York Times*, 6 July 1983.

2. THE BOARD AND ITS IMAGES

1. Raymond M. Hughes, *A Manual for Trustees* (Ames: The Iowa State College Press, 1943), 161–62.

2. Kay Longcope, "Lady Bird Turns 70, Makes Gift to US," *Boston Globe*, 23 December 1982.

3. Leonard Silk and Mark Silk, *The American Establishment* (New York: Basic Books, 1980), 170.

4. Cyril O. Houle, *The Effective Board* (New York: Association Press, 1960), 20–21.

5. Chris Welles, "Nonprofit Institutions," in *Abuse on Wall Street: Conflicts of Interest in the Securities Markets* (Westport, Conn.: Quorum Books, 1980), 499.

6. Grace Glueck, "Power and Esthetics: The Trustee," *Art in America* (July 1971): 81.

7. G. William Domhoff, *Who Rules America?* (Englewood Cliffs, New Jersey: Prentice Hall, 1967), 156.

8. Robert A. Liston, *The Charity Racket* (New York: Thomas Nelson, 1977), 60.

9. Alfred R. Stern, "Instilling Activism in Trustees," *Harvard Business Review* 58 (January/February 1980): 24.

10. Marts, *Generosity of Americans*, 170.

11. Ibid., 171.

12. John McPhee, "A Room Full of Hoving's," *New Yorker*, 20 May 1967, 129.

13. Glueck, "Power and Esthetics: The Trustee," 78.

14. Henry Wriston, *Academic Procession: Reflections of a College President* (New York: Columbia University Press, 1959), 44.

15. Frank Emerson Andrews, *Philanthropic Foundations* (New York: Russell Sage Foundation, 1956), 81–82.

16. Wriston, *Academic Procession*, 84.

17. Roy Sorenson, *The Art of Board Membership* (New York: Association Press, 1950), 14.

18. Lynch v. Spilman, 642.

19. Austin Wakeman Scott, *The Law of Trusts* (Boston: Little Brown, 1967) § 348.3.

20. President and Fellows of Harvard College, *Story of Harvard*, 2.

21. A. Lawrence Lowell, "The Relation between Faculties and Governing Boards," in *At War with Academic Traditions in America* (Cambridge: Harvard University Press, 1934), 281–82.

22. Howard L. Oleck, *Nonprofit Corporations, Organizations, and Associations*. 4th ed. (Englewood Cliffs, N.J.: Prentice Hall, 1980), 84 n. 117.

23. Andrews, *Philanthropic Foundations*, 302.

24. Ibid., 302–03.

25. Karl E. Meyer, *The Art Museum: Power, Money, Ethics* (New York: William Morrow, 1979), 211.

26. State of Oregon, Department of Justice, "An Open Letter from Attorney General Dave Frohnmayer on Responsibilities of Charitable Trustees and Directors," January 1985; citing Lane County v. Wood, 691 P.2d 473 (Oregon 1984).

27. Meinhard v. Salmon, 164 N.E. 545, 546 (New York 1928).

28. *Black's Law Dictionary*, 484 (5th ed., 1979).

29. Scott, *Law of Trusts* § 1.

30. Leonard D. DuBoff, *Art Law* (St. Paul, Minn.: West Publishing, 1984), 269–74.

31. *Restatement (Second) of Trusts* (Philadelphia, Pa.: American Law Institute, 1959) § 348, comment "f", 212.

3. HOSPITALS

1. Editorial, "The Prognosis for McLean," *Boston Globe*, 28 August 1983.

2. Bricker v. Sceva Speare Memorial Hospital, 281 A.2d 589, 592 (N.H. 1971).

3. Queen of Angels Hospital v. Younger, 136 Cal. Rptr. 36 (Cal. Ct. App. 1977).

4. Ibid., 39.

5. Ibid.

6. Ibid., 42.

7. Lizabeth A. Moody, "Nonprofit Corporations—A Survey of Recent Cases," *Cleveland State Law Review* 21 (September 1972): 39.

8. Fulton National Bank v. Callaway Memorial Hospital 465 S.W.2d 549 (Mo. 1971).

9. Ibid., 552.

10. Ibid.

11. Scott, *Law of Trusts* § 348.1, 2771.

12. Holt v. College of Osteopathic Physicians and Surgeons, 40 Cal. Rptr. 244, 247 (1964).

13. Scott, *Law of Trusts* § 391, 3002–03.

14. *In re* Pruner's Estate, 136 A.2d 107 (Pa. 1957).

15. Scott, *Law of Trusts* § 391 (Supp. 1984), 106–07.

16. Attorney General of Illinois, Charitable Trusts and Solicitations Division, "Common Law Powers of the Attorney General as Applied to Charitable Trusts," Springfield, Illinois, 1977, 16.

17. Holt v. College of Osteopathic Physicians and Surgeons.

18. Cal. Corp. Code § 5230 (West Supp. 1986), Nonprofit Corporation Law effective January 1, 1980. *See also* Carole Ritts Kornblum, "Trustees', Directors' and Officers' Responsibility," in *Non-Profit Cultural Organizations*, ed. Harvey Horowitz (New York: Practicing Law Institute, 1979), 43, 47.

19. Holt v. College of Osteopathic Physicians and Surgeons, 249.

20. Ibid.

21. Ibid., 250.

22. Ibid, 247.

23. Pepperdine Foundation v. Pepperdine, 271 P.2d 600 (Cal. Dist. Ct. App. 1954).

24. Ibid., 605.

25. Kenneth L. Karst, "The Efficiency of the Charitable Dollar: An Unfulfilled State Responsibility," *Harvard Law Review* 73 (January 1960): 444.

26. Holt v. College of Osteopathic Physicians and Surgeons, 246.

27. Ibid.

28. Ibid., 249.

29. Ibid., 248; citing Karst, "Charitable Dollar," 444.

30. Ibid., 248–49.

31. Karst, "Charitable Dollar," 436.

32. Holt v. College, 248.

33. Scott, *Law of Trusts* § 16A, 162–63.

34. Ibid. § 326.3, 2565.

35. Fremont-Smith, *Foundations and Government*, 435.

36. Holt v. College of Osteopathic Physicians and Surgeons, 249.

37. Massachusetts Health and Educational Facilities Authority, Revenue Bonds, McLean Hospital Issue (R.B., MHI), Series B, 1 December 1985, A–1.

38. Jean Dietz, "McLean Hospital Sale Rejected," *Boston Globe*, 4 November 1983.

39. Editorial, Arnold S. Relman, "Investor-Owned Hospitals and Health-Care Costs," *The New England Journal of Medicine* 309 (August 11, 1983): 370–72.

40. Robert V. Pattison and Hallie M. Katz, "Investor-Owned and Not-for-Profit Hospitals," *The New England Journal of Medicine* 309 (August 11, 1983): 347–53.

41. Dietz, "McLean Hospital Sale Rejected."

42. Ibid.

43. Editorial, "The Prognosis for McLean," *Boston Globe*, 28 August 1983.

44. Queen of Angels Hospital v. Younger, 39.

45. Massachusetts Health and Educational Facilities Authority, R.B., MHI, 3.

46. Ibid., A–12, A–18.

47. McLean Hospital/AMI, news release, 27 February 1986.

48. Ibid.

49. Jean Dietz, "Calif. Firm, Belmont Hospital Join in Venture," *Boston Globe*, 28 February 1986.

50. Massachusetts Health and Educational Facilities Authority, R.B., MHI, A–18, A–19.

51. Ibid., B–8.

52. Oleck, *Nonprofit Corporations*, 38–42, 80–83, passim.

53. Welles, "Nonprofit Institutions," 499.

54. Commonwealth v. Barnes Foundation, 159 A.2d 500, 504 (Pa. 1960).

55. Attorney General v. Hahnemann Hospital, No. S–3984, Slip op. (Mass. 2 July 1986) (494 N.E.2d 1011).

56. Anne Vilen, "Hitch in the Plan," *The Tab*, 26 February 1985.

57. Ibid.

58. The Attorney General's Complaint and Petition for Declaratory Judgment at 7–8, Bellotti v. Hahnemann Hospital. (Mass. 13 Feb. 1985).

59. Attorney General v. Hahnemann Hospital, 15.

60. Attorney General's Complaint and Petition for Declaratory Judgment at 6.

61. Attorney General v. Hahnemann Hospital, 18–19.

62. Greisman v. Newcomb Hospital, 192 A.2d 817 (N.J. 1963).

63. Ibid., 824.

64. Greisman v. Newcomb Hospital, 183 A.2d 878 (N.J. Super. Ct. 1962).

65. Greisman v. Newcomb Hospital, 820 (1963).

66. Ibid., 821.

67. Ibid., 821.

68. Ibid., 822.

69. Greisman v. Newcomb Hospital, 886 (1962).

70. Ibid., 823.

71. Ibid., 825.

72. Scott, *Law of Trusts* § 391.

73. Connecticut Bank and Trust Company v. Hartford Hospital, 276 A.2d 792 (Conn. Super. Ct. 1971).

74. Ibid., 794.

75. Ibid., 796.

76. Donald R. Young and Wilbert E. Moore, *Trusteeship and the Management of Foundations* (New York: Russell Sage Foundation, 1969), 34.

77. Connecticut Bank and Trust Company v. Hartford Hospital, 795.

78. Ibid., 796.

79. Mercantile Trust Company National Association v. Shriners' Hospital for Crippled Children, 551 S.W.2d 864, 867 (Mo. Ct. App. 1977).

80. Ibid., 868.

81. Ibid., 867.

82. Stern v. Lucy Webb Hayes National Training School for Deaconesses and Missionaries, 381 F. Supp. 1003 (D.D.C. 1974).

83. Ibid., 1011.

84. Ibid., 1015.

85. Ibid., 1014.

86. Ibid., 1007.

87. Ibid., 1015.

88. Ibid.

89. Ibid., 1016.

90. Ibid.

91. Ibid., 1018.

92. Ibid., 1019.

93. Ibid.

94. Ibid., 1013–14.

95. Steven H. Gifis, *Law Dictionary* (New York: Barron's Educational Series, 1984), 87.

96. Fremont-Smith, *Foundations and Government*, 136; citing Winter v. Anderson, 275 N.Y.S. 373 (1934).

97. Scott, *Law of Trusts* § 2.5, 39.

98. Oleck, *Nonprofit Corporations, Organizations, and Associations*, 595–96.

99. Gilbert v. McLeod Infirmary, 64 S.E.2d 524 (S.C. 1951).

100. Ibid., 525.

101. Ibid., 526.

102. Ibid., 529.

103. Ibid., 530.

104. Ibid., 531.

105. Ibid., 528; citing 1 *Bogert on Trusts* 61.

106. Franzblau v. Monardo, 166 Cal. Rptr. 610 (Cal. Ct. App. 1980).

107. Ibid., 612.

108. Ibid., 613.

109. District Attorney for the Northern District v. Board of Trustees of the Lenorad Morse Hospital, 452 N.E.2d 208 (Mass. 1983).

110. Ibid., 210.

111. Ibid., 209.

112. Ibid., 210.

113. Ibid., 210–11.

114. Judy Foreman, "Mass. Woman, 23, Gets New Heart; 5th Recipient in N.E.," *Boston Globe* 15 September 1984.

115. Ibid.

116. Mark Miller, "Hospitals' Bid to Cut Care for Poor Rejected," *Boston Globe*, 29 June 1984.

117. Richard A. Knox, "Hospitals Seeking Leeway on Transplants," *Boston Globe*, 2 May 1984.

118. Richard A. Knox, "Hub Aim: Cut Infant Deaths," *Boston Globe*, 26 May 1984.

119. Richard A. Knox, "Panel Urges 1 Hospital Do Heart Transplants," *Boston Globe*, 16 May 1984.

120. Richard A. Knox, "Debate: Hospitals' Free Care Budgets vs. New Technologies," *Boston Globe*, 26 June 1984.

121. Knox, "Panel Urges 1 Hospital."

122. Richard A. Knox, "No Heart Transplants for MGH," *Boston Globe*, 9 February 1980.

123. Ibid.

124. Ibid.

125. Richard A. Knox, "A Reluctant 'No' at MGH," *Boston Globe*, 17 February 1980.

126. Fox Butterfield, "Massachusetts' Opposition to Heart Transplant Eases," *New York Times*, 7 January 1984.

127. "Transplant Drug Called Dangerous for Kidneys," *Boston Globe*, 13 September 1984.

128. Robert Frost, "The Road Not Taken," in *The Poetry of Robert Frost* (New York: Holt, Rinehart and Winston), 1969, 105.

4. COLLEGES AND UNIVERSITIES

1. Otto Heller, "The Passing of the Professor," *Scientific Monthly* 24 (January 1927): 35.

2. William H. Cowley, *Presidents, Professors, and Trustees* (San Francisco: Jossey-Bass, 1980), 23–24.

3. "The Governance of the Universities II," *Daedalus* (Fall 1969): 1117.

4. Susan White, "Announcement to Close Stuns Wilson Body," *The Billboard*, 23 February 1979.

5. Ibid.

6. Gretchen Van Ness, "Statement," *The Billboard*, 23 February 1979.

7. Wilson College, news release, 19 February 1979, 2.

8. Elisabeth Hudnut Clarkson, "Ten Misconceptions about the Wilson College Case," *AGB Reports* 22 (July/August 1980): 7.

9. Zehner v. Alexander, [no docket no.] slip op. 14–15 (Pa. Orphans' Ct. of Franklin County, 29 May 1979).

10. "A Statement by the Board of Trustees of Wilson College," 2 April 1979, 11.

11. "Save Wilson Committee Files Class Action Suit," *Wilson College Alumnae Newsletter*, no. 3, 21 April 1979, 1.

12. Zehner v. Alexander, 1–2.

13. "Save Wilson Suit Heard, Ruling Expected Before End of May," *Wilson College Alumnae Newsletter*, no. 4, May 1979, 1.

14. Zehner v. Alexander, 14–33 passim, 73, 80.

15. Ibid., 78–79.

16. Ibid., 70.

17. Ibid., 59.

18. Clarkson, "Ten Misconceptions," 7.

19. Ibid.

20. Ibid., 8.

21. Fred M. Hechinger, "Wilson College, A 'Lost Cause,' Looks Lively," *New York Times*, 11 November 1980.

22. *AGB Reports* 22 (July/August 1980): 3–15.

23. Joseph C. Gies, "The Wilson College Case," *AGB Reports* 22 (July/August, 1980): 4.

24. Lorrie Brooks, "Wilson—Pioneer in Women's Education," *Public Opinion*, 31 August 1979.

25. Houle, *Effective Board*, 51–52.

26. G. Philip Anderson, "Trustee Responsibility: Conflict of Interest," *Lex Collegii* (Spring 1979): 6.

27. Zehner v. Alexander, 77.

28. Ibid., 83.

29. "Save Wilson Suit Heard," 1.

30. Zehner v. Alexander, 82.

31. Ibid., 82–83.

32. Ibid., 77.

33. Ibid., 74–75.

34. Ibid., 70.

35. "Save Wilson Suit Heard," 2.

36. Zehner v. Alexander, 32–33.

37. Ibid., 33.

38. Ibid.

39. Ibid., 71.

40. Ibid., 70.

41. Hechinger, "Wilson College."

42. Zehner v. Alexander, 45–46.

43. Ibid., 46.

44. Ibid., 34.

45. Ibid., 84.

46. Catherine Myers, "Pa. Judge Bars Closing of Private College," *Chronicle of Higher Education*, 18 June 1979, 10.

47. Zehner v. Alexander, 84.

48. Myers, "Pa. Judge Bars Closing," 10.

49. Zehner v. Alexander, 84.

50. Clarkson, "Ten Misconceptions," 10.

51. Zehner v. Alexander, 84.

52. Dave Dunkle, "Judge's Decision Was Not an Easy One to Make," *Public Opinion*, 31 August 1979.

53. "The Little College That Could," *Trenton Tmes*, 7 June 1979.

54. Zehner v. Alexander, 83.

55. Ibid., 81.

56. Board of Regents of the University of the State of New York, Hearing Committee, "Report," 24 May 1979, 8. (Typewritten.)

57. Ibid., 2.

58. N.Y. Educ. Law § 216 (McKinney's Supp. 1986).

59. "Faculty Members Ask Mannes Music College to Halt Merger Talks," *New York Times*, 20 January 1979.

60. "Mannes Merger Is Voted, But Opposition Remains," *New York Times*, 23 February 1979.

61. Ibid.

62. Ibid.

63. Board of Regents, "Report," 6.

64. Ibid., 6–7.

65. Ibid. 7.

66. Ibid., 4.

67. Jack Magarrell, "Public Board's Ouster of Private Trustees Keeps Mannes College of Music Alive," *The Chronicle of Higher Education*, 5 November 1979, 9.

68. Ibid.

69. Grace v. Grace Institute, 226 N.E.2d 531, 532, (New York 1967).

70. Ibid., 534.

71. Ibid.

72. Ibid.

73. Ibid.

74. Ibid.

75. *Restatement (Second) of Trusts* § 107.

76. Grace v. Grace Institute, 535.

77. Glen Macnow, "Schools' Chief Given Control of Troubled Mich. College," *The Chronicle of Higher Education*, 11 January 1984, 3.

78. Editorial, "WCCC: A New Board of Trustees Can Put Infighting and Inefficiency Behind It . . . ," *Detroit Free Press*, 3 August 1984.

79. Macnow, "Schools' Chief Given Control."

80. Macnow, "WCCC Scholarships, Jobs a Family Affair," *Detroit Free Press*, 15 January 1984.

81. Michigan, House of Representatives, House Committee on Colleges and Universities (HR, HCCU), *Report of the Special Committee to Study Wayne County Community College*, Lansing, Michigan, 1 December 1983, 2–3.

82. Michigan, HR, HCCU, Letter of Transmittal, *Report of the Special Committee*, 1.

83. Letter from Phillip E. Runkel to Doris J. Miller, 10 January 1984.

84. Memorandum from Phillip E. Runkel to Members of the Michigan Legislature, "Report on Monitoring Activities at Wayne County Community College," report no. 1, 7 March 1984, 4.

85. Susan Goldberg, "WCCC Board Self-serving, Report Says," *Detroit Free Press*, 24 May 1984.

86. Ibid.

87. Memorandum from Phillip E. Runkel, "Report on Monitoring Activities," report no. 4, 15 February 1985, 2.

88. Mike Wowk, "WC3 Board Shift Wins Runkel OK," *Detroit News*, 13 April 1984.

89. Cassandra Spratling, "Rebuilt WCCC Makes a Fresh Start," *Detroit Free Press*, 22 February 1985.

90. Kent M. Weeks, ed., *Legal Deskbook for Administrators of Independent Colleges and Universities* (Notre Dame, Indiana: Center for Constitutional Studies, Notre Dame Law School, 1982), I–2.

91. Derek Bok, *Beyond the Ivory Tower* (Cambridge: Harvard University Press, 1982), 29.

92. Vidal v. Girard's Executors, 43 U.S. (2 How.) 127 (1844), 129.

93. Girard Estate, 4 Pa. D & C2d 671, 721 (Pa. Orphans' Ct. of Philadelphia County 1955).

94. Trustees of the Philadelphia Baptist Association v. Hart's Executors 17 U.S. (4 Wheat.) 1 (1819).

95. Vidal v. Girard's Executors, 202.

96. Ibid., 192.

97. Scott, *Law of Trusts*, § 348.

98. Vidal v. Girard's Executors, 155–61.

99. Ibid.

100. Brown v. Board of Education of the City of Topeka, 347 U.S. 483 (1954).

101. Plessy v. Ferguson, 163 U.S. 537 (1896).

102. Commonwealth of Pennsylvania v. Board of Directors of City Trusts of City of Philadelphia, 353 U.S. 230, 231 (1957).

103. Commonwealth of Pennsylvania v. Brown, 270 F. Supp. 782, 785 (1967).

104. Ibid., 786.

105. Scott, *Law of Trusts* § 399.4, 3128.

106. Commonwealth of Pennsylvania v. Brown, 270 F. Supp. 782, 790 (1967).

107. Oliver Wendell Holmes, *The Mind and Faith of Justice Holmes: His Speeches, Essays, Letters and Judicial Opinions*, selected and edited with introduction and commentary by Max Lerner (Boston: Little, Brown, 1946), 172–79.

108. Endress v. Brookdale Community College, 364 A.2d 1080, 1084 (1976).

109. Ibid., 1088.

110. Ibid., 1089.

111. Ibid., 1085.

112. Ibid., 1099.

113. Ibid., 1094.

114. Ibid., 1098–99.

115. Ibid., 1098.

116. Ibid.

117. "Brookdale Study Finds No Conflict," *The New York Times*, 20 October 1975.

5. MUSEUMS

1. Meyer, *Art Museum*, 20.

2. Ibid.

3. Commonwealth v. Barnes Foundation, 503.

4. Ibid., 501.

5. Ibid., 502.

6. Ibid., 504.

7. Wiegand v. Barnes Foundation, 97 A.2d 81 (Pa. 1953).

8. Commonwealth v. Barnes Foundation, 502–03.

9. Ibid., 503.

10. Ibid., 505.

11. Conway v. Emeny, 96 A.2d 221 (Conn. 1953).

12. Jean C. Harris, *The Hill-Stead Museum* (Farmington, Conn.: Trustees of the Hill-Stead Museum): n.p.

13. Roderick Cameron, "Hill-Stead," *House & Garden*, April 1985, 189.

14. Ibid., 196.

15. Conway v. Emeny, 224.

16. Ibid., 222.

17. Ibid., 223.

18. Ibid., 224.

19. Ibid.

20. Ibid.

21. Ibid., 225.

22. Ibid., 224.

23. Ibid., 225.

24. Ibid.

25. Ibid., 224.

26. Ibid.

27. Luis Kutner, *Legal Aspects of Charitable Trusts and Foundations* (Chicago: Commerce Clearing House, 1970), 164.

28. Art Institute of Chicago v. Castle, 133 N.E.2d 748 (Ill. App. Ct. 1956).

29. "Gives $1,000,000 for Chicago Art," *Chicago Tribune*, 15 April 1905.

30. Ibid.

31. Lorado Taft, "Address," *Dedication of the Ferguson Fountain of the Great Lakes* (Chicago: Art Institute of Chicago, 1913), 29.

32. Charles L. Hutchinson, "Address," *Dedication of the Ferguson Fountain of the Great Lakes*, 35.

33. Complaint for Greene at 7, Greene v. Art Institute of Chicago, 147 N.E.2d 415 (Ill. App. Ct. 1958).

34. Art Institute of Chicago v. Castle, 752.

35. Complaint for Greene at 11–12, Greene v. Art Institute of Chicago.

36. Kutner, *Legal Aspects*, 163.

37. Complaint for Greene at 6, 10, Greene v. Art Institute of Chicago. *See also* Greene v. Art Institute, 417.

38. Elinor Richey, "Accused," *FOCUS/Midwest*, September 1972, 11.

39. Ibid., 9.

40. Greene v. Art Institute of Chicago, 418.

41. Ibid., 417–18.

42. Richey, "Accused," 12.

43. Kutner, *Legal Aspects*, 167.

44. Luis Kutner and Henry H. Koven, "Charitable Trust Legislation in the Several States," *Northwestern University Law Review* 61 (1966): 411, 417–18 n. 32.

45. B. F. Ferguson Monument Fund, Art Institute of Chicago, *B. F. Ferguson Monument Fund: A Growing Gift to the City of Chicago*. Chicago, Illinois: Art Institute, 1980, n.p. (Typescript.)

46. Art Institute of Chicago v. Castle, 751.

47. Austin W. Scott, "The Fiduciary Principle," *California Law Review* 37 (December 1949): 540; citing Josiah Royce, *The Philosophy of Loyalty* (New York: Macmillan, 1908).

48. Kutner, *Legal Aspects*, 161.

49. Meyer, *Art Museum*, 217; citing Attorney General's Conference of Museum Representatives, transcript, 29 October 1973, 4.

50. Ibid., 58–59 and Meyer, 217.

51. William James, *The Principles of Psychology* (New York: Dover Publications, 1890), 125.

52. Leah Gordon, "Trading a Museum's Treasure—a Very Hazardous Business," *The New York Times*, 31 March 1974.

53. Ibid.

54. Ibid.

55. Ibid.

56. Leonard D. DuBoff, *The Deskbook of Art Law,* (Washington, D.C.: Federal Publications Text, 1977), 887.

57. Gordon, "Trading a Museum's Treasures."

58. Ibid.

59. Fred Ferretti, "State Investigates American Indian Museum," *New York Times*, 3 October 1974.

60. DuBoff, *Deskbook of Art Law*, 888.

61. Lefkowitz v. Museum of the American Indian, no. 41416/75 (N.Y. Sup. Ct. 1975). *See also* DuBoff, *Deskbook of Art Law*, 888–92.

62. Grace Glueck, "Museum of Indian: The Troubles's Over?" *The New York Times*, 17 January 1980.

63. Douglas C. McGill, "Perot Seeks to Move Indian Museum," *New York Times*, 21 February 1985.

64. McGill, "Indian Museum to Seek Perot Pact; State Wary," *New York Times*, 23 February 1985.

65. "The Fogg Dilemma," *AVISO*, April 1982, 1.

66. Ethics and Standards Committee, "Deaccessioning Policy Resolution," (Montreal: Association of Art Museum Directors, 26 January 1982).

67. Robert Levey, "Harvard 'Botches' a Job," *Boston Globe*, 21 February 1982.

68. Massachusetts Health and Educational Facilities Authority, Revenue Bonds, Harvard University Issue (RB, HUI), Series I, 1 April 1985, A–2.

69. Levey, "Harvard 'Botches' a Job."

70. "Canceling of Fogg Wing Is Criticized," *New York Times*, 9 February 1982.

71. Levey, "Harvard 'Botches' a Job."

72. "Canceling of Fogg Wing Is Criticized."

73. Harvard University, *Financial Report to the Board of Overseers of Harvard College for the Fiscal Year 1984–85*, Cambridge: The University, 1985, 19, 57. *See also*, Massachusetts Health and Educational Facilities Authority, RB, HUI.

74. Levey, "Harvard 'Botches' a Job."

75. Ibid.

76. Harvard University, *Financial Report to the Board of Overseers of Harvard College for the Fiscal Year 1984–1985*, 21.

77. Levey, "Harvard 'Botches' a Job."

78. Patricia Failing, "The Maryhill Museum: A Case History of Cultural Abuse," *Art News* (March 1977): 83.

79. Ibid., 84.

80. Ibid., 87.

81. Ibid., 84.

82. Complaint for Specific Performance for Maryhill Museum at 4, Maryhill Museum v. Gorton, Civil Action 11777 (Wash. Super. Ct. of Klickitat County 1977).

83. Steve Gordenier, "Committee Removes Museum Trustees," *The Goldendale Sentinel*, 3 March 1977.

84. Stipulation, Maryhill Museum v. Gorton, Civil Action no. 11777; and State of Washington *ex rel.* Gorton v. Leppaluoto, no. 11781 (Wash. Super. Ct. of Klickitat County 1978).

85. Complaint for Specific Performance at 4, Maryhill Museum v. Gorton.

86. The Attorney General's Petition at 1, State of Washington *ex rel.* Gorton v. Leppaluoto, Civil Action 11781 (Wash. Super. Ct. of Klickitat County 1977).

87. Ibid.

88. Ibid., 2–6.

89. People *ex rel.* Scott v. Harding, 374 N.E.2d 756 (Ill. App. Ct. 1978).

90. "Harding Leaves Art Collection to the People," *Daily News*, 6 April 1939; citing The Attorney General's Amended Complaint at 4 and Exhibit C, People *ex rel.* v. Silverstein, case no. 76-CH–6446 (1982).

91. Jerry Crimmins, "Museum Director Used Funds Improperly: State," *Chicago Tribune*, 2 March 1982.

92. Attorney General's Amended Complaint at 12, People *ex rel.* v. Silverstein.

93. Attorney General's Amended Complaint at 2, People *ex rel.* v. Silverstein.

94. William Currie, "Harding Museum Hoard: Shh, It's a . . . . . . Secret," *Chicago Tribune*, 8 August 1976.

95. Final Pre-Trial Order at 2, People *ex rel.* v. Silverstein, case no. 76-CH–6446 (Illinois 1981).

96. Comments, "Trusts—Trustees—Investment Duties of Trustees and the Problem of Unduly-Conservative Trust Investment," *Michigan Law Review* 61 (1963): 1551.

97. Final Pre-Trial Order at 2, People *ex rel.* v. Silverstein.

98. Ibid., 4.

99. Ibid., 36.

100. Editorial, "Harding Case Only Half Settled," *Chicago Tribune*, 27 May 1982.

101. *Restatement (Second) of Trusts* § 170, comment 1, 369.

102. Final Pre-Trial Order at 2, People *ex rel.* v. Silverstein.

103. Attorney General's Amended Complaint at 5–7, People *ex rel.* v. Silverstein.

104. Ibid., 5–6 passim.

105. Scott, *Law of Trusts*, § 170.

106. Final Pre-Trial Order at 2, People *ex rel.* v. Silverstein.

107. Ibid., 3.

108. Attorney General's Amended Complaint at 12, People *ex rel.* v. Silverstein.

109. William Currie, "Scott to Court: Halt Harding Antiques Sale," *Chicago Tribune*, 28 October 1976.

110. Currie, "Harding Art Item Auctioned for $135,000," *Chicago Tribune*, 27 October 1976.

111. Final Pre-Trial Order at 5, People *ex rel.* v. Silverstein.

112. Currie, "Plan to Auction Two More Harding Treasures Revealed," *Chicago Tribune*, 20 November 1976.

113. Final Pre-Trial Order at 36, People *ex rel.* v. Silverstein.

114. Attorney General's Amended Complaint at 7–8, passim, People *ex rel.* v. Silverstein.

115. Currie, "Judge Allows Auction of Harding Collection," *Chicago Tribune*, 30 October 1976.

116. Jerry Crimmins, "Harding Records Admitted," *Chicago Tribune*, 4 March 1982.

117. Ibid.

118. Editorial, "The Harding Museum in Court," *Chicago Tribune*, 24 December 1976.

119. Currie, "New Charge Clouds Row over Museum," *Chicago Tribune*, 20 April, 1977.

120. Ibid.

121. Meyer, *Art Museum*, 197.

122. Edgar J. Driscoll, "Raphael's Eleanora Awaits Italy's Move," *Boston Globe*, 28 March 1971. *See also* Paul Hoffman, "Italy to Press Charges over a Raphael," *New York Times*, 23 March 1971.

123. Editorial, "The Maltese Falcon Revisited," *Boston Globe*, 12 February 1971.

124. Driscoll, "Raphael's Eleanora Awaits Italy's Move."

125. Currie, "New Charges."

126. Hoffman, "Italy to Press Charges."

127. Greg Mcdonald, "Italy Regains Painting from Hub Museum," *Boston Globe*, 11 September 1971.

128. Meyer, *Art Museum*, 197.

129. Currie, "Judge Drops Ex-Museum Chief as Appraiser of Harding Art," *Chicago Tribune*, May 19, 1977.

130. Ibid.

131. Ibid.

6. SCHOOL AND PUBLIC LIBRARIES

1. Benjamin Franklin, *Autobiography* (New York: Walter J. Black, 1941): 107.

2. Massachusetts, Free Public Library Commission, *Ninth Report*, public document no. 44 (1899): 131.

3. *A History of Franklin's Libraries*, exhibition catalog prepared by John A. Peters, Franklin, Mass., n.d., 5.

4. Arthur W. Peirce, "History of the Franklin Public Library, Franklin, Mass.," Peirce Papers, Franklin Public Library, Franklin, Massachusetts, 2–3. (Typescript.) *See also* Mortimer Blake, *A History of the Town of Franklin, Mass.; from Its Settlement to the Completion of Its First Century, 2d March, 1878* (Franklin, Mass.: The Committee of the Town, 1879), 71.

5. Jesse H. Shera, *Foundations of the Public Library* (Chicago: University of Chicago; reprint ed., Hamden, Conn.: Shoe String Press, 1965), 205.

6. *A History of Franklin's Libraries*, 5.

7. Carleton Bruns Joeckel, *The Government of the American Public Library* (Chicago: University of Chicago Press, 1935), 15.

8. Ibid., 18.

9. Linda Lewis, "Protecting the True Treasure," *Boston Globe*, 12 December 1979.

10. Ibid.

11. Ibid.

12. Ibid.

13. Trustees of Dartmouth College v. Woodward, 17 U.S. (4 Wheat.) 518 (1819).

14. Richard N. Current, "The Dartmouth College Case," in *Quarrels That Have Shaped the Constitution*, ed. John A. Garraty (New York: Harper & Row, 1964), 15–29.

15. Trustees of Dartmouth College v. Woodward, 518.

16. Ibid.

17. The Trustees of Rutgers College v. Richman, 125 A.2d 10.

18. Trustees of Dartmouth College v. Woodward, 636.

19. Shera, *Foundations of the Public Library*, 161–62.

20. Ibid.

21. Ibid., 170–81.

22. *In re* Application of Charles K. Jones, 415 A.2d 202 (Vermont 1980).

23. Ibid., 205.

24. Ibid.

25. Ibid.

26. Ibid.

27. Ibid.

28. Ibid.

29. Ibid., 206.

30. Ibid.

31. John Milton, *Complete Poetry and Selected Prose of John Milton*, introduction by Cleanth Brooks, *Areopagitica* (New York: Modern Library, 1950), 681.

32. "Librarians' Rights," *Newsletter on Intellectual Freedom*, January 1980, 12.

33. Ibid.

34. Pete Giacoma, "When Librarians Fight, the Media Respond: Intellectual Freedom Faces 'Crossfire,' " *Newsletter on Intellectual Freedom*, July 1980, 73.

35. Ibid.

36. "Librarians' Rights," *Newsletter on Intellectual Freedom*.

37. Layton v. Swapp, 484 F. Supp. 958 (N.D. Utah 1979).

38. Ibid., 959.

39. "Utah Librarian Wins Her Job Back," *Newsletter on Intellectual Freedom*, March 1980, 29.

40. "FTRF Reports Success of Jeanne Layton Challenge," *Newsletter on Intellectual Freedom*, January 1981, 32.

41. "Jeanne Layton Wins Downs Award," *Newsletter on Intellectual Freedom*, November 1980, 125.

42. Right to Read Defense Committee v. School Committee of Chelsea, 454 F. Supp. 703, 706 (D. Mass 1978).

43. Ibid., 708; citing Miller v. California, 413 U.S. 15 (1973).

44. Ibid., 706.

45. Ibid., 714.

46. Jack Thomas, "An Obscenity Beyond Words," *Boston Globe*, 1 August 1977.

47. Right to Read Defense Committee v. School Committee of Chelsea, 706.

48. Ibid., 707; citing "Special School Board Meeting on Book," *Chelsea Record*, 20 May 1977.

49. Right to Read Defense Committee v. School Committee of Chelsea, 707.

50. Thomas, "Obscenity Beyond Words."

51. Right to Read Defense Committee v. School Committee of Chelsea, 707.

52. Ibid.

53. Ibid., 708.

54. Ibid., 711–12.

55. Carol Hutton, "Chelsea Board Bans Poem from Schools," *Boston Globe*, 29 July 1977.

56. Right to Read Defense Committee v. School Committee of Chelsea, 714.

57. Ibid., 711

58. Ibid.

59. Ibid., 712.

60. Ibid., 714.

61. Ibid.

62. Ibid., 714–15; citing Tinker v. Des Moines School District, 393 U.S. 503, 511.

63. Ibid., 715.

64. "Chelsea and Its Aftermath," *Bay State Letter*, September 1978.

65. Ibid.

66. Right to Read Defense Committee v. School Committee of Chelsea, 714–15.

67. Board of Education, Island Trees Union Free School District No. 26 v. Pico, 457 U.S. 853 (1982).

68. Austin Broadhurst, "A Legal Opinion: Island Trees v. Pico," *Massachusetts Association of School Committees Journal* 16 (September 1982): 14.

69. Board of Education, Island Trees Union Free School District No. 26 v. Pico, 855–56.

70. Ibid., 872.

71. Ibid., 862.

72. Ibid., 856.

73. Ibid., 853.

74. Ibid., 857 n. 4.

75. Ibid., 858–59.

76. Ibid., 875.

77. Ibid., 854.

78. Michael Winerip, "L.I. School Board Ends Its Fight to Ban Books," *New York Times*, 31 January 1983.

79. Board of Education, Island Trees Union Free School District No. 26 v. Pico, 863–64.

80. Ibid., 864–65.

81. Ibid., 865.

82. Ibid.

83. Ibid., 867.

84. Ibid., 868.

85. Ibid., 870–71.

86. Broadhurst, "Legal Opinion," 16.

87. Board of Education, Island Trees Union Free School District No. 26 v. Pico, 874.

88. Ibid., 875.

89. Howard Sterling and the Ad Hoc Committee Against the Sale of "In the Park" v. Board of Library Trustees of the Paterson Free Public Library, Civil action no. C-641–82 (N.J. Super. Ct. Ch. Div. of Passaic County 1982). *See also* Garry Duffy and

Diane Haines, "Chase Painting Saved from Auction Block," *Paterson News*, 21 October 1982.

90. Denise Gellene, "Budget Paints a Dim Picture of Paterson Library's Future," *The Sunday Record*, 31 January 1982.

91. Frank Kingdon, *John Cotton Dana: A Life* (Newark, N.J.: The Public Library and Museum, 1940): 52.

92. Gellene, "Budget Paints a Dim Picture."

93. Editorial, "No Choice: Sell the Painting," *The Record*, 19 October 1982.

94. Michael C. Pollak, "Despite Pinch, Library Won't Sell Art," *The Record*, 20 January 1982.

95. Gellene, "Budget Paints a Dim Picture."

96. Ibid.

97. Ibid.

98. Pollak, "Despite Pinch."

99. Editorial, "Painful Choice in Paterson," *The Sunday Record*, 14 March 1982.

100. Brief for Howard Sterling at [6], Howard Sterling and the Ad Hoc Committee Against the Sale of "In the Park" v. Board of Trustees of the Paterson Free Public Library.

101. Kathleen Meehan, "Art Goes, Libraries Close," *Paterson News*, 30 September 1982.

102. Ibid.

103. Tom Groenfeidt, "Library Cutting Back," *The Record*, 30 September 1982.

104. Howard Sterling and the Ad Hoc Committee Against the Sale of "In the Park" v. Board of Library Trustees of the Paterson Free Public Library.

105. Garry Duffy, " 'Ransom' for City Painting," *The News*, 18 October 1982.

7. PRO BONO PUBLICO

1. James, *The Principles of Psychology*, 121.

2. Research and Forecasts, "The Touche Ross Survey of Business Executives on Non-Profit Boards," (Eric doc. no. ED 188 511) July 1979, 1–5.

3. Stephen E. Weil, *Beauty and the Beast* (Washington, D.C.: Smithsonian Institution Press, 1983), 134–35. *See especially* Mr. Weil's "A Checklist of Legal Considerations for Museums," in *Beauty and the Beast*, 143–50.

4. Council of Better Business Bureaus, *The Responsibilities of a Charity's Volunteer Board* (Arlington, Va.: CBBB, PAS Division, 1986), 16–17.

5. *Composition of Governing Boards, 1985* (Washington, D.C.: Association of Governing Boards of Colleges and Universities, 1986), 15.

6. "Hospital Trustees' Role Grows Tougher as Financial and Charitable Goals Clash," *Wall Street Journal*, 18 March 1986.

7. Laurence Vail Coleman, *Manual for Small Museums* (New York: G.P. Putnam's Sons, 1927), 24.

8. *Composition of Governing Boards*, 1985, 3.

9. Houle, *Effective Board* (see chap. 2, n.4), 163.

INDEX

About the Author

JAMES C. BAUGHMAN is Professor and Coordinator of the Media Program, Graduate School of Library and Information Science, Simmons College, as well as an independent consultant to nonprofit organizations. Among his many accomplishments, Dr. Baughman was the recipient of the Research Roundtable's Research Competition Award for his work on knowledge control for interdisciplinary research.